COUNTRY COOKING
Around The World

Marika Hanbury-Tenison
and Rosa Mashiter

COUNTRY

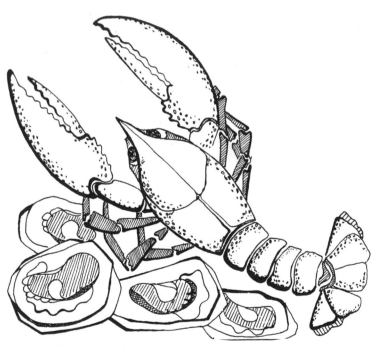

with line illustrations by Gill Hayles

COOKING
Around
The World

DAVID & CHARLES
Newton Abbot   London   North Pomfret (Vt)

British Library Cataloguing in Publication Data

Hanbury Tenison, Marika
  Country cooking around the world
  1. Cookery, International
  I. Title
  641.5   TX725.A1

ISBN 0-7153-8893-2

Typeset by Typesetters (Birmingham) Ltd,
Smethwick, West Midlands
and printed in Great Britain
by Redwood Burn Limited, Trowbridge, Wilts
for David & Charles Publishers plc
Brunel House   Newton Abbot   Devon

Published in the United States of America
by David & Charles Inc
North Pomfret   Vermont 05053   USA

Contents

Foreword

Some months after the tragically early death, from cancer, of Marika Hanbury Tenison her husband Robin handed me the incomplete manuscript of *Country Cooking Around the World* . Marika had never had time to finish it; some sections were complete, others had not even been started and it had been her last project. 'She would have wanted you to have it, and to make use of it if you can,' Robin told me. I was deeply touched by this gesture, and took the manuscript home, but planned to do nothing with it then – it was all too soon.

I first met Marika when I applied for the job as her PA. I went for an interview at Maidenwell, her beautiful home on Bodmin Moor. It was a misty Cornish night, and I was more than relieved when I found myself at the front door, after negotiating seemingly endless long narrow lanes. I knocked on the front door which was quickly opened by a slim, attractive fair-haired young woman, who greeted me in a distinctive and unusual gravelly voice. We sat and talked in her tiny, low-beamed sitting room, surrounded by books, her massive partners desk strewn with manuscripts taking up most of the space. I found an immediate rapport developing between us. She was passionate about her writing, her journalism and her books and the world of cookery and food. When I eventually left I had my fingers crossed that I might work with this dynamic woman – and I did.

I spent nearly five years working with and for Marika. I did all her secretarial work, researched her articles and books, travelled round the country with her, organising and helping her at the many demonstrations she gave for charity. She introduced me to the world of sophisticated eating out in London, giving me the chance to meet some famous names in the cookery world and

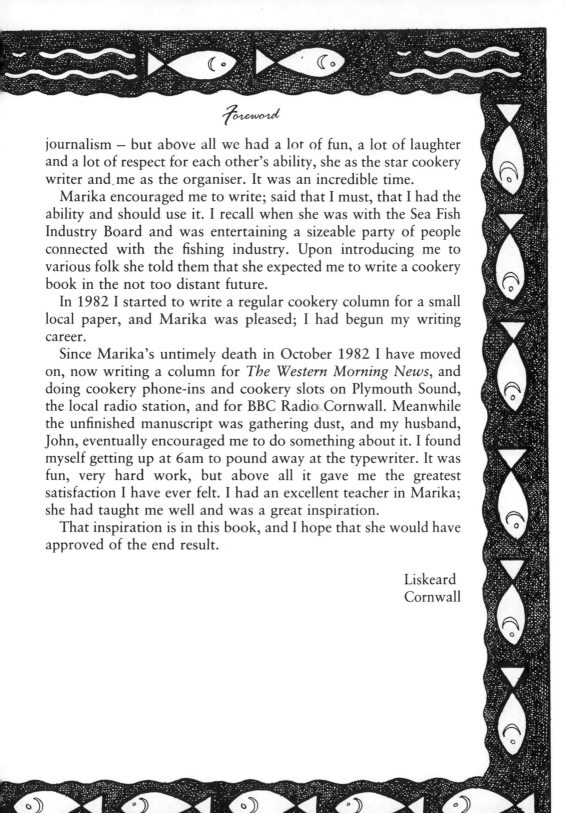

Foreword

journalism – but above all we had a lot of fun, a lot of laughter and a lot of respect for each other's ability, she as the star cookery writer and me as the organiser. It was an incredible time.

Marika encouraged me to write; said that I must, that I had the ability and should use it. I recall when she was with the Sea Fish Industry Board and was entertaining a sizeable party of people connected with the fishing industry. Upon introducing me to various folk she told them that she expected me to write a cookery book in the not too distant future.

In 1982 I started to write a regular cookery column for a small local paper, and Marika was pleased; I had begun my writing career.

Since Marika's untimely death in October 1982 I have moved on, now writing a column for *The Western Morning News*, and doing cookery phone-ins and cookery slots on Plymouth Sound, the local radio station, and for BBC Radio Cornwall. Meanwhile the unfinished manuscript was gathering dust, and my husband, John, eventually encouraged me to do something about it. I found myself getting up at 6am to pound away at the typewriter. It was fun, very hard work, but above all it gave me the greatest satisfaction I have ever felt. I had an excellent teacher in Marika; she had taught me well and was a great inspiration.

That inspiration is in this book, and I hope that she would have approved of the end result.

Liskeard
Cornwall

FOR JOHN, WITH MY LOVE

*A percentage of the royalties from this book
will be donated to the Cancer Research Campaign
in memory of Marika Hanbury Tenison*

Introduction

Marika called this book *Country Cooking Around the World*, meaning that it contains information about a country and the recipes used by ordinary people in their homes.

There are so many cookery books giving recipes for the classic dishes of the world. However, most of these books contain recipes for foods that you would eat out of, rather than in, the home. I have, for example, included Fiji, mainly because I lived there and have never seen a Fijian cookery book. I have eaten in restaurants in Fiji, but none serves the Fijian food that you will only find in a Fijian home.

Country cooking concerns the ordinary housewife, wherever her kitchen may be; Indonesia, or New Orleans, the Highlands of Scotland or the warmer climes of Western Australia. It is what she would cook in her kitchen, for her family, her friends and guests.

The ingredients, therefore, are by necessity indigenous. But let me say this: I feel strongly that cookery should never run along unbending or unalterable lines, and following a recipe word for word can take away the creativity. There is no reason why two cooks, on opposite sides of the world should not cook the same dish, the only difference is that one or both may find it necessary to improvise with ingredients. To my mind that is what the joy, the fun and the creativity of cooking is all about.

I do hope you enjoy the culinary journey that this book is designed to encourage you to take through the kitchens of many countries around the world.

Australia

When researching the foods of Australia, I got in touch with my husband's aunt and uncle, Ed and Jean Knowles, who live in Perth in Western Australia.

The magnificent glass-walled skyscrapers of this city which sits on the banks of the Swan River, contrast dramatically with the Victorian style of the older buildings with their sweeping pillars and ornate mouldings. This is an outgoing city with large shopping centres where the housewife can buy every conceivable ingredient under one roof. Parking is simple too and most supermarkets operate a system whereby purchases can be delivered to the car, which means no struggling with bulky carrier bags and getting hot and bothered before arriving home to cook for the family.

Ed and Jean live in the spaciously laid out suburbs of Perth. Australians take great pride in their gardens; everywhere brilliant splashes of colour can be seen; bougainvillaea, hibiscus, roses, marigolds and petunias contrast with the lush green lawns. Most Australian homes also have a barbecue, either a permanent brickbuilt structure, or one that can stay out doors throughout the dry summer.

Australian cookery has developed from the European and Asian tastes of the early settlers. At first they made mistakes and found life very hard indeed; they tried to produce crops unsuited to soil and climate which therefore took a long time to grow. The pioneering women still had to feed their families and during that time damper, or Bushman's bread as it was known, was created. A simple dough of flour and water was moulded into flat cakes and cooked in the hot ashes of the fire; at times it was moulded into small balls, speared on the end of a stick and poked straight into the fire. Those pioneers should perhaps have learnt from the indigenous Aborigine, a competent hunter gatherer who lived on fish from the rivers, cooked kangaroo meat in underground ovens and found a plentiful supply of wild fresh fruit in the bush.

Today, no matter where you go in Australia, you will find a casual outdoor lifestyle made possible by long hot summers

10

and mild winters. Most Australians want to enjoy as much as possible the wide variety of outdoor pursuits, from a day on the beach, a fishing trip, barbecue or football match.

When I asked Jean about Australian cookery she told me that the favourite dishes are probably universal. In Western Australia, top of the list is roast lamb, served in the traditional way with gravy and mint sauce, accompanied by lots of vegetables – roast pumpkins, parsnip, onion, potatoes and white or yellow turnips, usually cooked with the meat.

No selfrespecting Aussie will be without his tomato sauce and Vegemite. Vegemite is a vegetable extract and is used daily in sandwiches, for school combined with a banana or perhaps some hard boiled eggs, or lettuce and cheese, and it is popular too at breakfast time when it is liberally spread on toast and topped with scrambled eggs.

In Western Australia, where the weather is predictable, at least more so than in the east, barbecuing is the hot weather form of cooking. Lamb, beef, chicken, fish and seafood are barbecued and served with a wide variety of fresh salads. Ed enjoys nothing more than going off on a fishing trip and many of his catches end up on the barbecue in the family's 'back yard'.

Tropical fruits abound too, and a favourite with the Knowles family, particularly to round off a barbecue, is a fresh fruit platter with a rum dip.

Arrange a large platter of peeled and sliced fresh fruit, in medium chunks, using cateloupe or honeydew melons, mango, pineapple, pawpaw (papaya), peaches, kiwi fruit, black and green grapes, strawberries, and even good quality dried fruit mixed in with the fresh. Bananas, apples and pears can also be used provided they are added last after dipping in lemon juice to avoid discoloration. Chill the fruit. To make the rum dip you will need 1 tbsp of brown sugar and 2 tbsp dark rum to every 200g (7oz) carton of sour cream; beat until smooth and creamy, then chill well.

Like most dips it is eaten with the fingers, but you could provide toothpicks, and fingerbowls are useful too – though the dip is so good that people are more likely to lick their fingers than to wash them!

Christmas is a time when Australians turn back to their roots for the food they eat, particularly the older generation when, despite the blazing heat of midsummer, housewives will spend hours in the kitchen preparing roast turkey, mince pies and Christmas pudding. The younger Australians are more likely to spend the day at the beach, with a picnic lunch and ice-cold beer – plus Christmas crackers and funny hats. There is also the 'modern' Christmas pudding, a mixture of dried fruits in a sherry or wine jelly set in a pudding basin, turned out and decorated with whipped cream. That is likely to be adorned with a sprig of plastic holly.

Australia has a wealth of fresh ingredients which the Australian cook uses eagerly, whether cooking for her family, or more formally for guests, the most popular form of entertaining in Australia today.

Western Australia Seafood Chowder
(Serves 4)

450g (1lb) firm fleshed white fish fillets
250g (8oz) scallops
1 onion
1 carrot
1 parsnip
50g (2oz) butter
900ml (1½pt) fish stock
2tsp flour
450ml (16fl oz) milk
Salt and freshly ground black pepper
2tbsp finely chopped fresh parsley

Poach the fish in a little water until just cooked, remove with a slotted spoon and allow to cool, then remove any skin, and flake the flesh.

Cut the scallops into thick slices. Peel the onion, carrot and parsnip and dice roughly.

Melt the butter in a large pan, and add the onion and cook over a medium heat until the onion is golden, but not brown. Add the carrot and parsnip and cook for a further 2min. Pour over the fish stock, lower the heat, and cook until the vegetables are tender. Blend the flour with a little milk and add to the stock, together with the remainder of the milk. Bring to the boil, stirring. Add the flaked fish and sliced scallops, lower the heat and cook for about 10min, when the scallops will be cooked. Season with a little salt and some freshly ground black pepper. Serve the soup into warmed bowls, garnishing with a generous sprinkling of finely chopped fresh parsley.

Beer Soup
(Serves 4)

A widely acclaimed soup
as you may imagine.

425ml (¾pt) milk
1 stick cinnamon
Zest of a lemon
1tbsp soft brown sugar
2tbsp cornflour
50ml (2fl oz) water
350ml (12fl oz) beer
1 egg yolk
1tbsp finely chopped fresh parsley

In a large saucepan heat the milk, cinnamon, lemon zest and sugar until it comes to the boil. Lower the heat to simmer and cook for 10min. Mix the cornflour with the cold water to form a smooth paste and stir into the soup, stirring continuously until the soup has thickened and is smooth.

Stir in the beer. Beat the egg and mix it with a tablespoonful of the hot soup, add to the saucepan, stirring well.

Remove from the heat and strain through a sieve. Serve hot or cold, garnished with a good sprinkling of fresh parsley.

Sesame Grilled Prawns
(Serves 4)

These are delicious served
with crusty herbed bread
p16.

1kg (2.2lb) large king prawns
3 large shallots
125ml (4fl oz) red wine
125ml (4fl oz) sunflower oil
1tsp lemon pepper
100g (4oz) toasted sesame seeds

Peel and devein the prawns, leaving the tail shell intact. Peel and finely chop the shallots and combine them with the red wine and sunflower oil, season with the lemon pepper and mix well to form the marinade.

Thread the prawns, about 4, onto bamboo skewers. Pour the marinade into a large shallow dish (or a tray with a raised rim) and lay the skewers in it. Use a small brush to coat the prawns and put aside for at least 1hr to marinate.

Put the toasted sesame seeds onto a plate, remove the skewers from the marinade and roll them well in the toasted sesame seeds. Refrigerate for 20min.

Lightly oil the grill pan, and grill the prawns for 2–3min only, brushing lightly with the marinade.

Sea Bream Stuffed with Dried Fruits
(Serves 2–4)

50g (2oz) sultanas
50g (2oz) dried apricots
50g (2oz) raisins
100g (4oz) fresh white breadcrumbs
½tsp ground ginger
1tsp ground coriander
Juice of 1 lemon
2 medium sea bream, scaled and cleaned
½ cut lemon
Orange and lemon slices for garnish

Roughly chop the dried fruits and mix with the breadcrumbs and spices, adding enough lemon juice to bind the stuffing.

Spoon the stuffing into the cavity of the fish and lay on a lightly greased sheet of foil. Rub the cut lemon all over the top of the fish, then fold the foil into a neat parcel.

Cook in the oven at 180°C (350°F, Gas mark 4) for 25–30min.

Transfer the fish carefully from the foil onto a warmed serving dish and garnish with alternate layers of orange and lemon slices along the back of each fish.

Extremely popular method
of cooking lamb in
Western Australia, using a
variety of marinades.

Ask your butcher to bone
out the lamb, and cut to a
butterfly shape for you.

Barbecued Lamb
(Serves 8–10)

leg of lamb (2–3kg [4½–6½lb])

Marinade:

1 small onion
2 cloves garlic
1tsp mixed dried herbs
1tsp dried thyme
1tsp dried oregano
125ml (4fl oz) sunflower oil
Juice of a large lemon
Freshly ground black pepper

Peel and grate the onion, peel and finely chop the garlic.
Combine all the marinade ingredients and mix well before
pouring over the lamb. Leave to marinate for 3–4hr, turning
occasionally.

Ensure that the barbecue is white hot, then cook the lamb,
turning frequently, and basting with the marinade.

Serve with jacket potatoes
and a green tossed salad.

When cooked, remove from the barbecue and slice across
the grain.

Crusty Herbed Bread

A delicious
accompaniment to
barbecues, a favourite
method of cooking in
Western Australia.

100g (4oz) softened butter
2tbsp finely chopped fresh parsley
2 cloves garlic, crushed
1tsp lemon juice
Freshly ground black pepper
1 crusty French style long loaf

In a food processor or blender combine the butter, parsley,
garlic and lemon juice, and a good grind of black pepper until
well mixed.

Using a sharp knife cut the bread, into slices, but leaving a
small hinge of bread, so that the slices are still all attached
together. Spread the slices with the herbed butter, then wrap
in foil, and heat through on the barbecue.

Pickled (Salt) Pork
(Serves 6)

2 carrots
1 onion
1.5kg (3lb) pickled belly or hand of pork
8 black peppercorns
2 whole cloves
Bouquet garni
45ml (2fl oz) white wine vinegar

The best way to serve this dish is cut into thin slices with hot mustard to accompany, English or Dijon being the best.

Peel and slice the carrots and onion.

Soak the pork in cold water for 4–5hr, then drain and put in a large saucepan. Add enough water to well cover the meat and add the remaining ingredients. Over a gentle heat bring slowly to boiling point, then lower the heat and simmer for 1½–2hr until quite tender. Remove any scum that forms at regular intervals during the cooking time. Drain the pork, and allow to cool enough to handle, then remove any bones. Put the pork into a shallow bowl; it should fit quite snugly, cover with foil, and then weight down, until it becomes cold. Chill for 2–3hr before serving.

Carpet-Bag Steak
(Serves 4)

675g–900g (1½–2lb) thick rump steak
Freshly ground black pepper
12 oysters
2tbsp salad oil
2tsp lemon juice
2tsp onion juice
1tbsp chopped parsley
2tbsp dry sherry

Serve the steak with a good tossed salad and sauté potatoes.

Trim the surplus fat from the steak, then using a very sharp knife make a slit ⅔ through the side of the steak to form a pocket. Season the pocket with freshly ground black pepper, and fill with the oysters. Fasten the pocket with small skewers or cocktail sticks. Mix the oil, lemon juice and onion juice and pour over the steak. Leave to marinate for at least 1hr, turning once during that period.

Grill the steak either under a preheated hot grill, or on a barbecue, basting frequently with the marinade. Take care when turning the steak not to pierce the meat. When the steak is cooked, transfer to a warm serving dish and keep hot. Mix well the chopped parsley into the cooking juices, stir in the sherry and pour over the steak.

Passionfruit Pavlova
(Serves 6–8)

This could almost be considered Australia's national dish and is certainly popular throughout the country. The tale is told that a well known Australian hostess who entertained the ballerina, Pavlova, during her tour of Australia, named it after her famous guest.

4 egg whites
100g (4oz) castor sugar, sifted
100g (4oz) granulated sugar
½tsp white vinegar
1tsp cornflour
300ml (½pt) whipping cream
8 passionfruit

Brush a sheet of baking parchment lightly with oil, and place on a baking sheet. Preheat the oven to 140°C (275°F, Gas mark 1). (You may find it helpful to mark out a circle in pencil on the baking parchment before greasing.)

Beat the egg whites until stiff, but not dry; you should be able to turn the basin upsidedown without the egg whites moving. Add the sugars, 2tbsp at a time, beating well between each addition until all the sugar is incorporated. Now add the vinegar, drop by drop, and sift the cornflour over the mixture, folding in gently, with a metal spoon.

Turn the mixture onto the paper lined baking tray, and form into a round, slightly hollowing out the centre. Put into the lowest position in the oven and bake for 1½–2hr.

Check the meringue at regular intervals to make sure that it does not colour too much, it should be a pale cream in colour. When crisp remove from the oven, and remove the paper carefully so that you do not damage the meringue, as it is very brittle. Place on a serving dish and allow to cool completely.

Cut the passionfruit in half, and scoop out the flesh and seeds with a teaspoon. Whip the cream until thick, and fold in a little of the passionfruit pulp. Fill the centre of the pavlova with the fruit pulp and top with the whipped cream mixture.

Anzac Biscuits

175g (6oz) rolled oats
175g (6oz) plain flour
175g (6oz) desiccated coconut
175g (6oz) soft brown sugar
1½tsp baking powder
200g (7oz) butter
2tbsp golden syrup

Mix all the dry ingredients together in a bowl. Melt the butter and pour over the flour mixture, adding the syrup at the same time, mixing well with a wooden spoon. Shape the mixture into small balls, about the size of a walnut.

Lightly grease a baking sheet, and arrange the balls, flattening with the back of a fork onto the sheet and bake in a preheated oven 150°C (300°F, Gas mark 2) for 15–20min.

A recipe dating from World War I, hence its name.

Aussie Damper

225g (8oz) self raising flour
Pinch of salt
25g (1oz) butter
150ml (5fl oz) milk

A sustaining bread, often cooked in the outback over an open camp fire.

Sift the flour and salt into a bowl, cut the butter into small pieces and rub into the flour with the fingertips. Using a palette knife, mix in the milk until a dough is formed. Turn onto a well floured board and knead quickly and lightly. Shape into a large flat cake, brush the top lightly with a little sifted flour and bake in a preheated oven 190°C (375°F, Gas mark 5) for about 25min, or until brown.

Brittany

I have wonderful memories of my first trip to Brittany, some years ago. Living as I do in the South West, some 20 miles from Plymouth, with a regular ferry service operating to Brittany, it is an ideal region of France for me to visit. In spring, before the tourist season, is the time to visit this fascinating region. My husband and I had decided to spend a week in a *gîte* – a French holiday home. *Gîtes* vary considerably, from a modern apartment on the seafront to a converted farm building. We were lucky; we stayed in a delightfully converted barn, on a small working mixed farm some 8 miles or so from the medieval town of Vannes, near the inland sea of the Gulf of Morbihan. On our visits to Vannes we enjoyed nothing more than sitting outside one of the pavement cafes, sipping coffee, eating delicious raisin *galette*, a local speciality, and watching the world go by, and the boats bobbing up and down in the harbour.

The rugged coastline of Brittany reminds me of Cornwall, where I have lived for nearly 20 years, with the very similar inhospitable coast, dotted with warning lighthouses which are a constant reminder that the sea is dangerous and can be a formidable enemy to those who fish her waters. There is a great variety of fish and shellfish all around the coast, and in all the harbours, be they big like Lorient, one of the largest fishing ports in France, or one of the hundreds of little ports from St. Malo to St. Nazaire.

St. Malo is famous for its oysters, served raw on a half shell with a vinegar sauce spiked with finely chopped shallot. Shellfish abound, and include lobsters, langoustines, prawns, clams and scallops; the same boats will bring in wet fish such as sole, turbot and the flavoursome seabass. A famous Breton fish dish is *cotriade*, a substantial fish stew using a plain white fish, such as whiting or cod, with potatoes and onions, and perhaps a few mussels to give a more robust flavour. Mussels are another popular dish, cooked in a little white wine with parsley and some chopped shallot, and served piled high into earthenware bowls. *Moules à la marinière* can be found in

most little cafes in Brittany accompanied by crusty bread to mop up the delicious juices. The best way to eat mussels is to remove the first one with your fingers, then use the shell as pincers to remove the others, one at a time, there is a certain knack to it, but it is definitely great fun.

Most tuna is landed at the fishing port of Concarneau and sent for canning. We visited a canning factory where tuna was not only simply packed in oil as fillets or steaks, but was transformed into gourmet dishes such as tuna with artichoke hearts, tuna *à la grecque* and *à la jardine*.

We spent a day in Quimperle, which is twinned with my home town of Liskeard, where we were guests of a fellow Rotarian of my husband. Paul Cochin and his wife, Madeline, made us feel very much at home when we arrived around midday and immediately offered us aperitifs, or perhaps you would prefer a cognac! Madeline's mother, who must have been well into her 70s, was an English teacher, and spoke beautiful English. She had lived in England many years before, and spoke with great affection of her time in London, and how she still missed English sausages.

Madeline had cooked a typical family lunch for us, consisting of *Kig-ha-Farz* (meat in pudding), a tasty dish of meat, vegetables and gravy with a sweet pudding made from buckwheat flour and water. This was followed by thin slices of peppery, spiced *andouilettes* – tripe sausages, a regional speciality. We enjoyed some cheese, eaten with a knife and fork, and finished our meal with a rich, chocolate cream pudding.

There is much to see and enjoy in Brittany, and we meandered, unhurried, to little coastal towns like Trinite sur Mer, where on a wet and miserable day, with the sea a forbidding grey, we discovered the pleasures of the Breton *galettes*, better known perhaps as *crêpes*. In every little town in Brittany you will find a crêperie, and we found a delightful one tucked away in the backstreets. It was obviously very popular with the local inhabitants as, by 1pm, it was packed, and the patron was having to turn people away. We sat enthralled watching the *galettier* spread the thin batter, using a type of spatula and a rake, over the big gas-fired *galettieres* or griddles; somehow as she ladled the batter not a drop spilled over the sides. Eggs were broken onto the crêpe, chopped ham was sprinkled on top together with sliced spicy sausages, herbs, and freshly ground black pepper, and with a flip of the spatula the crêpe was folded and slid deftly onto a plate, ready to be served.

Crêperies usually boast a good variety of fillings, both savoury and sweet. Crêpes are made with either buckwheat or wheat flours, eggs and milk, although buckwheat, because of its more earthy flavour, generally is used for savoury crêpes. We gorged ourselves that day, washing down the crêpes with local cider and we emerged, full to bursting, then ambled along the seashore under a watery sun, totally and utterly replete.

Inland, farming is the way of life. Around Roscoff, onions are a main crop, together with some garlic (though the garlic of Brittany fails to compete with the flavoursome Provence variety due to the lack of sun). Fields and fields of cauliflower stretching as far as the eye can see, are a familiar sight, as are the flowerlike globe artichokes which fill the fields when the cauliflower season is over. To cook artichokes, soak them upside down for about an hour in cold salted water to help remove any soil lodged between the leaves. Take out of the salted water, cut off the stalks close to the leaves and put into a large saucepan of boiling water, to which you have added about 3 tbsp vinegar; return the water to the boil and cook for about 30min. To test whether the artichoke is cooked, remove from the pan with a slotted spoon and pull out a lower leaf; if the base of the leaf is tender — a kind of wedge of creamy consistency when you bite into it — then it is done; if not done, cook for a further 10min before testing again.

I like artichokes served hot accompanied by melted butter with a little lemon juice added. Artichokes are eaten with the fingers. Pull out a leaf at a time, dip the inner end into the butter and then scrape the tender base between your teeth. When all the leaves are gone, you will be left with a thick saucer of artichoke, topped by an inedible fibrous round and flat 'choke' which is best removed by taking small sections of the fibres between thumb and forefinger and pulling out sharply until all the fibres have been cleared from the base. The artichoke bottom, deliciously succulent, should be eaten with a knife and fork and lots of melted butter.

Agriculture plays an important part in Breton life. A Breton speciality is the famous saltmarsh lamb raised on the marshes of the Bay of St Michel. Further inland where there is mixed farming, every farm will have a few animals, chickens and ducks, some vegetable crops and perhaps some dairying. The only salted butter in France comes from Brittany, and if you order oysters in France you will inevitably find they are served with Breton lightly salted butter.

The Breton housewife looks for quality and variety in whatever she buys. Friday is still the traditional day for eating fish, and the main markets in Brittany (and in fact throughout most of France) are held on Friday mornings to allow the housewife to buy fresh fish.

Go to Quimper, a bustling town renowned for its sweet *crêpes dentelles*. In the indoor market you will find a dazzling array of shellfish and wet fish – lobster, langoustine, spider crabs, cockles, winkles and clams alongside sole, cod, red and grey mullet or perhaps monkfish tails, the latter being very popular in this region where it is known as *lotte de mer*. Other stalls beckon you to buy *Lobster à l'américaine* (lobster with garlic and tomatoes), and little tray of *palourdes farcies* (clams stuffed with herb butter) or brochettes of scallops and monkfish, or the well known *Coquille Saint-Jacques*, all ready prepared – a little expensive perhaps, but all looking so mouthwatering that it is difficult to resist. Shiny sardines are sold by the kilo, to be cooked at home over hot charcoal and served with a squeeze of fresh lemon – heavenly.

Sunday lunch is a great occasion in Brittany, whether the meal is taken at home or in a restaurant. More often than not the starter is a large platter of *fruits de mer* (fruits of the sea). Generally the housewife asks her fishmonger to prepare the platter for her, telling him how much she wishes to spend on how many people. Mussels, clams, oysters, whelks, winkles and langoustine are arranged around the platter, with a brilliant red spider crab as the usual centrepiece. A bowl of homemade mayonnaise, a basket of crusty bread and the lightly salted Breton butter is served with the platter accompanied by chilled Muscadet, or perhaps local cider, with much conversation and enjoyment.

The Bretons love poultry, especially chicken or duck, and this often forms the main course, simply cooked and served with just one vegetable and followed by a salad. Cheese follows the main course, and perhaps a *far breton*, a batter pudding with prunes.

The area around Nantes, at the mouth of the Loire, produces Muscadet, a main ingredient of the famous Breton sauce, *beurre blanc*. Equal amounts of wine and white wine vinegar, flavoured with a little chopped shallot are reduced, then the lightly salted butter is whisked in a little at a time to produce this classic sauce.

I thoroughly enjoyed my many visits to Brittany; there was always something new and always the old favourites, but each visit left me wanting very much to return there – and soon.

Salade de Moules au Safran (Mussels with Saffron and Mayonnaise)
(Serves 4)

2qt mussels
4tbsp wine
Pinch saffron
450g (1lb) new potatoes
300ml (½pt) mayonnaise made with lemon juice
(see page 00)
Salt and freshly ground black pepper
2tbsp finely chopped chives
Pinch paprika

An attractive starter that brings out the best flavour of fresh mussels and new potatoes with homemade mayonnaise. Very simple. Serve at room temperature with crisp French bread.

Wash the mussels under cold running water. Scrape the shells with a small sharp knife to remove any dirt and barnacles, then scrub with a stiff brush or wire brush to remove any sediment and wash them again under cold running water until they are clean, discarding any that close up while being washed. Place the mussels in a large saucepan without water but add a little wine. Bring to the boil with a saucepan firmly covered and shake over a high heat for about 6min, until the mussels have half opened. Leave until cool enough to handle. Strain 2tbsp of the cooking wine into a bowl, add the saffron and leave to infuse until cold.

Clean the potatoes and cook in boiling, salted water until they are just tender. Drain well, leave until cool enough to handle and then remove the skins. Blend the saffron liquid mixture into the mayonnaise, mixing well. Cut the potatoes into thin waxy slices with a small, sharp knife and toss them lightly with the mayonnaise. Season with salt and pepper.

Remove the mussels from their shells making sure you pull out any wiry barbs that may be left in the inside. Add the mussels to the potatoes and mix gently so as not to break up any of the ingredients but to lightly coat the mussels as well as the potatoes with the mayonnaise.

Pile into a bowl, sprinkle with chives and a little paprika.

Brittany

A tasty Breton fish soup. To serve, place some slices of French bread in a soup tureen and pour over the broth.

Cotriade
(Serves 4–6)

3 large onions
50g (2oz) butter
1 bouquet garni
1kg (2lb) potatoes
1.5kg (3lb) firm fleshed white fish (cod, haddock, whiting)
Freshly ground black pepper

Peel and finely chop the onions. Melt the butter in a large saucepan and sauté the onions until soft and transparent, pour over 2l (3½pt) water, add the bouquet garni and bring to the boil. Meanwhile peel the potatoes and cut into large chunks, and add to the saucepan. Season well with freshly ground black pepper, and cook for 20min.

Cut the fish into large chunks, and add to the broth, lowering the heat to simmer, and cook for about 10min. Lift the fish with a slotted spoon onto a serving dish, and surround with potato chunks.

Coquille Saint-Jacques au Muscadet (Scallops with Muscadet)
(Serves 4)

Fresh, good quality mussels placed in a bucket, covered with cold water and sprinkled with a large handful of oatmeal oats, can be left in a cold room overnight to clean themselves through and plump up with great success.

8 scallops
1 small onion or shallot
125g (4oz) button mushrooms
25g (1oz) butter
300ml (½pt) Muscadet
1tbsp butter
1tbsp plain flour
2tbsp double cream
Salt and white pepper
Chopped parsley

Cut the scallops into 2 or 3 diagonal slices. Peel and finely chop the onion or shallot. Thinly slice the mushrooms. Sauté the onion and mushrooms in 25g (1oz) butter over a very low heat until the onion is soft and transparent. Add the Muscadet and the scallops, bring to the boil, then lower heat to as low as possible and cook for 10min. Transfer the scallops with a slotted spoon to a gratin dish and keep warm.

Bring the liquids in the pan back to the boil, and boil hard to reduce by 1/3. Blend the tablespoon of butter and the flour together and add a little at a time to the pan, stirring well to mix, until the sauce is thick and smooth. Season to taste. Lower the heat and stir in the cream, do not allow to boil. Finally, add the scallops. Serve immediately garnished with chopped parsley.

Salad St Pierre (Fish Salad)
(Serves 4–5)

Butter
4 small John Dory fillets (or use small seabass fillets, lemon sole or some other firm fleshed white fish)
2 hardboiled eggs
Salt and freshly ground black pepper
1/2tsp dry English mustard
6tbsp olive or sunflower oil
1tbsp white wine vinegar
1/2tsp very finely chopped or minced parsley
1 cucumber
2 artichoke bottoms
(I buy these in a tin, they are not overly expensive)
175g (6oz) very small, thin French beans
1 small tin asparagus tips (225g [8oz])
150g (5oz) cooked small peas
1tsp very finely chopped chives

Why do we not eat more fish salads? They are so good, so easy to make, they look so nice and fresh and, for anyone who is (or wants to be) figure-conscious, they make ideal eating. One of the best fishes with which to make a fish salad is the John Dory, if you can get it.

Lightly butter a steaming pan, place it over a saucepan half filled with boiling water and steam the fish for about 6min until it is just tender. Remove from the steamer and leave until cool enough to remove any skin. Coarsely flake the fish.

Remove the egg yolks and mash them to a paste with a fork, season with salt, freshly ground black pepper and dry mustard and gradually beat in the oil. Add the vinegar and mix in the parsley.

You can also give the top of the salad a fine sprinkling of paprika pepper just to give a hint of red but go easy as this is a hot spice.

Peel and halve the cucumber, scoop out the seeds, sprinkle the cucumber with salt and leave to drain upside down for 30min. Pat dry on kitchen paper and cut into thin slices.

Thinly slice the artichoke bottoms. Chop the French beans. Combine all the vegetables with the fish and the egg whites, roughly chopped. Add the dressing and toss lightly to mix. Pile on to a serving dish and garnish with finely chopped chives. Serve chilled.

Caneton aux Olives
(Duck with Olives)
(Serves 8–10)

We all know about roast duck and duck with cherries, but both are rich and expensive dishes. What I wanted to find is a way of cooking duck that stretches your average sized bird into enough for 10 rather than 4 persons and which will provide a substantial, not too fatty or rich dish, but will still be interesting and flavoursome. I wanted to get the tastiness and texture of the duck without it being overly lavish. Finally I found it. There is help from onions and vegetables and from a good sauce with the addition of olives to provide something different. I found it in a small restaurant in France and it worked.

1.8kg (4lb) duckling
Salt and freshly ground black pepper
4tbsp sunflower oil
2 celeriac
Juice of ½ lemon
2 carrots
2 sticks celery
2 onions
2tbsp cornflour
300ml (½pt) dry white wine
450ml (¾pt) consommé
30 pimento stuffed olives
4tbsp pistachio or pine nuts
Rice

Season the duck all over with coarse salt and freshly ground black pepper and place on a rack in a roasting pan; dribble over half the oil and roast in a moderately hot oven 190°C (375°F, Gas mark 5) for 1¼hr, basting every now and then.

Remove the duck, prick its skin, drain off all the oil, and leave the bird to cool. Remove and retain the skin of the duck. Cut into thin strips all the flesh from the carcass, after removing any fat.

Peel the celeriac, cut into matchstick strips and leave to stand in water to which lemon juice has been added (1tbsp).

Peel the carrots and cut them into thin julienne strips. Cut the celery into julienne strips about 5cm (2in) long. Peel and chop the onions.

Heat the remaining oil in a casserole dish. Add the vegetables and cook over a moderate heat, stirring every now and then, until the vegetables are nicely soft and tender. Add the cornflour and stir well. With the heat raised high, stir the vegetables and flour until the flour is a nutty brown. Gradually add the wine and consommé, stirring all the time until the sauce is thick, smooth and satiny. Season well with salt and freshly ground black pepper and add the duck. Stir all the ingredients over a moderate high heat until the duck is hot through.

Cut the olives in slices, add to the dish with the chopped pine or pistachio nuts and heat through – check seasoning.

Serve the ingredients in a ring of fluffy white rice.

Poulet à la Bretonne (Chicken with Onions and Cream)
(Serves 4)

2 large onions
1.75kg (3lb 10oz) chicken, jointed
75g (3oz) salted butter
Salt and freshly ground black pepper
150ml (5fl oz) double cream

Peel and very finely chop the onions. Melt the butter in a heavy bottomed fireproof casserole, or cocotte, and brown the chicken pieces. Add the finely chopped onion and season with salt and pepper. Cover and cook over a low heat for 35min. Pour in the cream, and heat through, without boiling.

Andouillettes – Pommes en l'air (Sausages made of Small Chitterlings, with Apples)
(Serves 6)

6 andouillettes
1.5kg (3lb) eating apples
75g (3oz) butter
Salt and freshly ground black pepper

Slice the andouillettes in 2 lengthwise. Peel and core the apples and cut into quarters.

Melt half the butter in a large frying pan and cook the andouillettes until crisp. Remove with a slotted spoon and keep warm.

Add the remaining butter to the pan and sauté the apples until lightly browned. Season with salt and freshly ground black pepper. Place on a heated serving dish, and arrange the andouillettes on top.

Gigot de mouton à la bretonne (Leg of Lamb with White Haricot Beans)
(Serves 6–8)

2–3 cloves garlic
2kg (4lb) leg of lamb
50g (2oz) salted butter
1 onion
3tbsp tomato purée
300ml (½pt) chicken stock
1 large tin (450g [1lb]) white haricot beans
Salt and freshly ground black pepper

Peel the garlic cloves, and cut into thin slices. Using a very sharp pointed knife, make incisions in the lamb and slide in the garlic slices. Soften the butter a little, spread all over the

30

lamb and season with freshly ground black pepper. Place the lamb in a roasting tin and put in an oven preheated to 190°C (375°F, Gas mark 5), allowing 1hr/kg (2lb) cooking time.

Half an hour before the end of cooking time, peel and finely chop the onion. Melt the remaining butter in a frying pan, and gently fry the onion until golden brown. Stir in the tomato purée and chicken stock and mix well. Drain the haricot beans and add to the sauce. Cook gently for 4 or 5min, season with salt and freshly ground black pepper, spoon into a large serving dish and keep warm. When the lamb is cooked, place it on top of the beans and sauce, and serve at once.

Galetous aux Pommes (Apple Pancakes)
(Serves 6)

1kg (2lb) cooking apples
225g (8oz) sugar
2tbsp calvados
400g (14oz) buckwheat flour
100g (4oz) wheat flour
1 egg
100g (4oz) salted butter, melted
300ml (½pt) dry cider

Peel core and chop the apples, and put into a saucepan with the sugar and (2tbsp) water. Cook over a low heat until the apples are cooked and soft and breaking apart. Purée the apple in an electric blender, food processor or through a sieve. Add the calvados and keep the purée warm.

In a food processor or electric blender combine the flours, egg, melted butter and cider, then add enough water to make a pouring batter, and process again. Allow the batter to stand for at least 2hr.

Smear a large heavy bottomed frying pan with a little oil and heat it until a haze rises, swirl some batter in the pan, moving it so that the batter flows and completely covers the base; cook until bubbles pop up over the surface, flip over and cook the other side for about 2min. Put a good tbsp or so of apple purée in the middle of the pancake, roll up and serve at once, sprinkled with a little sugar.

Of course the French housewife prefers ingredients that are as fresh and as unadulterated as possible. However, she, like us, suffers from the recession and she is the last person to throw anything away that could be used. For this recipe any bits of stale cheese are used for a dessert to serve with crisp French bread and apples and it is always a triumph.

The Great Icecream Cheese
(Serves 6)

2tbsp Boursin cheese
25g (1oz) Brie
100g (4oz) cottage cheese
4tbsp double cream
1tbsp finely chopped chives
1 clove garlic
Salt and freshly ground (or a few crushed green peppercorns) pepper
Pinch cayenne pepper
2tbsp pine nuts

Mash with a fork or mix in a food processor the cheeses until they are smooth. Add the cream and mix well. Add the chives and crushed garlic, season with salt, pepper and a pinch of cayenne and mix well. Pack into a small damp, mould. Place in a deep freeze for about 2hr until solid and dip the mould in water to turn out. Return to the freezer until ready to use. Roast the pine nuts in a moderately hot oven 190°C (375°F, Gas mark 5) until they are golden brown and leave to cool. Remove the mould from the freezer 20min before serving and stud the top of the cheese with the nuts.

Sprinkle over a little more cayenne and serve at once in slices like a cake.

Far Breton Avec Cerises Fraiches
(Serves 4)

Raisins, prunes or dried apricots, soaked overnight, are also used in Far Breton, but fresh cherries to my mind are the most delicious.

225g (8oz) fresh cherries, stoned
100g (4oz) caster sugar
100g (4oz) flour
3 eggs
600ml (1pt) milk
A little butter

Lightly grease a 2l (3½pt) shallow baking dish with the butter and scatter the cherries evenly over the base.

Put the flour into a mixing bowl, make a well in the centre and pour the milk into the well, whisking the flour from the sides into the centre, until a smooth batter forms. Add the eggs, one at a time, beating in lightly. Mix in the sugar. Pour the mixture over the cherries and bake for 1¼–1½hr in a preheated oven at 180°C (350°F, Gas mark 4) until golden brown. Serve warm cut into wedges or squares.

Caribbean

There is nothing in the world, that quite rivals the glorious, wonderful, warmth of a Caribbean island. You come from a British winter, all grey skies and gloom, strikes and economising on the heating; you have sat for seven or eight hours in a flying capsule eating plastic food and probably drinking too many martinis and you are still wearing your heavyweight tights. Then, from some ludicrous height in the sky you begin the descent and, suddenly, unbelievably, you see the magic of the Caribbean spread below you. The sea is a dazzling azure streaked with aquamarine and sapphire, broken here and there by creamy waves where a reef curves through the water. Circular bays are lined with palm trees, inner island vegetation is lush and exotic and colours are richer, brighter and more beautiful than any you have ever seen before.

But it's the moment you step from that airconditioned cabin into the fresh air that makes the most lasting impression. Heat, glorious soft, warm, balmy, heat hits you in a great wave, instantly making you forget you were ever chilled to the bone. Heat relaxes your muscles, eases your tensions, smooths away the frown lines and you find yourself smiling involuntarily at customs and excise officials and being ushered through immigration with the help of a complimentary ubiquitous rum punch.

In the beginning Arawaks and Caribs were in the West Indies, those islands described by Christopher Columbus as 'Paradise'. Their lifestyle was a simple one of hunter gatherer and small farmer. They grew maize, sweet potatoes and yams, caught fish and hunted small mammals and garnered the many wild fruits that grew in the Caribbean jungles. They discovered the miraculous allspice tree with seeds that taste like a combination of nutmeg, cloves and cinnamon and they relied heavily on hot peppers for flavouring. They preserved meat by smoking thin slices of wild pig and other animals over a low fire and called it *boucan* that gave its name to the pirates or bouchaneres who scourged the islands.

All the Arawaks and most of the Caribs (a few still live in

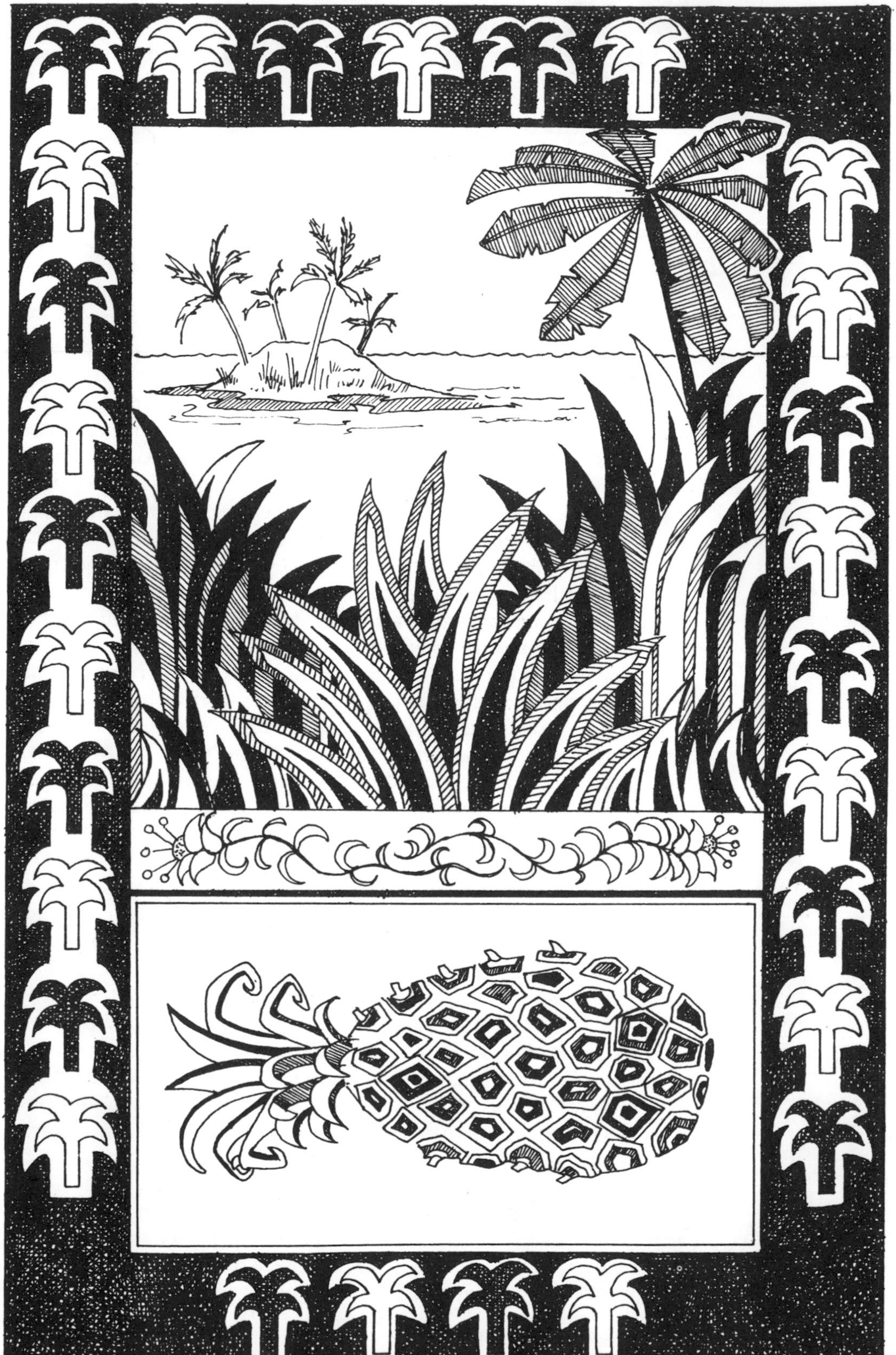

Dominica) were wiped out by those who followed Columbus, from Spain, Portugal, the Netherlands, France and Britain.

The era of the great sugar plantations began and with it came slavery, with slaves from Africa bringing with them the food and eating habits of their own countries. With the emancipation of the slaves, someone else had to be found to do their work and so Chinese and East Indians joined the community bringing, in their turn, their culinary preferences. The various cuisines have melded to become what is best in ethnic Caribbean food. They are still evident throughout the islands although, for the tourist, often hard to find. In Curaçao, for instance, a Dutch colonized island, you can still find a strange dish called *keshy yena* where an Edam or Gouda cheese is hollowed out and filled with chicken (or fish) and vegetables and baked in an oven; then there is *jug-jug* a form of Frenchstyle *cassoulet* which is made from millet and peas with ground meat. Curries abound in Trinidad and *callaloo*, a rich soup made from the vegetable of that name, is almost identical to the Creole soup found in Bahia in Northern Brazil.

It was the happiness of the people that impressed me most when I first went to the Caribbean. People danced in the street, they swung their hips as they waited in bus queues and tapped their toes as they waited to be served in supermarkets. Local shops were full of excitement for me, filled with wonderfully oldfashioned goods like Reckitt's blue (for use in rinsing white laundry), Old Uncle Edgar's Cough Mixture, miniature bananas, strange fruits, and curious items such as bags of chicken feet sold for about 20p to make delicious chicken soup.

Living on a sunny Caribbean island is cheap; all you need is a small wooden house with a leanto kitchen, a small plot of land, an open hearth and clay pot for cooking anything and everything in, and not much more. You can fish for your supper, when necessary kill one of the scraggy chickens that runs around outside, and you can grow enough fruit and vegetables to keep from starving by merely planting papaya pips, offshoots of banana or plantain and some callaloo and squash. The miracle is that from tiny wooden shacks, which may sleep 15 or more, there emerges in the morning children ready for school so cleanly and neatly dressed it is mind boggling.

Surprisingly most of today's fruits and vegetables of the Caribbean were introduced from other countries. Coconuts came from Africa, cassava came from South America, pineapples from the Canaries and even bananas and plantains were imported. All have established there happily together with a large variety of citrus fruit (even the grapefruit, which was developed in Jamaica, had as its ancestor the shaddock, brought by Captain Shaddock from China in the eighteenth century). There is the delightfully ugly soursop with its green warty skin and pulpy white flesh that tastes like a mixture of strawberries, lemon and pineapple. There is the delicate starapple (so named because its pips form a star pattern in the centre) which, combined with peeled and segmented oranges and whipped cream, make the delectable pudding *matrimony*; there are strange tasting naseberries, smooth, succulent pawpaws (papayas), and breadfruit, which can be fried into the most delicious chips.

✱ South American, Spanish and Indian influences have combined to provide the islanders with a taste for hot spices, and on any table, at any meal, West Indians will have their own version of hot pepper sauce which they love to offer to unsuspecting guests – and then burst into laughter at the reaction to the fiery strength of the sauce. Pepper sauces are made by combining pricked miniature sweet peppers with a little garlic and half vinegar and sherry or rum and leaving to steep for a time. A little, and I mean a *little*, is then added to all soups and stews. Most of the islands can provide some beef, pork, poultry, lamb and mutton but in fish and shellfish they are particularly abundant.

On feast days curried goat and roast sucking pig are popular throughout the islands and, although curried goat never really caught on with the colonists, roast sucking pig became a feature at great house or government parties. The meat was flanked by dishes of the hosts' countries, for most colonists stubbornly stuck to the food they would have eaten at home in preference to the more suitable local diet. I have had difficulty in finding local rather than tourist food while in the islands, but the effort is so worthwhile I try harder each time I visit the Caribbean.

Each island has its own cuisine and special dishes but there is a similarity throughout. The use of coriander and the pepper, for instance, is common, so are salt pork products and the ubiquitous rice and peas or rice and beans.

Islanders and island cooks island-hop from one gem to another taking their recipes with them. Pepperpot soup and pepperpot stew are popular throughout. The pepperpot can mean just *that* – sometimes the soup can burn your throat and send you running to the nearest rum punch. The basis of pepperpot soup is salt beef or pork and the vegetable *callaloo*, a personal favourite, which has a taste similar to kale but with rather mustardy overtones. The stew is also based on salt pork or beef made into a nourishing meal with *callaloo*, aubergine, tomato, onion, pumpkin or squash and plenty of herbs and seasonings.

Cooking oils vary with each island; some use groundnut (peanut) oil, some coconut oil and some palm or corn oil. Fried bananas and plantains are enjoyed throughout and so are crisply fried plantain chips to serve with drinks.

Fish provides the main protein; beautiful tropical fish such as snapper and grouper which are well fleshed and fat enough to be stuffed and baked. There are shrimps too, and lobsters; not the lobsters we know with claws but hard-shelled spiny lobsters with milky white flesh that is inclined to be tough. At the Old Yarde Inn, where I stayed on Virgin Gorda, one of the few hotels that serve local food, the chef tenderises the lobster by freezing it alive and then cooks it from the frozen state. A better answer, I found when I lived for a time in a beach house in Jamaica, was to insist on small fresh lobsters, and boil them immediately in seawater – their flesh was ambrosial.

As well as an amazing variety of smaller fish, there are king fish, with flesh like a firmly packed giantsized mackerel, and the dolphin which fortunately is unrelated to the mammal.

Fish is usually plainly cooked, baked or fried with tomatoes, onions, spices and herbs. As a friend of mine, Juanita from Puerto Rico, points out, 'If you have a good thing why spoil it?' Oily fish, like the king fish, is often grilled over an open charcoal fire and served with a dressing of freshly squeezed lime juice; most fish are lightly marinated in lime juice or vinegar and water before they are cooked.

Juanita taught me about the vegetables of the island. She is a compulsive gardener and her garden on the rather arid soil of Virgin Gorda is a never ending source of fascination. There I saw soya beans growing for the first time, her pigeon pea bush was laden with a heavy crop, tiny tomatoes grew beside cassava and sweet potatoes and a small patch of okra (gumbo) sprouted sticky lady's fingers. In the shade of mango, soursop and breadfruit trees goats that looked like sheep and sheep that looked like goats managed to survive on almost nothing.

On the whole the best West Indian dessert is the fresh local fruit, served as it is, although a little soursop icecream, rum and raisin icecream or a delicious mango fool is enjoyable too.

Fresh fruit, however, beats everything. The grapefruit are so sweet they need no sugar at all, small 'fig' bananas melt in your mouth and the pineapples are exquisite.

The drink throughout the Caribbean is rum, rum in all manner of flavours, colours and strengths. The locals drink it with Coca-Cola or ginger ale and make their own excellent ginger beer which goes well with it too.

Today you can find most West Indian ingredients on sale in Britain. Try roasting sweet potatoes and frying slices of plantain, experiment with pawpaw and fresh limes and please your family with a memorable guava or mango fool.

Caribbean

Spiced Baked Fish
(Serves 4)

8 fillets of fish (use whiting, plaice, sole, haddock, etc)
Salt and freshly ground black pepper
1 small onion
50g (2oz) fat pork or bacon
2 large tomatoes
1 medium onion
4tbsp fresh white breadcrumbs
1tsp white wine vinegar
25g (1oz) butter
2tbsp white wine vinegar
50g (2oz) butter

The idea behind the recipes in this book is to produce dishes from parts of the world which are perhaps not so well known and which provide nutrition, good flavour and interest relatively inexpensively. This is a typical example of a dish made from local ingredients and which has an excellent flavour. In this you have the rather unusual flavour of both meat and fish.

Season the fish fillets with salt and pepper. Peel and very finely chop or mince the small onion. Remove the rind from the pork or bacon and mince or very finely chop the flesh. Cover the tomatoes with boiling water for 3min, drain and slide off the skins. Slice the tomatoes. Peel and very thinly slice the medium onion and divide into rings.

Combine the breadcrumbs with the small onion, 1tsp vinegar and 25g (1oz) melted butter. Season with salt and pepper, spread the mixture over 4 of the fish fillets and sandwich with the other fillets (the skin sides of the fillets should be away from the centre).

Cook the pork or bacon without extra fat in a heavy frying pan over a medium heat until the fat runs from the meat. Add the large onion and cook over a low heat, stirring until the onion is soft and transparent. Add the tomatoes, season with salt and pepper, mix in the 2tbsp extra vinegar and cook for 5min. Spread this mixture in the bottom of a baking dish, top with the stuffed fish fillets and dot with the remaining 50g (2oz) of butter. Bake in a moderate oven 180°C (350°F, Gas mark 4) for 30min without covering. Serve at once.

Smothered fish and stuffed baked fish are dishes you will see time and time again on menus in everyday West Indian households. If you ask what fish are being cooked they often don't know or have local names which are incomprehensible to the Westerner; it depends what fish have been caught by local fishermen. The methods of cooking, however, remain simple but tasty, producing inexpensive nourishing meals in a relatively short time.

This dish gets its flavour from being steeped in lime juice before cooking.

Smothered Fish
(Serves 4–6)

900g (2lb) firm fleshed white fish fillets (use grouper, seabass, halibut, cod, hake, etc)
Salt and freshly ground black pepper
150ml (¼pt) water
2tbsp fresh lime or lemon juice
1tbsp white wine vinegar
1 large onion
2 cloves garlic
1 green pepper
1 egg
100g (4oz) fine fresh breadcrumbs
25g (1oz) butter
1tbsp sunflower oil
1 tin (425g [15oz]) tomatoes
2 bay leaves
Pinch cayenne pepper

Wash and dry the fish fillets and score them with diagonal cuts across the skin sides of the fillets. Season the fillets generously with salt and pepper. Combine the water and lime or lemon juice with the vinegar and pour the mixture over the fish. Leave to stand for 30min. Drain off the marinade and wipe the fillets dry with kitchen paper.

Peel and thinly slice the onion and divide into rings. Peel and finely chop the garlic. Remove the core and seeds from the pepper and thinly slice the flesh.

Dip the fish fillets in beaten egg and then coat them in breadcrumbs. Heat the butter with the oil in a large heavy frying pan. Add the fish fillets and cook over a moderately hot heat for 5–6min on each side until the fillets are golden brown. Drain the fillets on kitchen paper and keep them warm in a shallow baking dish. Add the onions and garlic to the juices in the pan and cook over a low heat, stirring every now and then to prevent sticking, until the onions are soft and transparent. Add the tomatoes, breaking them up with a fork, then add the pepper. Mix in the bay leaves, season with salt and cayenne pepper and bring to the boil. Boil, uncovered, stirring now and then for 15min. Add the fish to the sauce and heat through for 5min.

Serve the fish smothered with the sauce.

40

Sunday Salt Fish
(Serves 4)

675g (1½lb) salt fish
4 potatoes
2 large onions
4 rashers streaky bacon with the rinds removed
4 firm, unripe bananas
3 hardboiled eggs
1tbsp sunflower oil
Freshly ground black pepper
50g (2oz) butter

The use of salt fish in the West Indies shows just how versatile this product can be. This particular dish is traditionally served after church for a late breakfast on Sundays and has the merit of being able to be made the night before and heated up when the family gets back from church. I had it first one Sunday morning in Jamaica after having been to early morning service in the small coastal town of Falmouth. It was delicious and garnished with quarters of hardboiled eggs which were definitely very free range – their yolks were a magnificent orange golden colour.

Soak the fish in cold water overnight. Drain and rinse well in fresh cold water. Peel the potatoes, cut them into 0.5cm (¼in) thick slices and then into 0.5cm (¼in) wide matchstick strips. Peel and thinly slice the onions and divide into rings. Chop the bacon. Peel and halve the bananas and cut into 0.5cm (¼in) lengthwise slices. Quarter the hardboiled eggs.

Combine the fish and potatoes in a saucepan, cover with cold water, bring to the boil and simmer for about 15min until the fish and potatoes are tender. Drain the water, remove any skin and bones from the fish and flake the flesh.

Heat the oil in a frying pan, add the bacon and cook over a low heat until all the bacon fat has melted. Add the onions and cook over a low heat, stirring to prevent sticking, until the onion is soft and transparent. Add the fish, potatoes, and bananas, season with plenty of freshly ground black pepper and toss over a moderate heat until the ingredients are hot through. Add the butter, stir until the butter has melted, pile on to a serving dish and top with the hardboiled egg quarters.

Chicken Pie with Sweet Potato Crust

(Serves 6)

West Indian chickens are really tasty but rather scraggy creatures and before being topped by a pastry crust they are usually cooked in order to tenderize the flesh. In this dish vegetables are added to the chicken to supplement the meat, making a palatable but inexpensive main course.

1 small chicken
12 shallots or small onions
175g (6oz) carrots
175g (6oz) shelled peas
1 green pepper
40g (1½oz) butter
3tbsp flour
225ml (8fl oz) chicken stock
225ml (8fl oz) milk
Salt and fleshly ground black pepper
1tbsp finely chopped parsley
½tsp pepper sauce
100g (4oz) plain flour
Large pinch salt
1tsp baking powder
225g (8oz) cooked mashed sweet potato
100g (4oz) butter

Cut the flesh off the chicken into 1cm (½in) cubes (use the chicken carcass to make stock). Peel the onions and cook them in boiling water for 20min and drain well. Peel and dice the carrots and cook them in boiling water for 20min and drain well. Cook the peas and pepper for about 6min until just tender and drain well.

Melt 40g (1½oz) butter in a saucepan, add the chicken and cook over a low heat, stirring continually, until the chicken has turned opaque. Add 3tbsp flour and mix well. Gradually add the chicken stock and stir over a medium heat until the sauce is thick and smooth. Stir in the milk, season with salt and pepper. Mix in the parsley and pepper sauce and simmer gently for 20min. Add the onions, carrots, peas and peppers and turn into a pie dish. Leave to cool.

Sift 100g (4oz) of flour, a large pinch of salt and the baking powder into a bowl. Add the mashed potato and mix well. Add 100g (4oz) butter cut into small pieces and rub in with fingertips until the mixture forms into a stiff dough. Turn on to a well floured board and roll out lightly to the size of your pie dish. Damp the edges of the dish, press the dough firmly on to the edges of the dish and bake in a moderately hot oven 190°C (375°F, Gas mark 5) for 30min until the crust is golden brown.

Asapao (Chicken and Rice Stew)
(Serves 6–8)

1.1–1.4kg (2½–3lb) chicken
2 large onions
3 cloves garlic
1 large green pepper
1 large red pepper
3 rashers streaky bacon with the rinds removed
4 large ripe tomatoes
40g (1½oz) lard, dripping or 3tbsp sunflower oil
350g (12oz) long grain Patna rice
Salt and freshly ground black pepper
½tsp dried oregano
1.1*l* (2pt) chicken stock (or use water and stock cubes)
225g (8oz) fresh or frozen peas
4 small courgettes or zucchini

We in the West have for many years been spoilt for choice in what we eat and only recently have we had to look again at our menus and adjust them to inflation and a high cost of living. In this direction we have much to learn from those countries where stretching meat, poultry and fish ingredients is a way of life. In the West Indies chickens are usually scraggy and tough. Long, slow cooking, with rice, vegetables and other ingredients not only tenderizes the bird but also stretches the expensive protein ingredients to produce a cheap, satisfying dish.

Cut the legs and wings from the chicken, halve the carcass and, using a meat cleaver, cut into 5–7.5cm (2–3in) long pieces. Peel and coarsely chop the onions. Peel and finely chop the garlic. Remove the cores and seeds of the green and red peppers and chop the flesh. Chop the bacon.

Cover the tomatoes with boiling water, leave to stand for 3min, drain, slide off the skins and chop the flesh.

Heat the oil in a heavy casserole until a haze rises fom the oil. Add the chicken pieces a few at a time and brown them on all sides over a high heat. Remove the chicken with a slotted spoon. Lower the heat, add the onions, garlic, peppers and bacon and cook over a low heat, stirring to prevent sticking, until the onion is soft and transparent. Add the rice and stir well until the fat or oil has been absorbed. Season with salt and pepper, add the oregano and mix in the chicken stock and tomatoes. Bring to the boil, cover and simmer for about 30min until the rice is tender and most of the liquid has been absorbed. Add the peas and courgettes and continue to cook for a further 8–10min until the peas are tender. Check seasoning before serving.

One of the classic dishes of Jamaica is made from either pigeon peas or split green peas. The recipe varies from household to household and may be just the basic peas and rice or it may be augmented with flavourings provided by a small quantity of meat and other ingredients. This more elaborate version makes an inexpensive and nourishing supper dish.

Peas 'n' Rice
(Serves 4)

225g (8oz) split peas
Pinch bicarbonate of soda
225g (8oz) stewing beef (skirt is perfect for this dish)
2 bay leaves
Salt and freshly ground black pepper
350g (12oz) long grain Patna rice
1 onion
1 clove garlic
1 large tomato
25g (1oz) lard, dripping or 2tbsp sunflower oil
½tsp mixed herbs

Wash the peas, cover with cold water, add the bicarbonate of soda and leave to soak overnight. Cut the meat into thin slices and then into very thin matchstick strips. Combine the peas with the water in which they were soaked and the meat and bay leaves, bring to the boil, season with salt and pepper and simmer gently for about 1hr until the meat and peas are really tender and the water has been absorbed. Remove the bay leaves.

Wash the rice and drain well. Cover with enough water to come 2.5cm (1in) above the rice, season with salt, bring slowly to the boil and stir well. Cover tightly and cook over a low heat for 20min.

Peel and finely chop the onion. Peel and very finely chop the garlic. Cover the tomato with boiling water, leave to stand for 3min, drain and slide off the skin. Discard the tomato core and seeds and chop the flesh.

Heat the lard, dripping or oil in a large heavy pan, add the onion and garlic and cook over a low heat, stirring to prevent sticking until the onion is soft and transparent. Add the rice, peas and meat, stir in the herbs, season with more salt and pepper and toss over a high heat until the ingredients are hot through.

Stir well again, cover and leave to stand on the side of the stove for 10min, by which time the rice should be dry and fluffy.

Hopping John
(Serves 4)

225g (8oz) long grain or Patna rice
225g (8oz) split green peas
4 thin rashers streaky bacon
1 large onion
6 ripe firm tomatoes
1tbsp sunflower oil
Salt and freshly ground black pepper
Pinch allspice

'Hopping John' is the name given in the Bahamas to this excellent combination of rice, peas, bacon and tomatoes. It is good enough to serve by itself as a supper dish but may also be added to a dish of chicken, meat or fish.

Wash, then soak the rice in cold water for 20min. Drain well. Rinse the peas in cold water, combine them with lightly salted water in a saucepan, bring to the boil and simmer for about 40min until the peas are tender. Drain well.

Remove the bacon rinds and finely chop the rashers. Peel and finely chop the onion. Cover the tomatoes with boiling water for 3min, drain, slide off the skins, discard the cores and seeds and chop the flesh.

Heat the oil in a large heavy pan. Add the bacon and cook over a low heat, stirring, until the fat runs out. Add the onions and cook over a low heat, stirring, until the onion is soft and transparent. Add the tomatoes and stir for 3min. Add the peas, rice and 900ml (1½pt) of water. Season with salt, pepper and allspice, bring to the boil, cover and cook over a low heat for 20min. Remove the cover, stir the rice with 2 forks to get air into the grains, cover tightly again and leave to stand off the heat for 10min. Stir again so that the rice is fluffy before serving.

Fried Plantains
(Serves 4)

2 plantains
Groundnut or sunflower oil

It is often possible to buy plantains these days; fried as a vegetable they are delicious with pork or chicken. Plantains are large green bananalike fruits with a good flavour when cooked and a high vitamin content.

Remove the ends and cut each plantain in half across the middle. Using a small, sharp knife cut through the peel in four strips and gently ease the peel away from the firm flesh (with very green plantains it is easier to cut the skin right off the

Caribbean

flesh). Cut the plantains in 0.5cm (¼in) slightly diagonal slices.

Heat 0.5cm (¼in) oil in a large frying pan until a haze rises from the oil, add the plantain slices and cook over a high heat, turning every now and then, until they are tender and golden brown (about 8min). Remove the slices with a slotted spoon and drain on kitchen paper. Heat the oil again, add more oil to make up 0.5cm (¼in), and fry the plantain again until crisp. Drain again on kitchen paper.

Candied Sweet Potatoes
(Serves 4)

This is another sweet vegetable dish which crops up throughout the islands. Candied potatoes go especially well with boiled bacon or ham or with roast pork.

2 sweet potatoes
175ml (6fl oz) water
350g (12oz) sugar
25g (1oz) butter
1tbsp lime or lemon juice
Salt and freshly ground black pepper
Pinch allspice

Wash and boil the potatoes in lightly salted water until tender (about 30min) and leave to cool. Remove the skins and cut the potatoes into 1cm (½in) thick slices.

Combine the water with the sugar, butter and lime or lemon juice, a little salt and pepper and allspice, and heat in a saucepan until the sugar has melted. Add the potatoes and cook, stirring every now and then, until the syrup is thick and the potatoes are glazed (about 20min).

Banana Muffins

175g (6oz) plain flour
1tbsp cornflour
1tsp baking powder
½tsp bicarbonate of soda
Pinch salt
50g (2oz) butter
75g (3oz) castor sugar
1 egg
3 ripe bananas

West Indians draw their recipes from many corners of the world. There is a strong Latin American influence in many dishes; there are old favourites brought in by colonial settlers from England, Portugal and France and there are overtones of African cuisine. West Indians also have a strongly developed sweet tooth and teatime goodies are popular throughout the Caribbean with muffins, like this recipe which has its roots in America, being a typical favourite.

Sift the flour with the cornflour, baking powder, bicarbonate of soda and the salt. Beat the butter and sugar until light and fluffy. Beat the egg and add it, a little at a time, to the butter and sugar mixture, mixing well. Peel the bananas and mash them until smooth. Lightly fold in alternate tablespoonsful of the mashed bananas and flour mixture.

Half fill well greased patty tins and bake in a hot oven 200°C (400°F, Gas mark 6) for 20min until well risen and lightly golden brown. Serve hot with butter.

Rich Ginger Bread with Candied Peel

2tsp ground ginger
350g (12oz) plain flour
½tsp bicarbonate of soda
75g (3oz) chopped, mixed, candied peel
100g (4oz) butter
50g (2oz) soft brown sugar
225g (8oz) molasses
4tbsp milk
2 eggs

A popular gingerbread that is moist and keeps well.

Combine the ginger, flour, bicarbonate of soda and candied peel and mix well. Combine the butter, brown sugar and molasses in a saucepan and stir over a low heat until the sugar

Caribbean

has melted. Mix in the milk and leave to cool. Beat the eggs until smooth. Add the sugar mixture and the flour mixture and mix well.

Turn into a baking tin lined with Bakewell paper and bake in a very moderate oven 150°C (300°F, Gas mark 2) for 1¾hr until a skewer plunged into the cake will come out clean. Leave to cool in the pan, turn out, remove the paper and leave until completely cold.

Baked Pineapple
(Serves 4)

Most of the best West Indian puddings are based on fresh fruit. Often the fruit is cooked or flamed in rum making exotic, romantic sweets with which to end a meal.

1 medium, ripe pineapple
50g (2oz) castor sugar
Pinch ground allspice
4tbsp rum

Halve the pineapple lengthwise. Using a sharp, serrated knife, cut out the flesh of the pineapple leaving the shell intact. Discard the cores and chop the pineapple flesh retaining all the juice. Combine the pineapple, sugar and allspice in a bowl and mix well. Pile the pineapple back into the shell and bake in a moderately hot oven 190°C (375°F, Gas mark 5) for 30min. Heat the rum in a small saucepan, set it alight and pour it over the pineapple just before serving.

Preserved Fruit in Rum

I searched for years to find a really good recipe for preserving fruit so that one could buy fruit when it was inexpensive and keep it through the winter months. This is an excellent recipe from the West Indies and the joy of it is that you can strain off the liquor every now and then to use as the base for a good fruit punch.

2 tangerines, or 4 clementines
450g (1lb) firm strawberries
3 firm, ripe mangoes
1 small pineapple
1tbsp lime juice (or use lemon juice)
900g (2lb) soft brown sugar
900g (2lb) granulated sugar
5cm (2in) stick cinnamon
450ml (¾pt) rum

Peel the tangerines or clementines, divide into segments and remove all the white pith and pips. Hull the strawberries and cut them into thick slices. Thinly peel the mangoes and cut the flesh with a sharp knife into thin slices. Peel and core the pineapple and chop the flesh. Combine the fruit with the lime juice, sugars and cinnamon in a large ceramic bowl and stir lightly about once every 15min for 1hr. Pack the fruit in sterilized jars, pour over enough rum to cover to the top of the jars, seal tightly and leave in a cool dark place for at least 3 months before eating.

China

From China, that vast mystical continent, comes as many culinary secrets, subtleties and arts as there are edible ingredients. If the French purport to be the masters of cuisine, then the Chinese can surely claim to be its emperors and it is from their ancient knowledge and practical application to cooking that we can learn much today to help us produce better food for a lower cost.

Chinese food, whether on a low or high level is far more than just a matter of cooking and eating – it is a way of life, with recipes being handed down from mothers to daughters for generations with many being kept as closely guarded family secrets.

Not for the Chinese is the Victorian sentiment of not discussing food. For them, talking about food and the way it is cooked, the merits of 'aromatic crispy chicken' as served in the province of Kiangsi as opposed to that produced in the Spring Breeze Restaurant in Shanghai and the qualities of a soy sauce are what discussions about the weather are to us British. Even the everyday greeting consists of asking 'Have you taken rice?' 'Have you eaten?'

'To uphold the love of your dearest ones – serve them a good variety of food.' 'To expect your children to grow strong – give them appetite.' So said Confucius 2,500 years ago and for Chinese cooks these maxims still hold. The Chinese take pride in their family dishes; to entertain is to produce the best and most subtle marriage of flavours in order to outdo the Wongs next door and celebrations are occasions to cook recipes that, however humble the kitchen, are culinary masterpieces.

The Chinese love to eat. Good restaurants are always full because people would rather buy good food than anything else. Parties are screened from one another inside the restaurants, for you go to enjoy the food not the sight of others eating. They love snacks too and the quality of food sold by street vendors, with their little barrows from which savoury steamed buns, dumplings nestling in tiered bamboo baskets and rice or noodles are served, is often superb.

Breakfast in China is a relatively simple meal of *congee* rice with a little fish, other savoury ingredients or just soy sauce and perhaps peanut (groundnut) sauce. Snacks are often eaten throughout the day and the main meal comes in the evening with even the poorest family having at least 4 complementary dishes on the table.

To learn the basics of Chinese cooking you must look back through history. Most people were peasants, making what living they could from the soil and existing on little. Yet, unlike so many poor nations that developed a starch food as the staple diet (flavouring the starch but that is about all) the Chinese sought the most economical methods of cooking and used every available ingredient to provide contrast, texture and excitement in their dishes. Fuel was scarce, protein in the form of meat, fish and poultry was expensive and so they learnt how to cook it most economically, how to stretch food and how to produce necessary protein from the inexpensive soya bean.

Records show that by AD 500 the Chinese were using the *wok* as their basic cookery equipment. The wok, a large, round bottomed, frying pan which distributes a small amount of heat evenly around a large surface makes it possible to cook quickly and to save fuel. With a basic chopping knife, a small, razor sharp, cleaver, Chinese cooks perfected the art of chopping and thin slicing so that ingredients are stretched to the limit making it possible to perform miracles with a small amount of expensive protein and a few vegetables (cut a carrot into paper-thin slices and it looks like 3 carrots; cut a chicken breast into thin matchstick strips and it flavours a dish for 8 people). In their search for edible ingredients, taste and texture (the magic words of Chinese cooking) they found mushrooms with the flavour of meat, seeds and herbs that were richly aromatic, and pods and spices that together produce hot or sharp mixtures. Some items on an Eastern Chinese menu read like a list for a witch's brew (monkey's paws, dried fish lips, insect eggs, fish's stomach – the list is endless) but I am convinced that these now highly sought delicacies were, in fact, developed by Chinese housewives who would use anything edible to produce a good meal for their families.

Much of China suffers from severe winters and there are many pickled, salted, dried and preserved foods that Westerners have yet to discover. Fungi, in hundreds of varieties, are dried and used for flavouring; cabbage and other vegetables in vinegar and spices make both crisp and soft pickles, and meat is 'wind dried' or preserved in soy paste.

The *charouteris* of China is as varied as that of France with small highly spiced sausages, well flavoured meats and dried fruits, fish and vegetables of all kinds. Dried fish are especially important for flavouring (almost any fish however small or insignificant, salted and dried, make longlasting ingredients that look and smell unattractive but which, when added in small quantities can give a lift to meat, poultry or other fish dishes).

With a wok and a small charcoal or gas stove the Chinese can produce miracles in a matter of minutes. Using a steamer, over a relatively low heat, piled high with bamboo baskets through which steam rises and cooks different foods at different temperatures, energy is saved and several dishes are cooked together, cutting fuel costs yet again.

A Chinese cook uses the most humble herbs from the hedgerow, makes a rich broth from chicken feet and a banquet from duck's feet; she can give an insignificant dish of fried, wafer thin pork slices an elegance by combining the meat with quickly cooked shredded spinach and a sophistication by flavouring it with an oyster sauce but she insists on the *best* ingredients for, as the philosopher Yuen Mai declared, 'If an article of food is in itself bad, the greatest chef of all ages could not cook a flavour into it.'

Nothing is thrown away; the roots as well as the stalks of many vegetables are used and so are their leaves; scraps go into stock. Offal is venerated rather than being disdained and even cock's combs are transformed into a sought after delicacy. The smallest fish and crustaceans are salted, dried and ground into highly flavoured pastes and pig's fat is considered a culinary 'treasure'.

If the actual cooking process of many Chinese dishes is quick, the preparation of those dishes may be a fairly long and skilled affair. Vegetables are frequently cut in 3 or more different ways to give a variation in appearance and texture (carrots for instance, in one stir-fried dish, may not only be thinly sliced across the grain but also cut into matchstick lengths and sliced lengthways). The way fish and meat are cut alters the final flavour, texture and appearance of the dish and that indispensable Chinese cleaver comes into its own when a whole cooked chicken has to be chopped into small pieces, bones and all.

Mr. and Mrs. Poon who run the excellent Poon's Restaurant in Covent Garden have a glassed-in kitchen in the centre of the restaurant so that you can watch the chefs slicing and chopping ingredients at lightning speed and then tossing the food in giant sized woks over flaming gas jets – a strange, exciting sight. As well as the restaurant the Poons run cookery lessons for would be Chinese cooks and Cynthia Poon explained to me that they teach their students to *know* about Chinese food, to understand it and *then* to learn how to cook it.

'Cutting and preparation is very important. When you know how to do that then you can go into the art of stir-frying, the effect of heat, steaming, simmering and slow cooking.' I've learnt and I find it a most therapeutic and satisfactory procedure. I take pride in the thinness and evenness of my diagonally sliced celery stalks, my butterfly spread prawns and the delicacy of my shredded cabbage.

Cynthia Poon also pointed out how healthy the Chinese diet can be and when I complimented her on her beautiful, unlined and youthful skin, she said that was entirely due to diet. 'We eat a lot of vegetables and enough protein but not too much; we use little sugar and don't take alcohol – but we drink plenty of tea.

'I drink tea all day in lots of different flavours; green teas and red teas, jasmin tea, orange flavoured tea and one I like very much made from dried roses.'

In their restaurant the Poons serve exotics such as shark's fin and bird's nest soups but they also have a wonderful range of the more everyday Chinese dishes and some delicious countrystyle wind dried meats and sausages, cut into the thinnest slices and served at the start of a meal with the classic plum sauce and the inevitable 'dipping sauces' of chilli and soy.

The cooking of China has, like the cooking of India, been misused in the West. It is *not* the cuisine of '*chop suey*' (an invention of a Chinese–American) nor does it leave you feeling hungry after an hour; neither is it a collection of ingredients thrown together at random. On all levels the cuisine of China is an art, a joy and a ritual that makes each dish something cooked from the heart, with love.

Crab and Sweetcorn Soup
(Serves 4)

325g (11oz) tin whole kernel sweetcorn
1*l* (1¾pt) chicken stock
2tbsp medium sherry
2.5cm (1in) fresh ginger root, finely chopped
2tsp sesame oil
2tsp cornflour
100g (4oz) crabmeat
Salt and white pepper
4 spring onions, finely chopped

Drain the sweetcorn. Put the stock into a large saucepan, and bring to the boil. Add the sweetcorn, sherry, ginger and sesame oil and simmer for about 10min.

Mix the cornflour with a little water and slowly add to the soup, stirring, until the soup comes back to the boil. Add the crabmeat, and simmer for about 5min. Season with salt and pepper. Ladle into individual bowls and garnish with a sprinkling of finely chopped spring onion.

Steamed Seabass
(Serves 4)

1 whole seabass (about 1kg [2¼lb] in weight)
5cm (2in) fresh ginger root
Pinch of 5-spice powder
2tsp sesame oil
6 spring onions for garnish

A simply delicious dish, it should be presented on a large platter, then all help themselves to tasty little morsels using chopsticks.

Descale the bass under cold running water, and remove the large fin.

Peel and finely chop the fresh ginger root and mix it with the 5-spice powder and the sesame oil, then spread the mixture over the fish and in the body cavity. Lay the fish on a trivet in a wok (or you can use a steamer), adding water to just below the trivet; bring the water to boiling and vigorously steam the fish for about 15min only, until just tender. Finely chop the spring onions and sprinkle over the fish immediately before serving.

Prawn Toasts
(Serves 5–6)

These are usually served as part of a mixture of different first courses but my idea in calling on the best recipes from around the world is to adapt them to one's own particular use. These crisp toasts are gorgeous and I find them a happy first course to serve with a fairly strong homemade tomato sauce. Try them!

4cm (1½in) fresh green ginger root
1 spring onion
4 water chestnuts
450g (1lb) peeled prawns
2tsp very finely chopped parsley
1½tsp sherry or vodka
1½tsp cornflour
1 egg white
Salt and white pepper
Pinch cayenne pepper
4tbsp sesame seeds
6–7 slices white bread with crusts removed
Oil for frying

Peel and very finely chop or mince the ginger root. Trim and very finely chop or mince the onion. Very finely chop or mince the water chestnuts, mince the prawns to a paste. Combine the prawns, ginger, onion, sherry, cornflour, egg white and parsley, season with salt, pepper and a little cayenne and mix well (all this can be done in a food processor).

Spread the prawn mixture on the bread pressing it down generously and firmly. Cut each piece of bread into 3 fingers. Sprinkle over the sesame seeds and press them firmly into the paste.

Heat 0.5cm (¼in) oil in a frying pan until smoking. Add the prawn toasts (do not overcrowd), covered side down, until crisp and golden brown, turn over and continue to fry the bread slices until crisp and golden brown on the other side. Drain on kitchen paper and keep warm while frying the rest of the bread. Serve very hot.

Stir Fried Chicken and Vegetables with Almonds
(Serves 4)

Serve with fluffy boiled rice.

350g (12oz) chicken breast, skinned and boned
1 clove garlic
2.5cm (1in) fresh ginger root
1 onion
2 carrots
1 stick celery
1 green pepper
4 spring onions
1tbsp soy sauce
1tsp chilli sauce
1tbsp medium sherry
1tsp cornflour
3tbsp sunflower oil
50g (2oz) flaked almonds
150ml (¼pt) chicken stock

Using a sharp knife cut the chicken breasts into thin slivers. Peel and finely chop the garlic and root ginger. Peel and slice the onion and divide into rings. Peel the carrots and cut into thin matchstick strips. Chop the celery. Remove the core and seeds from the pepper and cut half into small squares and the other half into strips. Chop the spring onions. Mix the soy sauce, chilli sauce and sherry together with the cornflour in a small bowl.

Heat the oil in a wok and fry the chicken slivers, a few at a time, stirring all the time, until the flesh just turns opaque, remove with a slotted spoon onto kitchen paper until all the chicken is cooked.

Add the garlic and ginger to the wok and cook for about 1 min, add the onion and cook, stirring all the time, for 2min, add the carrot, celery and pepper, continuing to stir for 1min. Return the chicken slivers to the wok and mix in with the vegetables. Add the flaked almonds, stirring well. Add the soy sauce mixture and pour in the stock and mix well. Lower the heat under the wok and allow to simmer for about 5min. Pour into a serving dish and scatter the spring onions, roughly chopped, over the top.

Oyster sauce may be bought in Chinese foodshops or good supermarkets.

Beef with Oyster Sauce
(Serves 6)

350g (12oz) frying steak
½tsp salt
½tsp black pepper
25g (1oz) soft dark brown sugar
1tbsp light soy sauce
2tbsp dry sherry
1tbsp cornflour
1 egg
2.5cm (1in) fresh ginger root
10 spring onions
4tbsp sunflower oil
6tbsp oyster sauce

Using a very sharp knife cut the beef into thin waferlike strips. Mix the salt, pepper, sugar, soy sauce, sherry, cornflour and egg together, and pour over the beef strips. Leave to marinate for at least 1hr. Peel and finely chop the ginger root. Trim and chop the spring onions.

Heat the oil in a wok until really hot and stir-fry the ginger and onions for 1min. Add the beef and the marinade and fry for about 5min over a high heat, stirring all the time. Add the oyster sauce, mixing well and serve at once.

Shredded Beef with Green Peppers
(Serves 4)

450g (1lb) rump steak
1 medium onion
1 clove garlic
2.5cm (1in) fresh ginger root
2 green peppers
2tbsp sunflower oil
2tsp cornflour
2tsp soft brown sugar
2tbsp heavy soy sauce
300ml (½pt) chicken stock

Using a very sharp knife trim any fat from the steak and cut the lean meat into wafer thin strips. Peel and thinly slice half the onion, cut the other half of the onion into small squares. Peel and finely chop the garlic and ginger root. Deseed and thinly slice 1 pepper, deseed and cut into neat squares the remaining pepper.

In a wok or large frying pan, heat the oil and cook the garlic and ginger root until golden, add the slivers of steak, and cook, stirring all the time for 4–5min. Add the peppers, and cook, again stirring all the time, for a further 3min. Mix the cornflour, sugar and soy sauce together and mix into the chicken stock, then pour the sauce over the beef and peppers and stir to mix well. Simmer over a low heat for a further 5min. Serve with fluffy boiled rice.

Barbecued Spare Ribs
(Serves 8–10)

2.5cm (1in) fresh ginger root
3tbsp heavy soy sauce
1tbsp medium dry sherry
1tbsp vinegar
2tsp soft brown sugar
2 cloves garlic
Freshly ground black pepper
1.5kg (3lb) spare ribs

One of the most popular barbecue foods for my family and friends – be they 7 or 70, they eat these with great gusto.

Peel and finely chop the ginger root. Combine the soy sauce, sherry, vinegar, chopped ginger, sugar and the peeled cloves of garlic in a food processor, season with freshly ground black pepper and process until the garlic is finely chopped and all the ingredients are well mixed. Arrange the spare ribs on shallow dishes and brush all over with the marinade mixture, and allow to stand for at least 2hr.

Once the barbecue is red hot, and the coals are starting to turn white, cook the spare ribs, turning frequently, and basting with any leftover marinade, until they are a dark golden brown and cooked through.

Cantonese Sweet and Sour Pork
(Serves 6)

1kg (2¼lb) belly pork
1tbsp cornflour
Oil for deep frying
1 medium onion
1 red pepper
1 green pepper
1 carrot
1 stick celery
2tbsp sunflower oil

For the sauce
2tbsp dry sherry
2tbsp white wine vinegar
1tbsp cornflour
4tbsp chicken stock
2tbsp soft brown sugar
2tbsp orange juice
2tbsp pineapple juice
2tbsp soy sauce
2tbsp tomato purée

Cut the belly pork into small cubes and pile onto a large plate, and sprinkle all over with the cornflour, coating well. Heat the oil until a haze rises then deep fry the pork, in batches, for about 5min, until cooked; remove each batch with a slotted spoon and keep warm.

In a food processor or blender mix all the sauce ingredients together until well blended. Peel and roughly chop the onion. Deseed the peppers and cut into strips. Peel and cut the carrot into thin diagonal slices. Cut the celery into thin matchstick strips.

Heat the oil in a wok, or large frying pan, until really hot, add the onions and carrot and stir-fry for 1min, add the peppers and celery and fry for a further 3min, stirring all the time. Add the pork, and stir until the pork is heated through, pour over the sauce (if it appears too thick add a little water), and mix in well. Pile onto a dish and serve with fluffy boiled rice.

Special Fried Rice
(Serves 4–6)

1 small onion
50g (2oz) mushrooms
1 clove garlic
2.5cm (1in) fresh ginger root
½ red pepper
4 eggs
1tsp salt
3tbsp sunflower oil
450g (1lb) cooked rice
175g (6oz) shrimps
2tbsp light soy sauce
1tbsp medium sherry

Thinly slice the onion and mushrooms. Peel and finely chop the garlic and ginger root. Dice the red pepper. Beat the eggs with the salt.

Heat the oil in a wok and add the onion, garlic, ginger and red pepper and stir-fry for 1min, add the sliced mushrooms and cook for a further minute.

Push the vegetables to one side of the wok and pour in the eggs, cook for approximately 2min, or until the eggs are just starting to set and then stir in the rice, mixing well to break up the egg, add the shrimps and mix well, stirring all the time. Mix the soy sauce with the sherry and pour over the rice mixture, stirring until all the ingredients are well coated. Arrange on a warm platter to accompany your main dish.

China

Honeyed Pears
(Serves 4)

4 ripe but firm pears
50g (2oz) soft brown sugar
4tbsp clear honey
1tbsp sesame seeds

Peel and core the pears and stand in a steamer, and steam gently (about 25min) until tender, but still firm. Sprinkle the brown sugar over the pears and continue to steam for 10min. Remove with a slotted spoon and arrange in a shallow dish. Mix the honey and sesame seeds together and spoon over the pears. Chill well before serving.

Watermelon Bowl

(Serves 6)

1 medium watermelon
2 small oranges
2 peaches or nectarines
100g (4oz) preserved kumquats
1×225g (8oz) tin lychees
1 ripe, firm, pear
1 apple
100g (4oz) grapes

Cut off the top of the melon and scoop out the flesh, discarding the seeds. Cut the rind and pith from the oranges, then cut into segments between the skin. Cover the peaches with boiling water, stand for 1min, drain and slide off the skins. Cut in half and remove the stone, then dice the flesh. Drain the lychees. Peel the pear and remove the core, and cut into thin slices. Peel, core and chop the apple. Deseed the grapes.

Combine all the fruits together, mix lightly and then pile into the melon case. Chill well before serving.

England

So-called food experts have for years bemoaned English cookery as dull and uninteresting. In this green and pleasant land the variety of regional dishes and the plenteous fresh ingredients seem to me to be infinite. What is so exciting is that within a relatively small area, compared with many other countries, regional specialities abound.

Certainly there are dishes such as steak and kidney pie, the roast beef of old England, puddings, pies, stews and casseroles that have a nationwide appeal, but the variations in ingredients that, for example, the cook in the South may use in comparison with her Northcountry counterpart in Cumbria can make eating English food a memorable experience.

Fortunately in recent years traditional foods are gaining in popularity as we abandon the belief that foreign foods just have to be better than our own. Whilst knowing that you can't make a silk purse out of a sow's ear, the average family cook realises that excellent dishes can be produced using good quality, albeit inexpensive, cheaper cuts of meat and the more unusual and less expensive species of fish, mackerel being a good example.

Outside the big industrial cities the cookery of the Northern counties reflects the people and the landscape, hearty, economical and nourishing. Here is some of the most beautiful scenery in England, with the Cheviots, where hundreds of sheep dot the sweeping slopes, contrasting dramatically with the lushness of the Lake District where my husband was raised. The Yorkshire Dales are where one of England's most universally known and cooked dishes, the Yorkshire pudding, originated. It is now eaten as the traditional accompaniment to roast beef, but was intended as a first course to blunt the appetite so that less meat would be required. The city of York is famed for its hams, England's best so a Yorkshireman will tell you.

Across to the northwest lies Lancashire and Morecambe Bay; it is here that fishing boats trawl for those small

Morecambe Bay shrimps, so good when potted. To watch practised shrimp pickers is quite an experience, and you may well find that your eyes have a job keeping up with their fingers! My husband's Aunt Freda, who lives in Lancaster, is an accomplished picker, and there is nothing more pleasurable than to receive a pot of her Morecambe Bay shrimps, seasoned lightly with salt and pepper, potted in butter and eaten with thin slices of buttered brown bread and a crisp salad, they are deliciously 'moreish'.

From Worcester comes one of the most famous of cooking aids. Worcester Sauce, invented by Messrs Lea and Perrin some 150 years ago, is to be found in most kitchens, and adds that vital pep to stews, casseroles and soups.

The South West, where I have lived for some sixteen years, provides a rich source of quality ingredients for the cook. With the mildest climate in England, its luxuriant green pastures and fertile soil give an unending supply of milk, crusty topped clotted cream, plump fruits and vegetables including the new potatoes which in early June appear on every Westcountry table. South Devon beef is renowned for its excellence, both in flavour and texture and sheep and cattle graze on the vast areas of moorland throughout the South West. The coastline yields some of the best fish and shellfish in Britain.

One Saturday morning I left my home in southeast Cornwall to drive to Newlyn, one of the largest English landing ports, to watch the catches being laid out and sold in the market. Countless boxes of fish were to be seen; Dover and lemon soles, and the less known, but cheaper, megrim; boxes of coiled conger eel and barrels of red gurnard, hake and cod, and monkfish tails. Sadly, most of this fish goes to Europe and not onto English dining tables. The English housewife fails miserably in this respect and the fishing industry has as a result declined in recent years. Until the housewife is willing to learn the best ways to prepare and cook fish, she is missing out on the most natural and unadulterated food available. I took a large coolbox to Newlyn, and returned with it packed tightly with fish – a veritable treasure chest.

Today, supermarkets and shopping centres crammed with every conceivable convenience food, vacuum packs of vegetables and fruit, and cubed and trimmed meats, not only save the cook time and energy but they seem to have killed the desire to experiment and create new dishes.

It is reassuring to see some housewives bustling about the weekly markets buying their supplies of free range eggs and selecting vegetables from stalls run by local farmers or market gardeners. Other stalls offer home-baked pasties and pies and fat plump sausages, not mass produced, but made by local butchers using age-old secret recipes.

The country housewife still produces traditional foods for her family; she is becoming more aware of healthy eating; she takes care in her use of fats, bakes bread from wholemeal flour, and scorns the use of processed foods. More people now grow their own fruit and vegetables, experiencing the satisfaction of watching crops grow for harvesting at the right time to use not only in tested, traditional dishes, but to create new and enjoyable dishes.

Farmhouse Vegetable Soup
(Serves 6)

2 medium carrots
2 large onions
3 sticks celery
1 small cauliflower
50g (2oz) butter
1l (1¾pt) good chicken stock
Salt and freshly ground black pepper
125ml (4fl oz) cream or natural yoghurt

With the abundance of seasonal vegetables all year round, soups are popular for a quick farm lunch, served with chunks of homemade crusty bread.

Peel and finely chop the carrots and onions. Chop the celery and break the cauliflower into florets.

Heat the butter in a heavy bottomed saucepan and add the vegetables, cook over a low heat, stirring all the time, until the vegetables have softened. Add the stock, season with salt and freshly ground black pepper, bring to the boil and then simmer until the vegetables have cooked. Strain the vegetables, reserving the cooking liquid, and purée the vegetables (ensure that some texture is left in the vegetables, so do not overprocess). Return the cooking liquid and vegetable purée to a clean saucepan, and test for seasoning. Stir in the cream or yoghurt and reheat – do not boil.

Scalloped Fish Pie
(Serves 4)

675g (1½lb) white fish fillets, skinned (cod, coley,
haddock or hake)
300ml (½pt) milk
2 bay leaves
1tbsp lemon juice
Salt and pepper
1 small onion
100g (4oz) mushrooms
40g (1½oz) butter
25g (1oz) flour
3tbsp natural yoghurt
675g (1½lb) creamed potatoes

Poach the fish gently in the milk with the bay leaves and
lemon juice, seasoned with salt and pepper, for about 10min,
or until the fish is just tender. Drain off the cooking liquid and
make up to 300ml (½pt) again with milk or water if
necessary. Discard the bay leaves. Roughly flake the fish. Peel
and finely chop the onion, wipe and roughly chop the
mushrooms.

Melt the butter in a saucepan and cook the onion over a
low heat until soft and transparent, add the mushrooms and
cook for a further 2min. Stir in the flour over a medium high
heat and cook for 1min. Gradually add the reserve liquid,
stirring all the time until the sauce comes to the boil and is
thick and smooth. Take off the heat and stir in the yoghurt
and flaked fish.

Turn into a shallow ovenproof dish and top with the
creamed potatoes. Cook at 200°C (400°F, Gas mark 6) for
about 30min until piping hot and the potato is browned.

Mussels with Cheese and Parsley Topping
(Serves 4–6)

England

2.5kg (3½lb) mussels
100g (4oz) cottage cheese
50g (2oz) low-fat cream cheese
2tbsp natural yoghurt
2 cloves garlic
2tbsp finely chopped fresh parsley
Salt and freshly ground black pepper
50g (2oz) fresh white breadcrumbs
1tbsp finely grated Cheddar cheese

Mussels are one of the great specialities of the South West, and friends of mine make weekend treks along the Cornish coast to collect buckets of this tasty shellfish.

Scrub and wash the mussels, removing the beard. Put into a large saucepan, pour over about 450ml (¾pt) boiling water, cover the pan and boil for about 7–8min until the mussels have opened, discard any that remain closed. Break off the lid of each mussel at the hinge and arrange the bottom halves in a large shallow ovenproof dish.

In a food processor or electric blender combine the cottage and cream cheese, together with the yoghurt, crushed garlic and chopped parsley; season with freshly ground black pepper and a little salt and process until smooth.

Using a teaspoon put a dollop of the mixture on top of each mussel. Mix the breadcrumbs and Cheddar cheese together and sprinkle a little on each mussel.

Preheat the oven to 230°C (450°F, Gas mark 8) and cook the mussels until brown and the topping starts to bubble. Serve immediately with fingers of buttered toast.

Pan Haggerty
(Serves 4)

450g (1lb) potatoes
2 medium onions
175g (6oz) streaky bacon
100g (4oz) grated Cheddar cheese
Salt and freshly ground black pepper

Peel and thinly slice the potatoes and onions. Derind the bacon and chop the rashers. Cook the bacon, without fat, until all the fat runs out of the bacon. Remove the bacon with a slotted spoon.

Remove the pan from the heat and put a layer of potatoes in the bottom of the pan, followed by a layer of onions, the chopped bacon, a sprinkling of grated cheese and a good seasoning of freshly ground black pepper and a little salt. Continue layering up the pan, finishing with a layer of potatoes.

Cover the pan and fry gently, when nearly cooked (about 25min) remove the lid and brown under the grill.

Westcountry Herb Dumplings
(Makes about 12)

These are excellent popped on top of a savoury stew or casserole and cooked until light and fluffy.

75g (3oz) fresh white breadcrumbs
75g (3oz) self raising flour
50g (2oz) shredded suet
1 small onion
1tbsp finely chopped fresh parsley
½tsp dried mixed herbs
Salt and freshly ground black pepper

Put the breadcrumbs, flour and shredded suet into a mixing bowl and mix well. Peel and very finely chop the onion and add to the bowl together with the herbs, seasoning well with salt and freshly ground black pepper. Add sufficient water to make into a soft dough. With lightly floured hands form into about 12 balls and place on the top of the stew or casserole. They will take about 20min to cook.

Cornish Pasties
(To make 4)

50g (2oz) lard
50g (2oz) margarine
275g (10oz) plain flour
Pinch of salt
450g (1lb) beef skirt
1 large onion
3 medium potatoes, peeled
1 small swede
Salt and freshly ground black pepper
1 egg, beaten

I debated whether to include a recipe for this pastry-wrapped Westcountry speciality, as living in Cornwall, I risk the likelihood of hordes of Cornish ladies descending on me, brandishing their rolling pins, and telling me that their way is the *only* way to make a proper Cornish pasty. At the foot of the page is a fascinating little anonymous jingle I came across.

Using your fingertips rub the fats into the flour, mixing in a good pinch of salt, until the mixture resembles coarse breadcrumbs. Use sufficient cold water to form a firm, though pliable dough.

Trim any excess fat and sinew from the beef skirt, and dice it in small pieces. Peel and finely chop the onion. Cut the potatoes into small dice. Peel the swede and cut into small dice. In a mixing bowl combine the meat and chopped vegetables and mix well seasoning with salt and freshly ground black pepper.

Roll out the pastry on a well floured board, and cut out 4 circles, using a tea or breakfast plate. Divide the meat mixture evenly between the pastry rounds, moisten the pastry edges with water and draw the opposite sides of each round together over the top of the filling, pinching the edges together to form a good seal. Flute by pinching between finger and thumb, and then folding over the edge to form a double seal. Place on a baking sheet and brush with beaten egg. Bake in a preheated oven at 200°C (400°F, Gas mark 6) for 10min. Then put the pasties right at the bottom of the oven and allow to cook for a further 40min (cover the pasties with greaseproof paper if they start to brown too much).

Pastry rolled out like a plate
Piled with Turmut, tates and mate,
Doubled up and baked like fate,
That's a Cornish pasty.

71

Lancashire Hot-Pot
(Serves 4)

1kg (2.2lb) best end of neck lamb chops
2 lamb kidneys
1 large onion
450g (1lb) potatoes
Salt and freshly ground black pepper
600ml (1pt) stock
25g (1oz) butter

Trim any excess fat from the chops and skin, core and slice the kidneys. Peel and thinly slice the onion. Peel and thickly slice the potatoes.

Place a layer of chops in the bottom of a large heavy ovenproof casserole (I particularly like to use a cast iron one for this dish), cover with some of the sliced kidney, then sliced onion, and top with a layer of the potatoes, seasoning each layer with salt and freshly ground black pepper. Continue layering up the dish, finishing with a layer of potatoes. Pour over the stock, dot the potatoes with butter, cover and cook in a preheated oven at 170°C (325°F, Gas mark 3) for 2hr, remove the lid for the last 30min of the cooking time to brown the potatoes.

Buckinghamshire Clanger
(Serves 4)

225g (8oz) self raising flour
75g (3oz) shredded suet
Pinch of salt
225g (8oz) streaky bacon or bacon pieces
1 medium cooking apple
1 medium onion
1 large potato

Mix the flour, suet and salt together and mix into a firm dough with a little water. Roll out the pastry on a well floured board into a rectangle about 30cm (12in) by 25cm (10in); the pastry should be quite thick.

Remove the rind from the bacon and chop finely. Peel, core and dice the apple. Peel and chop the onion. Peel the potato and put through a coarse grater.

Mix the bacon, onion, apple and potato together and spread over the pastry, leaving a 5cm (2in) border around the edge. Roll the pastry up like a Swiss roll and seal the edge with water, fold over the ends and seal well.

Using a double thickness of greaseproof paper, the inner one lightly greased, wrap your 'clanger' neatly. Then wrap in foil, sealing well. Steam for 1½–2hr. Serve with seasonal green vegetables.

Steak and Kidney Pudding
(Serves 6)

100g (4oz) shredded suet
225g (8oz) self raising flour
Salt and freshly ground black pepper
675g (1½lb) chuck steak, trimmed
2 lamb kidneys
50g (2oz) plain flour
150ml (¼pt) beef stock
150ml (¼pt) red wine or brown ale

Traditionally the pudding should be served from the basin and not turned out. Serve with creamed mashed potatoes and Brussels sprouts.

Put the suet and flour into a mixing bowl, season with salt and freshly ground black pepper. Use sufficient water to mix to form a firm dough. On a well floured board roll out the pastry, and use ⅔ to line a lightly greased 1l (1¾pt) pudding basin.

Cut the steak into 2.5cm (1in) cubes, and trim the kidneys and slice thinly. Season the plain flour generously with freshly ground black pepper and a little salt. Toss the steak and then the sliced kidneys in layers, so that the kidney is evenly distributed. Mix the stock and wine or ale together and pour over the meat mixture so that the level of liquid is no more than ¾ of the way up the basin.

Use the remaining pastry to form a lid, moistening the pastry edges with water and sealing well. Cover securely with a double thickness of greaseproof paper, pleated in the middle to allow for expansion, and secure firmly with string.

Lower into boiling water and cook for 4hr, ensuring that the saucepan never boils dry; top up with hot water as necessary.

Pheasant shooting in season is popular in many regions of the British Isles. This is an ideal way to use a brace of older birds that would not be tender enough for roasting.

Pheasant Pie
(Serves 8–10)

A brace of pheasant, plucked, drawn and trussed
2tbsp oil
Salt and freshly ground black pepper
4 large leeks
8 rashers of streaky bacon, derinded
1 large cooking apple
50g (2oz) butter
50g (2oz) flour
600ml (1pt) chicken stock
½tsp dried thyme
4 juniper berries, crushed
2tbsp calvados
375g (13oz) pkt frozen puff pastry, thawed
1 small egg, beaten

Brush the pheasant with the oil, season with freshly ground black pepper and roast at 190°C (375°F, Gas mark 5) for 45min. Remove from the oven and allow to cool. Cut all the meat from the bones and cut into bite-sized pieces.

Trim and clean the leeks and slice thinly. Halve each bacon rasher and shape into small rolls. Peel and core the apple and cut into small dice.

Spread the leeks in a large baking dish and cover with the pheasant pieces, arrange the bacon rolls evenly around and then sprinkle over the diced apple.

Melt the butter in a saucepan, and when it just starts to foam stir in the flour, over a medium high heat. Gradually add the stock, stirring all the time until the sauce comes to the boil and is thick and smooth. Mix in the thyme, crushed juniper berries and the calvados and stir well, pour over the other ingredients, using a fork to lift the layers to ensure the sauce is evenly distributed throughout the dish.

On a well floured board roll out the pastry, quite thinly, and use to cover the pie (you may well find that you will need to use a pie funnel in the pie centre to support the pastry). Use any pastry trimmings to decorate the top of the pie, and then brush with beaten egg. Bake at 190°C (375°F, Gas mark 5) for about 45min.

Serve with game chips (see next recipe), broccoli spears and buttered carrots.

Game Chips

450g (1lb) potatoes
Oil for deep frying
Seasalt

Customarily served with roast game, they are also delicious served with drinks.

Peel the potatoes and slice very thinly (a food processor is excellent for this). Soak the slices in cold water for 1hr to remove excess starch. Drain and pat dry on kitchen paper.

Heat the oil in a deep fat fryer until a cube of bread dropped in turns golden brown and rises to the surface in 30sec. Cook the potato slices in batches, making sure you do not overcrowd the pan. When the potatoes turn a light golden brown lift them from the pan for a short while and then lower them again, when they will quickly turn a golden brown. Remove and allow to drain on crumpled kitchen paper, transfer to a warmed serving dish and keep in a moderately hot oven (this way they will retain their crispness). When all the chips are cooked sprinkle with a little seasalt.

Christine's Cornish Treacle Tart
(Serves 6–8)

225g (8oz) plain flour
Pinch of salt
100g (4oz) soft margarine
200ml (6fl oz) golden syrup
Grated rind and juice of a small lemon
75g (3oz) fresh breadcrumbs

Christine is cook for a well known Cornish family; cakes and desserts are her speciality, and this is one of them.

Serve with clotted cream, or whipped cream.

Sift the flour and salt into a mixing bowl. Cut the margarine into small pieces and rub into the flour with the fingertips until the mixture resembles coarse breadcrumbs. Add enough cold water to form into a soft, but firm, dough. Roll out on a well floured board and use to line a 25cm (10in) flan dish.

Heat the syrup in a saucepan until warm and runny, mix in the lemon rind and juice and the breadcrumbs, mix well and pour into the pastry case.

Use any pastry trimmings to make lattice strips to decorate the top of the tart, brush with a little milk. Then bake in a preheated oven 190°C (375°F, Gas mark 5) for 35–40min.

Summer Pudding
(Serves 6)

A firm family favourite that is repeated year after year when the soft fruits come into season.

675g (1½lb) mixed soft fruit (raspberries, blackcurrants, redcurrants etc)
50ml (2fl oz) water
225g (8oz) granulated sugar
8–10 slices of white bread

Pick over the fruit removing any stalks, and wash if necessary. Put the fruit, water and sugar into a saucepan and cook over a medium heat until the fruits are soft.

Cut the crusts off the bread, and line a 1*l* (1¾pt) pudding basin with the slices, reserving some for the top; pour in the fruit and juices while still warm, then use the remaining bread to make a lid, trimming the edges neatly with kitchen scissors. Put a saucer or teaplate on top of the pudding and weight down, either with metal weights or a few tinned products. Refrigerate overnight.

If you wish, you can decorate the pudding with whipped cream.

To serve, loosen around the edges of the pudding with a palette knife and turn onto a serving dish.

Spotted Dick
(Serves 4)

I doubt if there is a person in the whole of England who has not at some time or another enjoyed this traditional childhood sweet; lavishly topped with custard it is a real winter-time pudding.

75g (3oz) self-raising flour
Pinch of salt
75g (3oz) fresh white breadcrumbs
75g (3oz) shredded suet
50g (2oz) caster sugar
150g (6oz) mixed fruit
60ml (4tbsp) milk

Mix all the dry ingredients together in a large mixing bowl. Make a well in the centre and pour in the milk. With a wooden spoon mix well and form into a fairly soft dough (add more milk if necessary).

Form into a long roll on a well-floured board. Wrap in a double thickness of lightly greased greaseproof paper, and then in a double thickness of foil, ensuring that the 'parcel' is well sealed. Steam for 1½–2hr. Serve with custard.

Light Fruit Cake

175g (6oz) butter
175g (6oz) castor sugar
3 large eggs
100g (4oz) plain flour
150g (5oz) self raising flour
225g (8oz) mixed dried fruit
50g (2oz) glacé cherries
Grated rind and juice of ½ lemon
25g (1oz) walnut halves
13g (½oz) demerara sugar

Grease and line a 18cm (7in) cake tin. Cream the butter and sugar until light and fluffy. Beat the eggs into the mixture one at a time.

Combine the flours, dried fruit and cherries and fold into the mixture alternately with the lemon rind and juice. Spoon into the greased tin and top with the walnut halves, sprinkle over the demerara sugar and bake at 170°C (325°F, Gas mark 3) for 1½–1¾hr. The cake will be ready when it is firm to touch.

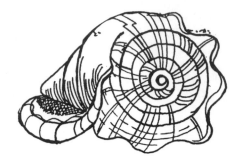

Fiji

I suppose the first shock to anyone visiting Fiji is to see men wearing skirts or sulus rather than trousers. The Fijians are an extremely handsome race, tall and muscular; they are also a happy people, with a ready smile. Fiji is not, as one imagines, one island; it is a group of more than 300 islands scattered across some 250,000 sq miles of the Pacific Ocean, with a land mass of about 7,000 sq miles.

I went to Fiji in 1974, landing at Nadi (pronounced *Nandi*) Airport on the dry side of the main island Viti Levu. After some 24 hours flying from London, I was exhausted and found myself in a tiny airport miles from Suva, where I was headed, and was told that I would then have to board another aircraft, this time a 12-seater, for my journey to the capital. The heat, and I can recall it now, was airless but dry. Sadly, I really was too tired that day to enjoy the flight, over a very blue Pacific Ocean, with the many reefs which run around the coast forming an endlessly moving pattern on the sea, several thousand feet below. Only when I was leaving Fiji some two years later did I see that magnificent aerial view of those islands scattered like jewels on a bed of blue velvet.

I lived in Suva, the capital, which is unfortunately on the 'wet' side of the island – almost as though an invisible line has been drawn across the centre. On the dry side, rainfall is minimal, whereas on the other it can rain nonstop for days – albeit warm rain.

Every small town has a market, and in fact market prices are a good indicator, changing continually with the economic state of the country, the climatic conditions and labour relations.

Suva has a very large municipal market, selling a dazzling variety of local crafts, these generally being for the benefit of the many cruise ships, mainly from Australia, which regularly visit the port of Suva. Handcarved wooden bowls are available, masks and turtle shells polished until they gleam (they make very good stools), miniature outrigger canoes symbolic of the first craft that carried settlers to the Fijian

Islands, or, if your feet are sore after sightseeing you may prefer a pair of Fijian slippers with pompoms on the front – extremely comfortable. You can also buy grass skirts and delicate filigree jewellery, the latter made by Indians.

The most important part of the market, however, for the housewife is the produce section. Here you will see high mounds of water melons, baskets of mussels, strings of fresh mud crabs and stalks of *dalo*, the leaves of which are cooked with a coconut cream sauce to make the classic Fijian dish, *palusami*. Hands of bananas sell for a few cents and sweet potatoes are sold by the bundle, and always there are piles of coconuts which form the basis of many Fijian dishes. A popular vegetable when in season is *duruka*, which looks rather like a stick of sugar cane; peeled and baked in coconut milk it is a flavoursome adventure. Another unusual ingredient is the *bêche-de-mer*, the elongated creature known as sea-cucumber, which is used in many soups, particularly by the small Chinese community in Fiji. Fresh fish are plentiful, glistening with rainbow hues, alongside heaps of Pacific prawns.

The Fijian housewife has, over the years, learnt to make full use of indigenous ingredients such as certain types of seaweed, rock snails and even spiny sea eggs. Mud crabs are enjoyed equally well by the Fijian and Indian population. The Indians use crabmeat in curry, while Fijians bake it in coconut milk.

Taro, a heavy textured root vegetable, like a potato, forms the basis of the Fijian diet, with careful cultivation taking almost a year to mature. Taro will keep for only a limited time once cut. To prepare taro, thinly peel, and bake in halves or the whole root, depending on size. It can also be sliced and boiled or steamed and any leftover cooked taro cut into thick sticks, makes excellent chips when deep fried. Taro beaten into coconut cream (*miti*) produces the classic Fijian dish *vakalolo*.

Yams are also popular for family meals; scrubbed, then baked whole in the oven, they are cut in half. The flesh is scooped out, mashed with butter, milk, salt and pepper, then returned to the yam case and heated through. Mashed yams are also used as baby food.

A much quicker growing root vegetable than taro or yam, *cassava* is another useful ingredient – but it is important when buying it to ensure that the roots have no strong smell of almonds, as these can be poisonous. To prepare cassava cakes Fijians mash or grate cooked cassava and mix it with butter and milk, season with a little salt and pepper, add some grated onion, and then form into small 2.5cm (1in) thick patties which are then fried until golden brown; alternatively, tablespoonsful of raw grated cassava are dropped into hot fat and fried until golden brown.

One culinary adventure not to be missed if you ever visit Fiji, is a *lovo*, these are usually only held on special occasions, and for celebrations. First, a large hole is dug in the ground, stones are laid in the hole and a fire is lit. Meat, lamb or pork, fish and a wide variety of local vegetables are laid on the red hot stones, then the hole is sealed with coconut fronds and banana leaves, earth is spread over the top to keep the heat in, and everything is left to steam for several hours. The hole is then opened, and the food lifted out, its unique aroma tantalising the palate.

Fijian food is not found in restaurants around the islands; there you will find westernised foods, and the inevitable steaks. But, for the Fijian, food is an integral part of celebration and hospitality. An essential part of the proceedings is the solemn ceremony of mixing and serving *yaqona*, made from the powdered root of a variety of the pepper plant, which if drunk in quantity can cause numbness of the tongue and lips. There is much ritual attached to the drinking of yaqona on ceremonial occasions. First it is mixed in a large wooden bowl called a *tanoa*, carved from a single piece of *vesi* or hardwood. Before receiving a small bowl of yaqona, the hands must be clapped, and then two or three small sips 'taken' – although strictly speaking the bowl should be emptied before it is placed on the ground. At home with the family, Fijians gather around the yaqona bowl and discuss life, its pleasures and problems and the ritual is very much a focal point of daily life.

A colourful people, the Fijians are dignified and proud, and they live happily alongside the Indians who first went to Fiji just over a hundred years ago. Together they produce a wealth of exciting dishes, using ingredients that are strange to the Westerner, but which beg to be sampled and enjoyed, and you will always be sure in any of the Fijian Islands to hear *Ni Sa Bula* or in English, 'Welcome', sincerely said and sincerely meant.

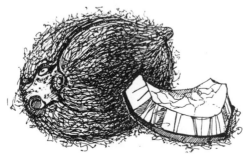

A deliciously different
Fijian way of serving lamb.

Pacific Roast Lamb
(Serves 6–8)

2kg (4½lb) shoulder of lamb
Salt and freshly ground black pepper
2 cloves garlic
2.5cm (1in) fresh ginger root
3tbsp light soy sauce
3tbsp sunflower oil
1 small pineapple

Using a sharp knife score the upper side of the shoulder in a diamond pattern, deep enough to go right through the fat layer into the flesh. Rub all over with salt and freshly ground black pepper. In a food processor or electric blender combine the garlic, peeled and crushed, the ginger, peeled and roughly chopped, and the soy sauce and oil, process to blend, then pour over the lamb.

Remove the top of the pineapple, cut off the skin and roughly chop the flesh, reserving all the juices that may come out of the fruit. Spread the fruit and juices over the lamb. Roast in a preheated oven at 190°C (375°F, Gas mark 5) allowing 25min/450g (1lb), basting frequently throughout the cooking time.

Fish Baked in Coconut Cream
(Serves 4)

450g (1lb) firm fleshed white fish fillets (cod,
haddock, whiting etc)
25g (1oz) flour
Salt and freshly ground black pepper
50ml (2fl oz) sunflower oil
225ml (8fl oz) miti (coconut sauce), see page 84
1 small onion
2 ripe, firm, tomatoes

Skin the fillets and cut into 5cm (2in) wide strips. Season the flour with a little salt and generously with freshly ground black pepper. Coat the fish pieces well with the seasoned flour. Heat the oil in a frying pan, and fry the fish until golden brown. Remove from the pan with a slotted spoon and arrange in a shallow ovenproof dish. Pour the coconut sauce over the top. Peel and finely chop the onion and sprinkle all over the fish and sauce mixture. Cover the dish tightly with foil and bake for 1hr at 140°C (275°F, Gas mark 1). Serve garnished with thin slices of tomato.

Coconut Kai Curry (Mussel Curry)
(Serves 4)

1kg (2.2lb) river mussels
1 small onion
Salt
1 large onion
2 cloves garlic
2.5cm (1in) fresh ginger root
2tbsp ghee or light oil
½tsp ground cloves
½tsp ground cinnamon
1tsp turmeric
1tsp hot chilli powder
225ml (8fl oz) miti (coconut sauce), see below
3 tomatoes

Kai, or river mussels as they are commonly called, are very popular, especially when served in a curry.

Serve with fluffy boiled rice.

Scrub the mussels and remove the beards, put into a large saucepan together with the peeled and chopped small onion and a little salt, pour over about 600ml (1pt) water, bring to the boil, covered. Shake the pan well and cook until all the mussels have opened, discard any unopened shells. Drain and remove the mussels from the shells, slice any particularly large ones.

Peel and finely chop the large onion, garlic and ginger root. Heat the ghee or oil in a frying pan and cook the onion, garlic and ginger until the onion is soft and transparent, not browned. Mix the spices together, add to the pan, mixing well and cook for 2min. Stir in the miti, and leave over a very low heat.

83

Cover the tomatoes with boiling water, leave for 3min and then slide off the skins. Deseed and chop the flesh, and mix with the mussels. Add this mixture to the pan and heat through.

Kokoda
(Raw Fish in Coconut Sauce)
(Serves 6)

To my mind this is the most delicious of all Fijian dishes. Once you have overcome any mental aversion to eating raw fish, you will find yourself eating this frequently; it is a culinary poem.

675g (1½lb) firm fleshed white fish (cod, haddock, whiting)
Salt
225ml (8fl oz) lemon juice
½ green pepper
2 tomatoes
225ml (8fl oz) miti (coconut sauce), see above
½tsp turmeric

Skin the fish fillets and cut the flesh into thin strips (about 1cm [½in]) and arrange in a shallow dish. Sprinkle over a little salt and then pour over the lemon juice. The fish must be completely immersed. Leave for 3–4hr, or overnight in the refrigerator, until the fish turns white, and has a 'cooked' appearance. Strain off the juice and squeeze excess moisture from the fish, and distribute evenly between 6 glass goblets.

Finely dice the pepper and blanch for 1min in boiling water, drain and pat dry. Put the tomatoes into boiling water, leave for 3min then peel off the skins, deseed and finely chop the flesh. Mix the peppers and chopped tomato together and spoon a little into each goblet. Mix the turmeric into the miti, before pouring over the rest of the ingredients, and serve well chilled with buttered brown bread.

(Do not overchill as the miti can harden.)

Miti (Coconut sauce)

Miti forms the basis of many Fijian dishes, as well as being a sauce for dipping.

1 small onion
1 lemon
1 hot chilli
1 coconut, grated
1tsp salt

Peel and finely chop the onion. Roughly chop the lemon. Finely chop the chilli. Put the coconut, onion, lemon, chilli and salt in a blender or food processor and mix well. Stand for 1hr, then strain through muslin, including the liquid that will have accumulated during the standing time, squeezing the muslin to produce the greatest amount of liquid.

Baked Bananas
(Serves 4)

4 large firm, but ripe, bananas
50g (2oz) butter
2tbsp lemon juice
50g (2oz) soft dark brown sugar
2tbsp dark rum

Serve with icecream.

Peel and thickly slice the bananas and arrange in a shallow ovenproof dish. In a food processor or electric blender mix the butter, lemon juice, sugar and rum together and spread evenly over the bananas. Cover the dish with foil and bake at 180°C (350°F, Gas mark 4) for 20–25min.

Mango Mousse
(Serves 4)

3 large ripe, but firm, mangoes
50g (2oz) castor sugar
1tbsp lemon juice
2tsp gelatine
75ml (3fl oz) hot (not boiling) water
450ml (¾pt) whipping cream

Don't forget to remove the mousse from the freezer about 10min before serving time.

Peel, then halve the mangoes and remove the central stone. Slice the flesh into a saucepan, add the lemon juice and sugar and cook over a low heat for about 10min, until the fruit is soft. Purée in a food processor or blender, then allow to cool.

Dissolve the gelatine in the hot water, and stir into the purée. Whip the cream until stiff and fold into the mango purée. Pour into a freezerproof dish. Cover with foil and freeze until firm.

Germany: The Rhineland

There appears to be a misconception that all German food is heavy and indigestible; not so! I feel sure that anybody visiting the Rhine region has a very pleasant surprise in store.

Rhinelanders are warm and friendly people and I have always visited them at Carnival time. This is in February, when the weather can be quite bitter, and snowfall heavy, but it certainly does not detract from the warmth and friendliness of the people.

Boppard is a small town, perched on the banks of the Rhine, and I arrived just a couple of hours before the carnival procession was due to start. The town was milling with people; everyone from babies in pushchairs to old ladies was dressed in every conceivable type of costume, and colourful clowns seemed to be the favourite. The atmosphere was electric, with expectancy and excitement. Then came the faint sound of a band, and into sight came the first of the many floats, marching bands and their supporters, all in costume, all smiling. As they passed they shouted *ellau* to the watching crowd, which roared in response. Showers of multicoloured sweets were thrown into the air from the floats, to be caught by children who scooped them into bags – many seemed to collect a month's supply for the entire family.

Everywhere were stands selling that enjoyable and warming concoction of hot red wine and spices called *Glühwein*, which warms you down to your toes. Sizzling hot *Bratwurst* sausages, served in a crusty roll with an enormous dollop of strong German mustard was simple food at its best.

In Boppard the carnival is a two-day event. On the second evening the men dress in funeral clothes with top hats, and ceremonially carry an effigy depicting the bad spirits of the wine to the bank of the river where it is put on a bonfire. Everyone sings the Bopparder Ham song (Bopparder Ham is the local wine) to ensure that the vines will grow strong and healthy and produce a good harvest, and the singing and dancing continue into the early hours of the morning.

I particularly enjoy the German custom of taking afternoon coffee and cake. Every small town has its coffee shop, and when you see the gorgeous looking goodies, you realise that the German pastry chef is a master. But the German Hausfrau is usually a good baker too, and to be invited to a German home for coffee and cake often means you will also be offered a glass of the German Asbach brandy – a little fiery for my taste, but most welcome on cold February afternoons.

I suppose when thinking of German food in general most people think of the many varieties of *wurst* (sausages) that are so much a part of German home cooking. There must be something like 1,500 different types of sausage ranging from *Brühwurst*, scalded sausages made of finely minced pork or beef that include the original *Frankfurter; Bierwurst*, an oval shaped pork and beef sausage; and if you like garlic try the *Fleischwurst*, or for something more spicy, the offal-based *Kochwurst* could be the one for you. But the favourite in the Rhineland must be *Blutwurst*, a black pudding, usually sliced and fried and scrumptious when incorporated into the popular Rhenish dish *Himmel und Erde* (literally translated it means heaven and earth). There are also smoked or air dried varieties of wurst and these include the well known German salami, *Zervelat*.

At the annual *Wurstmarkt* in Bad Durkheim, huge plates of wurst and sauerkraut are eaten washed down with large glasses of Rhine wine. But there is far more to the cookery of the Rhineland than sausages. Game is very popular, although quite expensive, with pheasant, partridge and woodcock being marinated in red wine vinegar, herbs and spices.

Dumplings are, of course, the basics of German cookery, from small fluffy ones served in a bowl of soup, to the tiny *spatzle* which are boiled and then fried.

Freshwater fish such as pike, carp and trout, poached in a court bouillon, go well with the light white wines of the Rhine Valley. Around October, kitchens in the wine region will be abuzz as onion, bacon and egg filled yeast tarts are baked to accompany the first tasting of the *Federweisser*, the new wine. People flock to wine festivals, not only to taste the wines, but to enjoy the simple, but delectable, peasant food which is served at these events.

Huge blazing log fires are used to cook thick succulent chops, or slices off a leg of pork; half chickens sprinkled with a few herbs are cooked until crispy golden brown and huge slablike steaks sizzle away. Most of this type of food, accompanied by chunks of crusty fresh bread, is eaten with the fingers and washed down with copious amounts of Rhine wine.

But perhaps the most famous and certainly my favourite Rhenish dish is *Sauerbraten*, a pot roasted marinaded joint of beef. Traditionally eaten on special occasions it needs to be marinaded for at least 48 hours before being cooked. Served with potato dumplings and red cabbage, it is outstandingly delicious.

The German Hausfrau is rather more spoilt than other Europeans in that well trained assistants in both the supermarkets and speciality shops know about the varieties, origins and traditions of the produce they sell. Beautifully clean and well laid out food markets offer fresh produce, cheeses, fruits and locally grown vegetables, and more than 200 varieties of fresh baked breads, rolls and buns.

Above all else the German housewife demands the highest quality and is prepared to pay for it. In recent years the trend has moved from the heavier, more starchy foods, such as dumplings, but on high days and holidays diet is cast aside in favour of traditional foods. Christmastime in the German home would not be Christmas without a roast goose; stuffed with prunes, raisins and apricots it is served with glazed apples and spicy red cabbage.

Rhenish cookery reflects the people, it is warm, wholesome and delicious; I hope you will enjoy it as much as I have.

Bochnensupple 'Rheinisch' (Green Bean Soup)
(Serves 6)

1.4kg (3lb) fresh green beans
450g (1lb) potatoes
1¼l (2pt) chicken stock
Bouquet garni
2tbsp flour
300ml (½pt) sour cream
Salt and freshly ground black pepper
4 frankfurters
1tbsp chopped parsley

Wash and trim the beans, and cut into bite-sized slices. Peel and dice the potatoes.

Put the stock into a large saucepan with the bouquet garni

and bring to the boil, add the beans and potatoes and cook until the vegetables are cooked. Mix the flour with the sour cream, add to the soup and stir all the time – do not allow to boil. Season with salt and freshly ground black pepper.

Thickly slice the frankfurters, add to the pan, and heat through. Serve the soup in warmed bowls garnished with a sprinkling of chopped parsley.

Gefuelltr Hecht (Stuffed Pike)
(Serves 4)

A tasty poached fish dish served with a béchamel sauce.

1 pike
2 onions
13g (½oz) butter
450g (1lb) firm fleshed white fish
2 slices of bread
150ml (¼pt) milk
2 egg yolks
Salt and freshly ground black pepper
Pinch of ground nutmeg
150ml (¼pt) white Rhine wine
150ml (¼pt) fish stock

Prepare and clean the pike. Finely chop one onion. Melt the butter in a large frying pan until golden and softened. Meanwhile poach the white fish until it starts to flake. Remove with a slotted spoon and allow to cool slightly. Soak the bread in the milk.

In a food processor combine the cooked onion and flaked fish. Squeeze out the bread and add to the fish and onion together with the egg yolks and seasonings. Process until well mixed.

Put the pike into an ovenproof dish, and spoon the stuffing into the belly cavity, and secure the opening with a skewer or toothpicks. Thinly slice the remaining onion and arrange around the pike. Mix the wine and stock together and pour over the fish. Bake at 180°C (350°F, Gas mark 4) for about 40min, basting frequently.

Sauerbraten (Pickled Beef)
(Serves 6)

1½kg (3lb) topside of beef
225ml (8fl oz) red wine
125ml (4fl oz) red wine vinegar
225ml (8fl oz) water
3 small onions
1 bay leaf
3 cloves
5 peppercorns
Salt and freshly ground black pepper
125g (4oz) streaky bacon
1tsp mixed herbs
150ml (5fl oz) hot beef stock
150ml (5fl oz) single cream
25g (1oz) flour
Pinch of sugar

Usually served with potato dumplings and a bowl of red cabbage.

Place the beef in an earthenware dish. Put the red wine, vinegar and water into a saucepan. Peel 1 onion and slice into rings and add to the wine mixture together with the bay leaf, cloves and peppercorns. Over a medium heat bring to the boil, leave to cool and then pour over the beef. Leave covered for 3 days, turning once. After 3 days remove the beef from the marinade and dry thoroughly. Rub in salt and freshly ground black pepper all over the beef.

Chop the bacon; peel and chop the remaining onions. In a large fireproof casserole, on top of the cooker, fry the bacon without additional fat until it is crisp and all the fat has run out. Add the beef to the pan and brown all over for about 10min, turning it until well sealed. Add the onions to the pan and cook for a further 10min. Strain the marinade through a sieve into the casserole, add the hot stock and the mixed herbs. Cover and simmer on a very low heat for about 1½hr.

Remove the meat from the pot, and put on a serving dish, keep warm in the oven. Sieve the meat juices into a saucepan and bring to the boil. Mix the cream and flour together in a small bowl until smooth and add to the meat juices, stirring all the time; season with salt and freshly ground black pepper and a pinch of sugar. Pour a little of the sauce over the meat and serve the remainder separately.

Dumplings are a basic ingredient of the German diet, served in soup, as an accompaniment to meat dishes and stews.

Leberknödeln (Liver Dumplings)
(Serves 4)

225g (8oz) calf liver
1 slice of bread
A little milk
1 small onion
1tbsp finely chopped fresh parsley
25g (1oz) flour
Salt and freshly ground black pepper
Grated rind of ½ lemon
1 egg
1*l* (1¾pt) stock or water
50g (2oz) butter

Mince or very finely chop the liver. Soak the bread in the milk. Finely chop the onion. In a mixing bowl combine the liver, onion, parsley and flour, then squeeze out the bread and add to the mixture. Season with the salt and pepper and stir in the lemon rind. Beat the egg, and add to the mixture a little at a time until the mixture becomes workable. Using lightly floured hands mould the mixture into small balls, refrigerate for 20min.

Bring the stock or water to the boil, drop in the dumplings and boil for 15–20min, remove with a slotted spoon into a warmed serving dish. Melt the 50g (2oz) butter and pour over the dumplings and serve.

Himmel und Erde
(Heaven and Earth)
(Serves 4)

1kg (2.2lb) potatoes
1tsp salt
1kg (2.2lb) cooking apples
1½tbsp sugar
125g (4oz) streaky bacon
2 medium onions
400g (14oz) black sausage

Boil the peeled potatoes until tender in lightly salted water. Peel and core the apples and stew in a little water, with the sugar added, until just cooked. Meanwhile derind and roughly chop the bacon, and peel and finely chop the onions. Cook the bacon, without any fat, until it is crisp; add the onions and allow to sauté until lightly browned and softened in the bacon fat.

Drain the potatoes and mash them, then fold in the cooked apples, bacon and onions and put in a warm serving dish; keep hot in the oven.

Skin and slice the black sausage, and fry till crisp. Arrange on top of the potato mixture.

Rheinischer Hasenpfeffer (Jugged Hare)
(Serves 6–8)

1 hare approx 3.5kg (7½lb)
2 medium onions
2 carrots
8 peppercorns
225ml (8fl oz) red wine vinegar
225ml (8fl oz) red wine
2tbsp cognac
225g (8oz) streaky bacon
2 onions
225ml (8fl oz) chicken stock
Bouquet garni
Salt and freshly ground black pepper
50g (2oz) ginger biscuits
3tbsp redcurrant jelly

This recipe was sent to me by a very dear German friend, Kristina, who told me that although it is rather expensive it is extremely delicious.

Wash the hare inside and out. Using a sharp knife cut it into 6 or 8 pieces. Peel the medium-sized onions and cut into very thin slices, and then into rings. Peel and cut the carrots into matchstick strips.

Arrange the meat, onion rings and carrot sticks together with the peppercorns in a shallow nonmetal dish. Mix the wine vinegar, wine and cognac together and pour over the ingredients in the dish. Cover with clingfilm and refrigerate for 4–5hr.

Remove the rind from the bacon and cut the rashers into strips. Peel and roughly chop the remaining onions. In a large flameproof casserole, on top of the stove, cook the bacon, without additional fat, until all the fat has run out. Add the hare pieces to the dish and brown all over. Add the onions and mix in well. Strain the marinade into the casserole, add the chicken stock and bouquet garni and season with salt and freshly ground black pepper. Cover the dish (preferably with foil and then the lid) and let simmer for about 1½hr. When cooked remove the hare pieces onto a warmed serving dish.

Crumble the ginger biscuits into the liquid left in the pan and stir in the redcurrant jelly, then pour over the hare pieces.

Rheinischer Apfelpie
(Serves 6)

Different variations of apple pie are baked from the North Sea to the Alps; this version comes from the Rhine region.

275g (10oz) plain flour
Pinch of salt
175g (6oz) butter
100g (4oz) castor sugar
1 pkt vanilla sugar
1 egg
750g (1¾lb) sourish apples
75g (3oz) sugar
½tsp ground cinnamon
100g (4oz) currants
Icing sugar to decorate

Put the flour into a large bowl together with a pinch of salt, cut the butter into small pieces and rub into the flour with the fingertips until the mixture resembles fine breadcrumbs; stir in the castor sugar and vanilla sugar, beat the egg and mix to form a smooth dough – adding a little water if necessary. Knead the dough gently then wrap in clingfilm and refrigerate for 30min before rolling out on a well floured board. Use the pastry to line a 25cm (10in) flan dish.

Peel, core and roughly chop the apples and put in a saucepan with the sugar and cinnamon. Cook without any further liquid, until the apples have softened, mix in the currants and use the mixture to fill the flan case. Cook at 190°C (375°F, Gas mark 5) for 35–40min. Sieve some icing sugar over the top before serving.

Gisela's Cherry Cake

250g (8oz) groundnuts
250g (8oz) brown sugar
4 eggs
A few drops of vanilla essence
250g (8oz) plain chocolate
1 large jar (approx 400g [14oz]) sour cherries
1 pkt gelatine
Whipped cream
Toasted flaked almonds

On one visit to Germany I persuaded my German friend to part with one of her many recipes for scrumptious German gateaux.

Mix the groundnuts and sugar together in a large bowl, and beat in the eggs, one by one, add the vanilla and stir in the melted chocolate, mixing well.

Spoon the mixture into a 22cm (9in) hinged cake tin and bake for 30min at 150°C (300°F, Gas mark 2). Remove from the oven and allow to cool. Drain the cherries, reserving about 150ml (¼pt) liquid. Arrange the cherries on top of the cake. Heat the reserved liquid to just below boiling and sprinkle in the gelatine, mixing until completely dissolved. Spoon carefully over the cherries; once set, decorate with whipped cream and toasted flaked almonds.

Rumtopf

1 bottle of dark rum
Soft fruits, such as raspberries, strawberries, gooseberries, cherries, apricots, peaches etc
225g (8oz) sugar to each 450g (1lb) fruit

You top up the *rumtopf* as the different fruits come into season. You can strain off some of the liquid and serve at Christmas time as a fruit liqueur.

Wash and pick over your fruit, dry and put in a shallow dish; sprinkle over the sugar and let stand for 1hr before spooning into your rumtopf. Pour over enough rum to cover and use a saucer or small plate weighted down, so the fruit is kept covered by the rum. Continue throughout the soft fruit season, adding the fruit and sugar in layers, covering with rum. After you have put in your last layer of fruit, seal the rumtopf with clingfilm or foil, and let stand for 3 months before using. Mix well and serve with whipped cream.

Greece

I made my only trip to Greece, so far, some six years ago. We chose Evia, which, according to the atlas is an island, but is in fact joined to mainland Greece by a drawbridge. Arriving in Athens on an August afternoon, is like stepping into a hot airless vacuum, so it was a relief to feel the sea breeze from the ferry before we arrived at the hotel. The place is secluded and across the bay from Athens. Although still warm, the air was balmy with a slight sea breeze; muted sounds of Greek music drifted on the night air — we had arrived.

Greek cooking is rooted in some of the most ancient of traditions, and Greeks will tell you that Turks and Europeans plundered Greek cuisine for their own countries. Greece was probably the first civilisation to record food recipes. It is said that Archestratus, a poet from Gela (circa 330BC), visited the civilized countries of the ancient world searching for their recipes, so fascinated was he by gastronomy.

The basic ingredients of Greek cookery, olive oil, herbs, spices and wine, play as important a part as they did thousands of years ago. The Greek housewife has plenty of fresh produce available. The olives of Kalamata (Kalamai) the melons of Argos, and the artichokes of Dalamanara are renowned. Fields of tomato plants can be seen in the season throughout Greece. Orange and lemons grow in Argolis, and groves of apple trees and walnut trees cover the mountainside of Cynouria. And then there are the vineyards which in summer are shimmering green carpets. Later in the year, the harvested grapes produce the wine so essential to many Greek dishes.

In Andros there is an abundance of game, hare, pheasant, partridge, quail and wild duck. Venison is available in Macedonia, and wild boar is hunted throughout the year.

With so much coastline, many Greek dishes contain seafood and the rivers of Greece provide many freshwater fish including trout, carp and eels, which are incorporated into regional dishes.

The Greeks enjoy their food, you only have to watch them

sitting in the tavernas, relaxing with glasses of *ouzo*, the distinctive aniseed flavoured national aperitif, nibbling olives and perhaps some cheese and bread. If you visit a taverna along the coast you will probably be served your *meza* (the nibbles that accompany drinks) in the form of little fried fishes, rather like whitebait, or perhaps some fried squid.

A Greek dish I enjoyed was stuffed tomatoes, with a filling of minced meat and rice subtly flavoured with oregano. And I enjoyed sitting drinking ice-cold ouzo topped up with lemonade and dipping small pieces of bread into a bowl of *tzatziki*, a deliciously sharp combination of yoghurt, oil, vinegar and crushed garlic to which some diced cucumber had been added – deliciously cooling.

Charcoal grills are used when eating out of doors. We spent a lot of our holiday on the beach, revelling in the sunshine, but in mid-August the midday sun could become almost unbearably hot, and at that time we would seat ourselves in the tree-shaded beach taverna, at the rough wood benches and tables. A tantalising smell would waft over from the charcoal grill while we sipped a glass of cool white Greek wine. *Souvlakia* was my favourite dish. Morsels of lamb or pork, marinaded in lemon juice and olive oil, and sprinkled with oregano are speared onto metal skewers and quickly cooked over hot coals; accompanied by thick chunks of crusty bread this is food for the gods. Bowls of crisply grilled little fishes (*marithes*) served with slices of fat, juicy tomato sprinkled with cubes of *feta* cheese (probably the best known Greek cheese, made from goat's milk) with an olive oil and vinegar dressing flavoured with fresh basil were also very enjoyable.

We spent a day in Athens, eating in one of the squares, crowded with tables set out under the trees. We even cycled along the coast to a fishing village, and on the quayside ate *dolmathes*, a concoction of meat, rice and herbs, encased in vine leaves, gently steamed and served with an egg and lemon sauce. We watched while the waiter, who had to bring the food from the restaurant across the road, dextrously negotiated any traffic, tray held high.

Herbs are important to Greek cookery, and many grow wild and are picked in spring. The one that I always associate with the food of Greece is oregano (*rigani*). Parsley is liberally used in most dishes and dill, fresh, rather than dried, is used in meat, fish and vegetable dishes. Bay leaves, for use either fresh or dried, grow profusely; many Greek housewives have a bay tree or bush growing in their gardens.

Our last night in Greece was spent sitting by the sea, under the stars, as our dinner of fresh lobster sizzled on the barbecue. At the next table a Greek party of family and friends was out for an evening of good eating and good company. Suddenly a bottle was set down on the floor, the men rose, clasped each other round the shoulder, and began to dance to the haunting strains of Greek music. A truly memorable end to a memorable holiday.

Fish Soup with Egg, Lemon and Rice
(Serves 4)

1.4kg (3lb) white fish
(choose seabass for preference, grey mullet, haddock, hake, whiting, etc, and allow 3lb of fish body in addition to heads)
1 onion
3 potatoes
1 carrot
1 stalk of celery with leaves
2 large, ripe tomatoes
Salt
4tbsp sunflower oil
1.1*l* (2pt) water
Freshly ground black pepper
3 bay leaves
Pinch mixed herbs
100g (4oz) long grain rice
2 egg yolks
Juice 1 large lemon
2tbsp finely chopped parsley

A lighter soup than most of the fish variety and more of a first course than a stalwart main course. It has a delectable flavour and it is worth removing the bones to make for less complicated eating. Good value.

Fillet the fish (or ask your fishmonger to do this for you, but you keep the heads and bones). Tie the bones and heads in a piece of fine muslin.

Peel and finely chop the onion. Peel the potatoes and cut them into small dice. Peel and cut the carrot into very small dice. Very thinly chop and dice the celery with leaves.

Cover the tomatoes with boiling water, leave for 3min, drain, then remove the skins, discard the core and seeds and finely chop the flesh. Cut the fish into large bite sized pieces and sprinkle generously with salt.

Heat the oil in a large saucepan, add the vegetables and cook over a low heat until the oil is absorbed, stirring to prevent sticking. Add the water, season with pepper, add the herbs and the bag of fish trimmings, bring to the boil and simmer over a relatively high heat until the vegetables are soft. Remove the bag of fish bones. Cook the rice until just tender, drain well and add it to the soup.

Beat the egg yolks with the lemon juice until smooth. Add a little of the hot soup to the lemon juice and egg and beat until smooth.

Add the fish to the soup and simmer gently for about 10–15min until the fish is almost tender. Lightly stir in the egg and lemon juice without boiling and stir gently until the fish is tender but still firm and the soup has pleasantly thickened. Add the parsley and serve at once.

Kalamarakia Tigita (Fried Squid)
(Serves 4)

900g (2lb) small squid
Flour
Salt and freshly ground black pepper
Deep oil for frying
Lemons
Watercress for garnishing

We need a breakthrough in this country over squid. Sadly, there are those who still turn up their noses at it, make a fuss about cleaning the fish, fail to recognize it as value for money and good nutritional material and refuse to discover how enjoyable it is. Do try it. Squid is remarkably cheap; once conquered it is not too time consuming to prepare and can be very versatile. You can get it fresh or frozen in many fishmongers and supermarkets these days. Fried squid makes a good first course or light summer main course and once tried will be enjoyed again.

Defrost the squid if necessary. Remove the heads and tentacles and cut off and discard the bottom of the heads behind the eyes. Put the bodies and heads in a large bowl under cold running water. Take out the bodies one by one, peel off with the fingernails the transparent, purplish skins from the bodies and wings and scrape out the whitish gunge from the centre of the bellies (if necessary turn the body inside out to do this or split it open). You will also need to remove the polythenelike back rib. Cut the cleaned squid into thin rings or strips and pat dry on kitchen paper.

Season some flour with a generous amount of salt and pepper and lightly coat the squid with the flour.

Heat the oil until a haze rises from the surface. Add the squid (do not overcrowd the pan, the pieces should not be allowed to stick to each other) and cook over a high heat until the squid is a crisp, light, golden brown. Lift in a basket or on a wire spoon and strain well. Then strain the squid on plenty of kitchen paper and keep warm while frying the next batch.

Pile on to a clean linen napkin and garnish with lemon wedges and watercress sprigs. Serve hot, at once.

Kreas me Patates
(Beef and Potato Stew)
(Serves 6)

900g (2lb) chuck beef
1 large onion
2 cloves garlic
900g (2lb) peeled potatoes
4tbsp olive or sunflower oil
4tbsp tomato paste
450ml (¾pt) water
4tbsp finely chopped parsley
1tsp dried savory or oregano
Salt and freshly ground black pepper

In Greece a lot of potatoes are used in everyday cooking and especially in a combination with meat where they soak up the rich gravy or stock from the meat to make hearty and nourishing dishes.

Cut the beef into 4cm (1½in) cubes. Peel and roughly chop the onions. Peel and crush the cloves of garlic. Peel and cut the potatoes into chunks and cover with water until ready to use.

Heat the oil in a flameproof casserole until a haze rises from the oil. Add the meat cubes without overcrowding the pan (better to cook the meat in smaller batches at a time). As soon as it has browned, remove the meat with a slotted spoon. Add the onion and garlic to the juices in the pan and cook over a low heat until the onion is soft and transparent. Stir in the tomato paste and 450ml (¾pt) of water, return the meat to the pan with the parsley, savory or oregano, season with salt and pepper. Bring to the boil and simmer for 30min. Add more water to the casserole and simmer for a further 30min until the meat is tender. Add the potatoes, cover tightly and continue to cook for a final 20min or until the potatoes are cooked but not falling apart.

Most of the liquid should be absorbed into the meat and potatoes and the stew, although still moist, should be fairly dry.

Serve with a crisp green vegetable like lightly shredded and cooked cabbage or beans.

Youvarlakia
(Meatballs with Lemon Sauce)
(Serves 6)

900g (2lb) lean lamb off the bone
1 large onion
1 egg white
3tbsp long grain or Patna rice
2tbsp finely chopped parsley
Pinch oregano
Salt and freshly ground black pepper
1.1*l* (2pt) chicken stock
(or use water and stock cubes)
50g (2oz) butter

Saltsa Avgolemono
4 egg yolks
4tbsp lemon juice

I find myself in something of a quandary over Greek meat balls. You may find it rather surprising that there are not more recipes in this book for some of the many hundreds (and I do mean hundreds) of ways meatballs are cooked and served by restaurants, large and small, and in private houses throughout the country. My problem, when I cook them at home, is that I find the best rather too time consuming to make and if I cut the corners they tend to be tough, especially when they are simple recipes quickly deep fried in oil. Either they are crisp on the outside and overcooked, therefore on the hard side, or undercooked and not of a particularly good colour. So, as this book is about the recipes I like to cook and have found successful from my adventures around the world, I have stuck to those meatballs and minced meat recipes which I feel happy to produce in my kitchen. This is one of them and the difference here is that you poach rather than fry the meatballs and serve them with that evocative and memorable truly Greek lemon and egg sauce, Saltsa Avgolemono.

It is the most lovely and subtle dish. You can serve it with mashed potatoes or cooked rice and with spinach or crisp French beans, although the Greeks usually have it entirely by itself with vegetables and salad dishes in the first course.

Mince the meat fairly finely or chop it in an electric food processor. Peel and very finely chop the onion.

Lightly beat the egg white with a wire whisk until smooth.

In a bowl, combine the egg white, meat, onion, uncooked rice, parsley and oregano, season with salt and pepper and knead with the hands until the mixture is smooth, well mixed and firm. Roll into small balls the size of a walnut and leave, separated, on nonstick paper in the refrigerator for at least an hour to firm up.

Combine the stock and butter in a saucepan and bring to the boil. Add each meatball. Lower gently into the rolling stock, lower the heat and simmer so that the stock is only just moving for 30min. Remove the balls gently with a slotted spoon and keep on one side while making the sauce.

Beat the egg yolks until smooth and foaming and gradually beat in the lemon juice, a little at a time, beating as you do so (this can be done with a wire whisk, an electric whisk or in an electric liquidizer or food processor). When all the lemon juice is incorporated, gradually blend in 3tbsp of boiling stock used to cook the meatballs. Transfer the sauce to a saucepan (large enough to take the meatballs). Add the meatballs to the sauce and cook over a very low heat, stirring (on no account must the sauce be allowed to boil).

Youvetsi
(Lamb with Noodles and Sauce)
(Serves 4–5)

900g (2lb) lean lamb off the bone
1 large onion
6 large firm, ripe tomatoes
150ml (¼pt) olive or sunflower oil
2 cloves garlic
1½tsp dried savory
Pinch oregano
Salt and freshly ground black pepper
225g (8oz) ribbon noodles

Very much a homely family dish which you are unlikely to find in any restaurant other perhaps than a working man's taverna.

Cut the lamb into fair sized cubes about 4–5cm (2in). Peel and chop the onion fairly finely. Cover the tomatoes with boiling water for 3min, slide off the skins and roughly chop the tomatoes. Peel and crush the garlic through a garlic press or with the back of a fork.

Heat the oil in a flameproof casserole until smoking. Add the meat without crowding the pan and brown the pieces quickly on all sides. Remove with a slotted spoon each batch of meat as it browns. Return the browned meat to the pan with the onions, tomatoes, herbs and garlic, season with salt and pepper, bring to the boil and cover tightly.

Simmer the ingredients over a low heat for 30min until the meat is just tender but not falling apart. If the mixture gets too dry (it should have a rich but not too runny sauce), add some water during the cooking time. Cook the noodles for about 5min in fast boiling, salted water and drain well.
Add the noodles to the lamb stew, mix well, check seasoning and pile all the ingredients on to a heated serving dish.

Hirino Avgolemono
(Pork Stew with Lemon and
Egg Sauce)
(Serves 4–6)

Another Greek dish that relies on the glory of egg and lemon sauce to take the richness out of pork and to complement the meat and make it into something special. I use tinned celery hearts because it is difficult to get even hearts, tenderly cooked and without strings at home. One of the few tinned vegetables, beside tomatoes, I do use. This is very much a warming winter dish.

900g (2lb) lean pork
1 large onion
2 cloves garlic
1 large tin celery hearts (450g/16oz)
4tbsp olive or sunflower oil
150ml (¼pt) dry white wine
2tbsp white flour
150ml (¼pt) water
150ml (¼pt) celery liquid
2tbsp finely chopped parsley
¼tsp dried oregano
Salt and freshly ground black pepper
(Avgolemono sauce see page 102)

Remove any fat from the meat and cut the meat into 4cm (1½in) cubes. Peel and chop the onion. Crush the garlic cloves through a garlic press or with the back of a fork. Quarter the drained celery hearts, draining and reserving the liquid they are preserved in.

Heat the oil in a large heavy saucepan until a haze rises from the oil. Add the pork (do not overcrowd the pan but cook the meat in batches) over a high heat until the meat is browned on all sides. Remove the meat when it is cooked with a slotted spoon. Add the onion and garlic to the juices in the pan and stir over a low heat until the onion is soft and transparent. Add the wine and mix well.

Mix the flour with the water until smooth, then add to the 150ml (¼pt) celery liquid and mix well until the sauce thickens and is smooth. Add the meat, parsley and oregano, season with salt and pepper, bring to the boil and simmer for about 45 min until the meat is cooked through but not yet fork tender.

Place the quarters of celery hearts over the meat in the frying pan, cover tightly with a saucepan lid or with foil and simmer for a further 30min. Make the avgolemono sauce and lightly stir it into the pork and celery heating through without letting the mixture boil.

Serve with rice and a green vegetable.

Lentil Salad
(Serves 4)

225g (8oz) brown lentils
4 cloves garlic
2 medium onions
900ml (1½pt) water
1tbsp dry light white wine
(in Greece it would be resinated 'domestica')
Freshly ground black pepper
3 bay leaves
1tsp oregano
Salt
3tbsp sunflower or light olive oil
1tbsp white wine vinegar
2tbsp finely chopped or minced parsley
6 firm, ripe tomatoes
100g (4oz) feta cheese

There is no reason not to eat salad during the winter. There is no reason not to follow hot dishes with salad or why salad should not be served as a starter. This salad is based on lentils, is easy to make, slightly different and full of flavour.

Rinse the lentils in cold running water and drain well. Stick the cloves of garlic into one peeled onion and finely chop the second onion. Combine the lentils and onion stuck with garlic in a saucepan, add the water and wine, some freshly ground black pepper and the bay leaves, bring to the boil (do not add salt) and cook over a medium heat for about 40min until the lentils are tender and almost all the water has been absorbed. Discard the bay leaves and onion and drain off any excess liquid.

Combine the lentils in a bowl with the chopped onion, season with salt, pour over the oil and vinegar, mix in the parsley and oregano and toss well to incorporate all the ingredients. Leave to cool. Cut the tomatoes into thin slices. Crumble the feta cheese. Add the tomatoes and cheese to the cooled ingredients, toss lightly and pile into an attractive serving dish and serve chilled.

Rothákina Komplósta
(Fresh Peach Salad)
(Serves 4)

Some of the fruit grown in Greece is the finest in the world, especially if you eat it in its own environment. If you can get what I call 'proper' peaches, those with pale skins and white flesh, so much the better, but the more common yellow fleshed peaches will do and so will those rather large and vulgar nectarines which are now being imported in such vast quantities. This is another of those beautifully plain and simple endings to a meal which both refreshes the palate and is delightfully fresh and cooling in hot weather.

6 ripe peaches
Juice 1 medium lemon
175g (6oz) castor sugar
150ml (¼pt) finely crushed ice

Cover the peaches with boiling water for 30sec, drain well, cool and peel off the skins. Halve the peaches, cut them into thick slices and pour the lemon juice over. Add the sugar and toss the peach slices lightly in the lemon juice and sugar until all the fruit is well coated. Cover tightly with plastic film and chill the fruit in a refrigerator for about 30min or more until it is icy cold.

Crush ice cubes into fine granules by wrapping the cubes in a clean tea cloth and banging the parcel on a stone surface until the ice is pulverized.

Transfer the peaches and any juices to 4 serving dishes, sprinkle over some ice granules and serve at once.

106

Rizógolon (Greek Rice Pudding)
(Serves 4)

75g (3oz) short grain rice
150ml (¼pt) water
1.1*l* (2pt) milk
175g (6oz) granulated sugar
1tbsp finely grated lemon peel
¼tsp ground cinnamon
Pinch ground nutmeg

This pudding you are likely to find in cafés throughout many of the Greek Islands and rural districts. It is served at the end of a meal but is also eaten as a form of elevenses or even at teatime to provide something for a sweet tooth.

The dish is usually served ice cold and can be found on vendors' stalls with little bowls of the rice pudding being kept chilled on crushed beds of ice. Although to our minds it might smack of nursery high tea it is, nevertheless, a most soothing and refreshing dish provided it is nicely chilled.

Place the rice in a saucepan, add 150ml (¼pt) water and leave to stand for 10min. Combine the milk and sugar in a saucepan, bring to the boil and stir until the sugar has melted.

Add the rice and water, stir well, bring to the boil, stir in the lemon peel and simmer gently until the rice is tender and the milk has been absorbed (30–40min). Transfer the rice to a serving dish (or use separate small bowls) and sprinkle the cinnamon and a small pinch of ground nutmeg over the top. Chill well before serving.

India

Think of India and what springs to mind? Burning curries, desiccated coconut, sacred cows, relatively inexpensive restaurants smelling strongly of spices, Indian colonels drinking *chota pegs* on wide verandahs and shades of *The Far Pavilions*? Well, of course, there is more to India and its cuisine than that; more in the use of flavourings and spices than comes from a commercial drum of mixed curry powder and far, far, more excitement and subtlety in the cuisine than tales of the British Raj would have us believe.

When looking at other nations' cuisines for what can be married to our wealth of quality ingredients to produce less expensive but exciting dishes, the cookery of India is an obvious choice; there is such variety, such colour, taste and texture combinations to experiment with, and such a wealth of ideas to draw on providing we can get away from the concept that Indian food is nothing more than 'curry'.

I talked to Mr Latif Tarafder who owns the Indian Khyber Restaurant in Plymouth (like most Indian restaurants it is popular because it is relatively inexpensive). Mr Tarafder is proud of the food he serves but saddened when his customers combine dishes which do not complement each other. 'Because it is an Indian food they think it must be hot and people often come in and order three or more hot dishes together. It is only in the south of India, from Madras, that the cooking is very highly spiced and there is much use of chillies. Further north much of the food is only mildly spiced, and in any case, only one hot dish is served at one time with other more mild dishes to complement it.'

'Curry powder,' said Mr Tarafder, 'should never be used'. Employ ground spices if you must but better still grind your own and add them carefully to suit your own taste.

I began to use cinnamon, cloves and nutmeg; I flavoured uninteresting river fish with crushed garlic, ginger, and cumin and learnt that if spices are roasted before use, their flavour would be increased and enhanced. I became fascinated by the rich colour contrasts of food flavoured with different spices

(the reds of chilli, the bright yellow of saffron, gold of turmeric and iridescent green of fresh coriander leaves) and I was intrigued by how some flavourings helped tenderize other ingredients – garlic, lemon or lime juice, fresh ginger root, vinegar and yoghurt.

The everyday cooking of India varies with the region and even with the village; recipes are not written down but pass by word of mouth from mother to daughter. Dishes are based on what fresh ingredients are available so that in the south much use is made of coconut milk, flesh and cream while in the north this is replaced by yoghurt and other curd mixtures. The somewhat runny dishes of the south are served with rice to absorb the liquid, while in the north breads of various varieties provide the starch for a meal.

Possibly the *true* Indian cuisine is found in the southern part of the subcontinent, in the hotter, more spicy foods and the mainly vegetarian dishes. In the north successive invasions by Aryans,, Parthians, Scythians, Kuskans, ending with the Moguls brought Central Asian Muslim cuisine and in the west, Goanese cooking shows a strong Portuguese influence.

It is wrong to believe that Indian cooks use spice to disguise food that has become 'high' or has 'gone off'. In fact Indians, and especially, Muslims, are very particular about the freshness of food; dishes are eaten at one sitting and not reheated (with the exception of some curries that are made in advance because they actually benefit from being reheated). Spices are used for tenderizing, flavouring and for their medicinal properties rather than as preservatives. The tenderizing properties of spices and other ingredients are perhaps of most use to us in Britain since with them we can take cheaper and tougher cuts of meat and frozen poultry, and flavourless frozen fish and make them tasty, tender and moist to eat.

Try this: score the skin of defrosted chicken joints or fish then rub the flesh with a combination of lemon juice, a little fresh ginger root and garlic, crushed through a garlic press, and salt. Leave to marinate for an hour or two before cooking and then taste the result – it's practically miraculous.

Try making your own *garam masala* (a mixture of spices that is a condiment, not a curry powder) from 4 parts black peppercorns, 4 parts coriander seeds, 3 parts cumin seeds, 1 part cloves, cinnamon and cardamon seeds all ground together. Add a 10ml (2tsp) to lightly cooked spinach, green beans, cauliflower or cabbage with a little oil and lemon juice, toss lightly for a few minutes over the heat and serve – deliciously different.

In India, for even meat eaters, vegetables form the basis of most dishes with meat, fish or poultry as a bonus rather than the main ingredient, a practice I frequently copy. Imagine being able to produce a main course dinner party dish for 6 people based on a *maximum* of 450g (16oz) of meat or poultry – I've done it often and can assure you that, budgetwise, it makes sense.

Mince or ground meat made into meat balls, patties or subtle, exquisitely flavoured curries can be a grand budget stretcher (one of my favourites combines minced lamb with onions and a quantity of the outside leaves of lettuces; another uses spinach to add bulk to the meat and, as well as spices, is flavoured with a little vinegar and finely chopped mint). Cubes of aubergine cooked with cubes of lamb, seasoned, spiced and moistened with yoghurt soak up the flavour of the meat and become indistinguishable from the lamb itself when the dish is cooked.

Flour is not used for thickening in Indian recipes so the dishes tend to have an attractive lightness of texture. Ground nuts and poppy seeds, lentils, coconut milk, yoghurt and other curd products produce natural rich creamy sauces; puréed raw onion and the plentiful use of tomatoes also result in rich, aromatic sauces.

Rice is never used as a bed for a main dish but is served on the side, cooked until white and fluffy and makes the perfect complement for both meat and vegetable dishes. Use Patna or Basmati rice for your Anglo–Indian dishes; I prefer the slightly more expensive Basmati variety because it has more flavour and is easier to cook to perfection (wash and rinse the rice, put it in a large pan with enough salted water to come 4cm (¾in) above the surface of the rice, bring slowly to the boil, stir well, cover tightly and cook over a very low heat for 20min. Remove from the heat, stir vigorously with a fork, cover tightly again and leave to stand for 15min by which time the rice should be tender but still firm and just right).

Apart from flavouring meat, fish poultry and vegetable dishes, spices can also, with other ingredients, be cooked with rice to make a great many inexpensive *pulaos*, enhanced by colourful saffron, cinnamon, cardamom, chilli, cumin and perhaps a little chicken, garlic, some peas, onions and small pieces of tomato.

For those interested in experimenting in the kitchen the dishes of India provide a wide horizon indeed and now that you can buy a wide range of spices, fresh green and red chillies, fresh ginger root, lentils and other ingredients, there is nothing to stop you doing so. Buy spices in small quantities and store them in airtight containers (it is cheaper to buy them in packets than in glass jars or drums); buy your spices ready ground or grind them in a coffee grinder if you have one and go easy with their use until you get used to their different attributes. Purée garlic, ginger and raw onions in an electric liquidizer or food processor and don't be afraid to be lavish with the use of onion, the longer it is cooked the milder it becomes.

Garam Masala

A mixture of spices, ground finely, which is used widely in Indian cookery. The spices are sprinkled over dishes at the last minute or added for the last 5min of cooking time; the flavours are particularly successful in vegetable dishes. The spices can be stored for a few weeks in a screw topped container.

25g (1oz) coriander seeds
20g (¾oz) cumin seeds
6 blades mace
15 cloves
10 green cardamom seeds, peeled
10 black cardamom seeds, peeled
5cm (2in) stick cinnamon
1tsp ground nutmeg

Roast the coriander, cumin, mace and cloves in a heavy frying pan without fat until they are crisp but browned; leave to cool. Combine all the spices in an electric blender or coffee grinder (the second gives the best results) and grind until fine but not powdery.

Tandoori Machi
(Baked Spiced Fish)
(Serves 4)

1kg (2.2lb) firm fleshed white fish fillets (cod, haddock etc)
Juice of ½ lemon
2 cloves garlic
150ml (¼pt) natural yoghurt
1tsp chilli powder
1tsp ground cumin
1tbsp vinegar
Salt

Place the fish fillets in a shallow baking dish, pour over the lemon juice, and leave for 10min.

Crush the garlic and add to the yoghurt together with the chilli powder, ground cumin and vinegar, season with a little salt and mix well. Pour over the fish and leave to marinade for 3hr. Cover with foil and bake at 190°C (375°F, Gas mark 5) for 20min, remove foil and baste fish and cook for a further 10min. Serve with fluffy boiled rice.

India

Green Peas with Herbs
(Serves 6)

1 medium onion
1 small chilli pepper
5cm (2in) fresh green ginger root
3tbsp water
5tbsp sunflower oil
¼tsp fenugreek
¼tsp turmeric
1tsp ground coriander
1tsp ground cumin
675g (1lb 8oz) shelled young green peas
4tbsp finely chopped fresh coriander leaves (or use parsley)
1tsp garam masala (see page 112)
Salt
3tbsp water

I am not a vegetarian but I do enjoy vegetarian meals and being fortunate in having my own vegetable garden I find I lean heavily on Indian vegetarian dishes for summer and autumn meals. With a choice of 3 or 4 vegetable dishes and a couple of side dishes who needs more expensive meat or fish? *An Invitation to Indian Cookery* by Madhur Jaffrey and the books of Jack Santa Maria have been a great inspiration in this direction.

Peel and finely chop the onion, remove the seeds from the chilli and finely chop the flesh. Peel and very finely chop, or mince, the ginger root. Combine the ginger and 3tbsp water in an electric liquidizer or food processor and process until they are well mixed.

Heat the oil in a large heavy pan. Add the ginger and water mixture (watch out for spitting from the pan) and the fenugreek and turmeric powder. Stir over a high heat until most of the water has evaporated. Add the onion, green chilli, ground coriander and cumin and cook over a moderate heat, stirring, for 5 min. Add the peas and cook for 5min, stirring occasionally.

Add the fresh coriander and garam masala, season with salt, stir in 3tsp of water and cook over a low heat for a further 5min.

I also make this dish with courgettes when they do their usual trick of providing an unmanageable glut in the garden. Take care not to overcook the courgettes.

113

India

Keema (Spicy Minced Beef with Vegetables)
(Serves 6)

(see page 112)

Visit Indian students for a supper party or get-together in England and one of the most popular forms of supper dishes will inevitably be some form of *keema*, inexpensive and relatively easy-to-produce curried dishes (very popular in the Pakistan areas of the sub-continent) which are filling and delicious. Serve keemas with rice and with *chapatis* and, if you like, with a lightly curried *dhal* or an extra vegetable dish. This particular variety has a strong overtone of tangy lemon and is not too heavy with a refreshing taste that encourages you to ask for second helpings. It also responds well, like many Indian dishes, to being made in advance and reheated.

The meat must be really tender when it is served, therefore the cheaper the cut of meat the more tough it is liable to be and the longer it will have to be cooked. If you can afford it, make the keema from minced chuck. It will be just as good from a cheaper cut like skirt or even shin, although the cooking time will be longer, providing you remove any gristle from the meat. Don't buy inferior commercially produced minced meat.

3 medium onions
3 cloves garlic
2.5cm (1in) fresh green ginger root
1 aubergine
450g (1lb) lean minced meat (use chuck, skirt, shin etc)
3tbsp sunflower oil
1tbsp garam masala (see page 112)
2tsp ground coriander
1tsp ground cumin
¼tsp chilli powder
½tsp turmeric
4 cardamom seeds
2cm (¾in) cinnamon stick
1 small tin tomatoes
Salt and freshly ground black pepper
300ml (½pt) chicken stock (or use water and stock cube)
Juice one large lemon
4 bay leaves
175g (6oz) frozen peas
Finely chopped parsley or
fresh coriander leaves for garnishing

Peel and finely chop 2 of the onions. Thinly slice the remaining onion and divide it into rings. Peel and finely chop the garlic and ginger. Coarsely grate or finely chop the aubergine.

Heat a large, preferably iron, frying pan without using any oil. Add the meat and stir over the highest heat until the meat is well browned. Remove the meat. Add the oil to the pan and fry the onion rings until they are golden brown. Remove the onion rings with a slotted spoon, drain on kitchen paper and set on one side for garnishing.

Add the chopped onion, garlic and ginger to the juices in the pan and cook over a high heat until the onions are golden brown, stir in the garam masala and cook for a further minute, mixing in well with the onion. Add the aubergine,

114

coriander, cumin, chilli powder, turmeric, cardamoms and cinnamon to the pan and stir for 3min. Add the tomatoes, mix well and cook over a moderate heat until reduced to a pulp. Add the meat, season with salt and pepper, stir in the stock, lemon juice and bay leaves, cover and simmer for about 40min until the meat is tender. Add the peas, check seasoning and cook for a further 3–4min until the peas are just tender.

Turn on to a serving dish, top with the fried onion rings and scatter with finely chopped parsley or fresh coriander. Serve with fluffy boiled rice.

Mhans Korma
(Lamb or Mutton Curry with Curds)
(Serves 4–6)

1 5cm (2in) fresh green ginger root
4 black peppercorns
3 green cardamom seeds
2.5cm (1in) piece cinnamon
¼tsp ground cloves
3 cloves garlic
225g (8oz) cottage cheese
6 thin slices lean lamb or mutton cut from the leg
¼tsp saffron strands
1tsp lemon juice
150ml (¼pt) hot water
2tbsp ghee or sunflower oil
Salt
75g (3oz) blanched almonds

Peel and chop the garlic and ginger root. Combine the garlic, peppercorns, cardamom seeds, ginger root, cinnamon and cloves in an electric liquidizer or food processor and process until the spices are coarsely ground. Add the cottage cheese and continue to process until the cheese is smooth. Spread the mixture over the meat and leave it to stand for 1hr. Steep the saffron in the lemon juice and water while the meat is marinating.

Heat the ghee or oil in a large, heavy, frying pan, add the meat slices and brown quickly on both sides over a high heat. Add the saffron and water it has been steeping in, stir in salt and any remaining marinade and simmer gently for about 30min until the meat is tender and the liquid has evaporated (add more water if the liquid dries out before the meat is fork tender).

Roast the almonds in a hot oven 200°C (400°F, Gas mark 6) for 3min until they are crisp and golden. Chop the almonds and sprinkle over the slices of meat.

Korma (Curried Meat)
(Serves 4)

Kormas are curries made from cubes of meat rather than minced meat and, like keemas recipes vary from household to household or restaurant to restaurant with most never having been written down. The sauce should be thick and richly flavoured.

900g (2lb) lean mutton or lamb
3 large onions
4 cloves garlic
2.5cm (1in) fresh green ginger root
4 tomatoes
3 green chilli peppers
3tbsp ghee or sunflower oil
4 cloves
4 green cardamoms
1tsp ground coriander
½tsp ground cumin
2.5cm (1in) cinnamon, crushed
2 bay leaves
600ml (1pt) water
Salt
2tsp garam masala (see page 112)
1tbsp finely chopped coriander or mint leaves

Cut the meat into 3.5cm (1½in) cubes. Peel the onions. Cut 1 onion into thin slices and then separate into rings. Peel and very finely chop or mince the garlic and ginger. Finely chop the other onions.

Cover the tomatoes with boiling water for 3min, drain, slide off the skins and chop and tomatoes. Remove the seeds from the chillies and finely chop the flesh.

Heat the ghee or oil in a large heavy frying pan. Add the meat and brown quickly on all sides over a high heat. Remove the meat with a slotted spoon. Add the onion rings to the ghee or oil in the pan and fry over a medium high heat, stirring, until the rings are crisp and lightly browned. Remove the rings with a slotted spoon. Add the remaining onions, garlic and ginger and cook for 2min over a medium low heat until the onion is soft and transparent. Add the cloves, cardamoms, coriander, cumin, cinnamon and bay leaves and stir over a moderate heat for 2min. Add the meat, chillies and tomatoes, mix well, pour over half the water and cook over a moderate heat, stirring every now and then, without covering, for 5min until most of the liquid has been absorbed. Add the remaining water, lower the heat and simmer slowly, stirring now and then, for about 30min until the meat is tender. Season with salt, stir in the garam masala and transfer to a heated serving dish. Top with the onion rings and sprinkle over the coriander leaves or mint before serving.

Mhans Phali (Lamb or Mutton with Green Beans)
(Serves 4)

450g (1lb) mutton or lamb
2 large onions
450g (1lb) French or runner beans
3tbsp ghee or sunflower oil
Salt and freshly ground black pepper
6tbsp water
1½tsp garam masala (see page 112)
1tbsp finely chopped fresh coriander (optional)

Cut the meat into small cubes. Peel and thinly slice the onion and divide into rings. Top and tail the beans and cut into thin diagonal slices.

Heat the ghee or oil in a large heavy frying pan. Add the meat and brown over a high heat on all sides. Add the onions and cook over a medium heat, stirring now and then until the onions are soft, transparent and a golden brown. Season with salt and pepper, add the water and cook without covering until the meat is tender and all the water has been absorbed. Mix in the garam masala for the last 5min of cooking time. Transfer to a heated serving dish. Sprinkle the chopped coriander over before serving.

The flavouring of keemas varies from one household to another and favourite recipes are usually handed down from mother to daughter. The secret lies in colouring the meat and producing a dish at the end that has a thick, rich sauce. Tomatoes, onions and peas or beans add bulk to the meat, stretching the more expensive protein ingredients.

Keema (Curried Minced Lamb)
(Serves 4)

450g (1lb) lean mutton or lamb
2 large onions
4 medium tomatoes
6 garlic cloves
2 green chilli peppers
0.5cm (¼in) fresh green ginger root
225g (8oz) shelled peas or trimmed beans
2tbsp ghee or sunflower oil
2.5cm (1in) cinnamon
5 cloves
1tsp ground coriander
½tsp ground cardamom
½tsp turmeric
3tbsp water
Salt
1tsp garam masala (see page 112)
1tbsp fresh coriander leaves (or use finely chopped parsley)

Mince the meat through the coarse blades of a mincing machine or finely chop it in an electric food processor. Peel and finely chop the onions. Cover the tomatoes with boiling water for 3min, drain, slide off the skins and chop the tomatoes. Peel and finely chop the garlic. Remove the seeds from the chillies and finely chop the flesh. Peel and mince the ginger. Chop the beans if they are being used.

Heat the ghee or oil in a large heavy frying pan. Add the onions, garlic, cinnamon and cloves and stir over a moderate heat to prevent sticking for 4min. Add the spices, raise the heat, stir in the meat and cook over a high heat stirring lightly until the meat is browned on all sides. Add 3tbsp of water and mix in the tomatoes; simmer, stirring every now and then to prevent sticking, for about 30min until the meat is tender (if the mixture gets too dry stir in a little extra water). Add the peas or beans and continue to simmer for about 6min until the vegetables are tender. Season with salt, stir in the garam masala and pile on to a heated serving dish. Sprinkle the keema with the coriander leaves or parsley before serving.

Tandoori Murg (Spiced Chicken)
(Serves 4)

1.4kg (3lb) chicken
Salt and freshly ground black pepper
½tsp cayenne pepper
3tbsp lemon juice
3 cloves garlic
5cm (2in) fresh green ginger root
2tsp coriander seeds
2tsp cumin seeds
4 cardamoms, peeled
2tbsp lemon juice
4tbsp yoghurt
1tsp red vegetable colouring
2tbsp ghee or sunflower oil

This dish from North India is baked in a clay oven and usually served on special occasions. The red colouring of the chicken is most distinctive (Indians love brightly coloured food, especially for festivals). Red colouring can be bought from supermarkets and Oriental food shops. You can buy prepared tandoori powder or paste from these shops too, but the spices you grind yourself will always taste better and the joy of all spiced dishes lies in altering the spices to suit your taste. In India customers go to a market to have spices freshly ground into powders or pastes to suit their family's particular desires.

Tandoori chicken is extremely good cooked over a barbecue.

Cut the chicken into 4 quarters and slash through the skin of the quarters at about 1cm (½in) intervals with a sharp knife. Rub the chicken pieces with salt, freshly ground black pepper, half the cayenne and half the lemon juice. Leave to stand for 1hr.

Peel the garlic and ginger. Combine coriander, cumin and cardamoms in an electric blender, food processor or coffee grinder and process until finely ground. Add the garlic and ginger, the remaining lemon juice, cayenne pepper, yoghurt and food colouring and blend until smooth. Rub this mixture all over the chicken pieces and leave to stand again for 24hr in a cool place or refrigerator, turning the pieces about 4 times.

Place the chicken pieces on a rack, spoon over any marinade from the dish and brush the pieces with melted ghee or oil. Roast in a preheated hot oven 200°C (400°F, Gas mark 6), turning frequently and basting with any juices in the pan, for about 30min or until the chicken is tender and crisp on the outside.

Rice, the staple food of India, is served at almost every meal. By the sixteenth century there were already more than 26 varieties of rice listed; today there are many more varying from brown rice to long grain Patna and the high quality Basmati rice. In some dishes the rice is served plain boiled, in others it is spiced and highly flavoured and in some the rice is fried with other ingredients.

Rice
Basic Plain Boiled Rice (Chawal/Chaval)
(Serve 6)

350g (12oz) white long grain Patna or Basmati rice
40g (1½oz) ghee
2tsp salt

Soak the rice in cold water for 30min; drain really well.

Melt the ghee in a saucepan, add the rice and stir over a moderate heat for 4min. Add enough water to come 2.5cm (1in) above the surface of the rice and stir in the salt. Bring slowly to the boil, stir well, cover tightly and cook over a low heat for about 20min until all the water has been absorbed. Stir the rice with a fork to separate the grains and beat air into the rice, cover tightly again and leave to stand for 10min.

A pulau in which spices and nuts are added to the rice to make an aromatic and savoury accompaniment for curries.

Rice
Navratan Chaval (Nine Gem Rice)
(Serves 6)

350g (12oz) long grain Patna or Basmati Rice
1 large onion
3 cloves garlic
5 green cardamoms
4 dried apricots
1 small cauliflower
50g (2oz) blanched almonds
1tbsp pistachio nuts
4tbsp ghee or sunflower oil
8 peppercorns
3 cloves
7.5cm (3in) cinnamon
100g (4oz) fresh or frozen peas
½tsp turmeric
Salt
2tbsp sultanas

Wash and drain the rice. Peel and finely chop the onion. Peel and very finely chop the garlic. Crush the cardamoms. Finely chop the apricots. Divide the cauliflower into small florets. Slice the almonds and pistachio nuts.

Heat 3tbsp of the ghee or oil in a large, heavy pan. Add the onion and garlic and cook over a medium heat until the onion is golden. Add the peppercorns, cloves, cardamoms and cinnamon and stir over a medium heat for 2min. Add the cauliflower and continue to stir for 3min. Mix in the rice and stir until the grains become transparent. Add enough hot water to come 2.5cm (1in) above the level of the rice and mix in the peas, apricots, turmeric and a good seasoning of salt. Bring to the boil, stir lightly, cover tightly and simmer for 20min. Remove from the heat, stir lightly again and leave, covered, for 5min. Heat the remaining tbsp of ghee or oil in a frying pan, add the nuts and fry over a medium heat until the nuts are crisp.

Pile the rice on to a serving plate and sprinkle over the nuts and sultanas before serving.

Rice and Spinach Ring
(Serves 6–8)

350g (12oz) long grain or Patna rice
675g (1½lb) fresh spinach
Salt
2 medium onions
6tbsp sunflower oil
Salt and freshly ground black pepper
25g (1oz) butter
1tbsp garam masala (see page 112)

To be honest I am not sure whether this is an authentic Indian dish or one that I have dreamed up for myself. Certainly its origins lie in India; what I have not been able to find out is whether the recipe is served in a ring mould like this one. The point about it is that it is an Indian dish which can be adapted most successfully to Western cooking. The ring looks very attractive and makes a perfect background to any number of simple minced, curried or creamed meat, fish, poultry or vegetable dishes.

Cover the rice with cold water and leave to soak for 2hr. Blanch the spinach in boiling salted water for 2min, drain well and press out excess water. Finely chop the spinach. Peel and finely chop the onions. Drain the rice. Heat the oil in a heavy saucepan, add the onions and cook over a low heat, stirring to prevent sticking, until the onions are soft and transparent. Add the spinach and stir for 2min. Add the rice and 600ml (1pt) of water, season with salt and pepper, bring to the boil and simmer for 15min. Drain off water and mix the butter and garam masala with the rice, onions and spinach.

Press the ingredients firmly into a buttered ring mould, cover with foil and bake in a moderate oven 180°C (350°F, Gas mark 4) for 30min. Uncover and leave to stand for 5min, remove the foil and invert the mould on to a serving dish.

Dum Gobi
(Baked Spiced Cauliflower)
(Serves 4)

1 medium sized cauliflower
1 large onion
300ml (½pt) natural yoghurt
2tbsp tomato purée
1tsp ground coriander
1tsp chilli powder
1tsp ground ginger
Salt
50g (2oz) butter, melted

Trim the cauliflower into florets and parboil for 8–10min. Peel and finely chop the onion and mix with the yoghurt, tomato purée, coriander, chilli and ginger, and season with a little salt. Put the cauliflower in a deep ovenproof dish, pour over the yoghurt mixture and cover loosely with foil. Bake at 190°C (375°F, Gas mark 5) for about 1hr, basting occasionally with the sauce. About 10min before the end of the cooking time, take off the foil and pour over the melted butter.

Crisp Fried Aubergine Slices

A most delicious accompaniment to other vegetable or chicken dishes. The aubergine should be very crisp and well drained on kitchen paper. The slices are often used to garnish other dishes and are always cooked at the last minute.

4 small aubergines
Salt and freshly ground black pepper
Flour
8 fenugreek seeds
½tsp fennel seeds
¼tsp cumin seeds
Oil for frying
Pinch cayenne pepper
1tbsp lemon juice

Cut the aubergine into thin slices, sprinkle with salt and leave to sweat in a colander or sieve for 20min. Wash the slices in cold water and pat dry on kitchen paper and lightly dredge the slices in seasoned flour.

Heat 5cm (2in) oil in a deep pan until smoking. Add the fenugreek, fennel and cumin and cook until the seeds begin to pop. Add the aubergine slices taking care not to overcrowd them in the pan and cook over a high heat until crisp and golden brown. Remove the slices with a slotted spoon and drain on plenty of crumpled kitchen paper. Serve as soon as they are ready with a sprinkling of lemon juice topped with a good pinch of cayenne.

Curried Potatoes with Yoghurt
(Serves 6)

1 large onion
3 cloves garlic
2 small chilli peppers
2 large, ripe tomatoes
8 medium potatoes
6tbsp sunflower oil
½tsp fennel seeds
2 bay leaves
½tsp mustard powder
Pinch sugar
½tsp ground nutmeg
½tsp ground cumin
Salt and freshly ground black pepper
300ml (½pt) water
5tbsp plain yoghurt
1tbsp finely chopped parsley

Potato recipes are abundant in India and a great joy they are, as boiled, mashed or chipped potatoes can become very boring during the winter. The other joy about these recipes is that, like so many curry dishes, they stand up well to being reheated.

Peel and finely chop the onion. Peel and finely chop the garlic. Remove the seeds from the chilli peppers and chop the flesh. Cover the tomatoes with boiling water, leave to stand for 3min, drain, slide off the skins and roughly chop the tomatoes. Peel the potatoes and cut them into thick 'chips'. Combine the onion and garlic in an electric liquidizer or food processor and process until the mixture is reduced to a purée.

Heat 5cm (2in) of oil in a frying pan, add the potatoes and cook over a high heat until the potatoes are golden brown but still very firm. Drain on kitchen paper.

Transfer the oil to a deep sided, heavy pan. Add the fennel, bay leaves and peppers, and stir over a medium heat until the bay leaves begin to turn colour. Add the onion, garlic purée and mustard and stir (take care to avoid spitting) over a medium heat for 4min. Add the tomatoes, sugar, nutmeg and cumin, season with salt and freshly ground black pepper, bring to the boil and simmer for 10min without covering. Add the fried potatoes with 300ml (½pt) of water and cook over a medium high heat, stirring lightly every now and then, for 20min until the potatoes are tender, well coated with the reduced sauce but are not broken up.

Add the yoghurt, mix well and heat through. Serve hot with a topping of finely chopped parsley.

Tamatar Bharta (Tomatoes and Spices)
(Serves 4 as a side dish)

1 small onion
2 cloves garlic
300ml (½pt) plain natural yoghurt
1 egg white
1 tin 425g (15oz) tomatoes
1½tbsp ghee or sunflower oil
2 bay leaves
1tbsp finely chopped fresh mint leaves
Salt and freshly ground black pepper

Peel and finely chop the onion and garlic. Combine the yoghurt and egg white in an electric liquidizer or food processor and process until smooth. Transfer the mixture to a saucepan and stir (in one direction only) over a low heat until the yoghurt has thickened and is smooth. Roughly chop the tomatoes.

Heat the ghee or oil in a heavy frying pan. Add the onion, garlic and bay leaves, stirring until the onion is soft and transparent. Add the tomatoes, yoghurt and mint and season with salt and freshly ground black pepper. Cook, uncovered, over a medium heat, stirring occasionally, until the liquid has dried out.

Channna Dhal
(Spiced Yellow Split Peas)
(Serves 4 with a meat or vegetable curry)

225g (8oz) split yellow peas
1 onion
3 cloves garlic
2 green cardamom seeds
1 green chilli pepper
2.5cm (1in) cinnamon
2tbsp ghee or sunflower oil
½tsp paprika
¼tsp turmeric
1tbsp lemon juice
Salt and freshly ground black pepper
1tbsp finely chopped coriander leaves or parsley

Dhals are the Indian lentil dishes that often provide hearty accompaniments to curries or rice and which provide inexpensive protein.

Soak the peas in cold water for 30min. Drain, cover with cold water, add a pinch of salt and bring to the boil. Simmer the peas for about 30min until soft and drain well. Peel and finely chop the onion and garlic. Crush the cardamoms. Remove the seeds from the chilli pepper and very finely chop the flesh. Crush the cinnamon.

Heat the ghee or oil in a heavy frying pan and add the onion, garlic and chilli and cook over a low heat until the onion is soft and transparent. Add the cardamom, paprika, cinnamon and turmeric and stir for 2min. Add the peas and lemon juice, season with salt and pepper and cook over a low heat, stirring, for 5min. Turn into a serving dish and sprinkle over the coriander leaves or parsley before serving.

Indonesia

The eating habits of the people of this enormous country (which comprises more than 3,000 islands) can be surprising. First, and difficult for the twentieth century Westerner to come to grips with, is *bojo kromo* which roughly translated means 'real hospitality', part of the *adat* (cultural tradition) of Indonesia. Sir Stamford Raffles, founder of Singapore and a great South East Asia traveller, wrote in his nineteenth century *History of Java*, 'By the custom of the country, good food and lodging are ordered to be provided for all strangers and travellers arriving at a village, and in no country are the rights of hospitality more strictly observed by custom and practice'.

Salamat makan ('good eating'), the daily greeting before any meal in Indonesia, is an encouragement to relax and enjoy your food, and to accept it as a gift. We met frequent examples of this hospitality in Indonesia and we tried to reciprocate whenever we could, but there were a few unexpected special meals that will always be memorable.

On one occasion, dead tired, we arrived at a policeman's lonely shack on the coast of the island of Ceram where we were trying to make contact with a little-known tribe of headhunters. The policeman was away but his wife, far from being frightened by the sight of us, lined up four giggling daughters and welcomed us with open arms. Turtle eggs the size of pingpong balls were quickly boiled to take the edge off our appetites (you suck out the white and yolk from a hole in the soft shell) while the daughters rasped coconut flesh on a grater made from a thorny bark; rice was boiled, a handful of vegetables fleetingly tossed in coconut oil over the high heat of an open fire, a light soup brewed from the ever present stockpot, and pieces of a mackerel-like fish were quickly fried. Supper was on the table in less than half an hour and mouthwatering it was too.

Take rice, for instance, which is used throughout Indonesia, not just as an appetite reducer but to absorb the flavours of more expensive protein ingredients and the liquid

they are cooked in. Simple vegetable soups provide nourishment at a small cost; vegetables are thinly sliced and lightly cooked or steamed on top of rice while it is cooking to conserve the goodness; fish, meat and poultry are often cut into the thinnest possible slices or shredded to make a little go a long way; highly flavoured sauces, often sweetened with dark brown palm sugar, with rice give body to a small amount of basic ingredients.

Indonesian food in the urban areas still reflects, to a certain extent, the influence of Dutch colonisers who arrived in the sixteenth century. Sugary confections remain popular and you often find breakfast in city hotels consisting of chocolate vermicelli served with slices of bread and butter and slices of Dutch type cheese. And there is, of course, the famed *rizsttafel* still being served to foreign tourists in larger hotels and restaurants.

Rizsttafel, translated means 'rice table' and really denotes the classic Indonesian style of serving the daily main family meal. A basic dish of boiled or fried rice is accompanied by several small dishes with emphasis on spices, sweet and sour flavourings and peanut based sauces. During the time of the Dutch colonisers this meal pattern was inflated to banquet proportions with the rice being accompanied by not just 4 or 5 savoury dishes but as many as 40 or 50 side dishes at a time.

Saté is very much a national dish which I serve frequently at home. In Indonesia satés are served at the smartest of cocktail parties, they form part of any respectable rizsttafel; most people nibble a few bought from favourite vendors, on the way to or from work. Satés are basically the South East Asian equivalent of the Middle Eastern kebab but the meat, fish or poultry is cooked on small bamboo skewers and usually cut into thin thin slices so that it cooks in a matter of minutes. In the more elaborate satés the ingredients are marinaded before being cooked and then served with a rich, peanut flavoured sauce; for the more simple variations the ingredients are brushed with the sauce as they cook over charcoal.

The marinade is usually a mixture of oil, lemon juice, soy sauce, spices and seasonings. The peanut sauce is made by frying finely chopped onion and garlic, finely chopped or ground chilli and fresh ginger root, adding ground peanuts or crunchy peanut butter, water or thin coconut milk, a little lemon or lime juice, 1tbsp of dark brown sugar and about 2tbsp of soy sauce with salt to taste. The mixture is boiled for about 5min and used for basting or as a dipping sauce.

I chill my meat or chicken in the deep freeze for 20min before cutting it into wafer thin slices about 2.5cm (1in) wide and threading the slices onto thin bamboo skewers (which can be bought from good kitchen shops or Chinese super-markets). I soak my satés overnight in a marinade flavoured with oil, lemon juice, cumin, coriander, salt and pepper, then I grill them quickly and serve the peanut sauce separately.

Much of the flavouring that makes Indonesian dishes so individual is the use of *sambals*, spicy pastes or thick sauces and *blanchans*, a seasoning based on ground, salted and dried fish or shellfish.

Since coconut milk is used so much in the making of Indonesian dishes here is how to produce it in your own kitchen. To make coconut cream which is thick and rich, grate the flesh of a mature coconut (you can buy these from health food shops) or use desiccated coconut; mix with an equal amount of boiling water, leave to stand until cool enough to handle and then squeeze through muslin. If you add warm water to the residue of the squeezed coconut and then squeeze again through muslin, you have coconut milk — combine equal quantities of both cream and milk and you have a liquid suitable for using in the place of stock for many Indonesian dishes.

Seen on many Indonesian dishes are crisply fried onion flakes. They can be made in bulk whenever you have time and then stored in an airtight jar. They are a tasty garnish for the top of vegetables, some salads, rice dishes and even on mashed potatoes. Chop up very finely as many peeled onions as you can bear to (a food processor is ideal for this), and pat them dry on kitchen paper. Heat some sunflower oil in a large frying pan until a haze rises from it, add the chopped onion and cook over a medium heat, stirring every now and then, until the flakes are crisp and dry (this always takes longer than one thinks, the onions must be very crisp and a good nutty brown colour). Remove the onion flakes from the pan with a slotted spoon and make them completely oil free on kitchen paper. Leave to cool; store in airtight, screw topped jars. Use only a tablespoon or two as needed.

Perhaps the most exciting thing about Indonesian food for me is the multiple influences which make up so many dishes. Add to that a climate in which almost anything will grow, the lush paddy fields and vegetable gardens of Sumatra; intensely terraced, breathtakingly beautiful country, the abundant harvest of the seas that surround the Indonesian islands; rich pasture lands for raising beef, forests for game and the results *must* be stunning.

Sweet toothed influences come from the Dutch; spices and a love of fish from Portuguese invaders; Arab influences appear too; curries and curry spices owe their popularity to the Indian communities; the Chinese (who arrived about

100BC) brought their own cuisine and finally, the indigenous peoples also had their own food culture, traditions and rituals. Religion plays a part in the food habits of many Indonesians; Muslims, for instance, eat no pork and keep their abattoirs separate from the other butchers; Hindus eat no beef but delight in sweet, sugared, roast suckling pig, and many tribal peoples still live as hunter gatherers.

Among the tribal peoples of Indonesia we ate well; if you can get it, I cannot recommend too highly wild pig, fresh crayfish and sago packed into green bamboo, sealed and baked over an open fire – as so often, the simplest food can be the best of all gastronomic delights!

Kacang Bawang
(Savoury Fried Peanuts)

6 cloves garlic
1 large onion
Oil for frying
4tbsp finely chopped celeriac or celery leaves
450g (1lb) blanched peanuts
Salt

These savoury peanuts are served as an accompaniment to rice and other dishes and also as a snack. They keep well in an airtight tin, but once you start eating them it is hard to stop.

Peel and very thinly slice the garlic. Peel and very finely chop the onion. Heat 3tbsp oil in a heavy frying pan, add the onion and cook over a moderately high heat, stirring every now and then, until the onion is crisp and well browned, drain on kitchen paper.

Heat 2tbsp oil in a clean frying pan, add the celeriac or celery and cook over a medium heat, stirring to prevent burning until the celeriac is crisp but not burnt. Drain well on kitchen paper.

Heat 3tbsp oil over a high heat, add the garlic and peanuts and cook, stirring until the garlic is pale golden and the peanuts are crisp; drain well on kitchen paper. Combine the peanuts, garlic, onions and celeriac, season with salt, shake to mix well and leave to cool.

130

Soto Ajam (Chicken Soup)
(Serves 4)

1 chicken approximately 1.5kg (3lb) with giblets
1 onion
4 cloves garlic
4 sticks celery
2tbsp oil
5cm (2in) fresh ginger root
100g (4oz) bean sprouts, washed
4tbsp medium dry sherry
4tbsp light soy sauce
Salt and freshly ground black pepper
6 spring onions

Put the chicken and giblets in a large saucepan, cover with water. Peel and roughly chop the onion and add to the pan. Bring to the boil over a medium heat, lower heat and allow to simmer until the chicken is tender (about 1½ hr). Remove the chicken from the stock, allow to cool a little then remove the skin and bones and chop the flesh into bitesized pieces. Strain the stock through a sieve and reserve. Peel and finely chop, or mince, the garlic. Finely chop the celery.

In a large saucepan heat the oil and gently sauté the garlic together with the fresh ginger root which you have squeezed through a garlic press, add the celery and cook until the celery has softened, pour over the stock, and mix in the chicken pieces and bean sprouts. Mix the sherry and soy sauce together and stir into the soup, simmer over a low heat for about 20min. Season with salt and freshly ground black pepper. Serve in individual bowls with a sprinkling of finely chopped spring onion as garnish.

131

Kari Udang (Curried Shrimps)
(Serves 4)

1 small onion
4 red chilli peppers
3tbsp vegetable oil
1tbsp lemon juice
½tsp shrimp paste
1tsp ground turmeric
4 candlenuts
450g (1lb) peeled shrimps
250ml (¼pt) thick coconut milk (see page 129)

Peel and finely chop the onion. Deseed and roughly chop the chillies.

Heat the oil in a large frying pan, or wok, and stir fry the onion and chillies for approximately 1min. Stir in the lemon juice, shrimp paste and turmeric, mixing in well. Finely chop or grind the candlenuts and add to the pan. Mix in the shrimps, stirring all the time, until they are just turning pink, pour over the coconut milk and allow to simmer for 10min. Serve immediately with some plain boiled rice.

Peanut Sauce for Satés

Peanut sauce is served with most satés and, in Indonesia, you will find the street vendors who sell many varieties of saté by the side of their charcoal fires making the sauce in a pan.

1 small onion or shallot
2 cloves garlic
1 small chilli pepper
1tbsp oil
300ml (½pt) water
5tbsp coarse peanut butter
½tsp sugar
1tbsp dark soy sauce
1tbsp lemon juice
Salt

Peel and very finely chop the onion and garlic. Very finely chop the chilli pepper (remove the seeds if you do not like too hot a taste). Heat the oil in a small frying pan, add the onion and garlic and cook over a low heat until the onion is soft and transparent. Add the chilli pepper and continue to cook, stirring for 3min. Add the water, peanut butter and sugar and mix well. Bring to the boil and cook over a high heat, stirring for about 10min until the sauce is thick. Add the soy sauce and lemon juice, season with salt, and serve hot or cold.

Beef Saté
(Serves 6)

1 onion
2 cloves garlic
5cm (2in) fresh green ginger root
1 chilli pepper
25g (1oz) peanuts
450g (1lb) rump steak or topside of beef
1tbsp sunflower oil
1tsp ground coriander
¼tsp ground turmeric
¼tsp soft brown sugar
¼tsp curry powder
Salt

Saté comes in all flavours and many varieties. You cut the meat into small cubes, but it is more successful and more economical if cut into very thin strips or slices.

Peel and chop the onion, garlic and ginger. Chop the chilli pepper. Combine the onion, garlic, ginger, chilli and peanuts in a food processor or liquidizer and process until the ingredients are reduced to a purée.

Chill the beef in a deep freeze for about 30min until firm. Cut into very thin slices and then into 5cm (2in) strips.

Heat the oil in a frying pan. Add the onion paste, coriander and turmeric and fry over a high heat for 3min. Add the sugar and curry powder, season with salt and continue to stir for 2min. Leave to cool. Spread the spices over the meat and leave to stand for 1hr.

Thread the meat onto small bamboo skewers and baste with any remaining marinade. Grill over hot charcoal or under a high grill, turning frequently for 5–6min until tender.

This is another recipe where, if you chill the chicken before cutting it, you can make a relatively small amount stretch a remarkably long way.

Saté Ayam (Chicken Saté)
(Serves 6)

450g (1lb) boned chicken breast
2 cloves garlic
2tbsp soy sauce
2tbsp water
Salt
Oil

Chill the chicken breast in a freezer for 30min until firm, and then cut into very thin slices and then into 3.5cm (1½in) wide strips. Peel and chop, or mince, the garlic, and combine with the soy sauce and water, season with a little salt. Marinade the chicken in the soy sauce mixture for 2hr.

Serve with the peanut sauce (see page 132).

Thread the chicken onto small bamboo skewers, brush with oil and grill over charcoal or under a hot grill for about 5min, turning frequently, until the chicken is just tender.

Indonesian Fried Pork
(Serves 4)

450g (1lb) pork, leg fillet or tenderloin preferably
1 medium onion
2 cloves garlic
3tbsp groundnut (peanut) oil
3tbsp heavy soy sauce
2tbsp medium dry sherry
2tsp soft brown sugar
2tsp lemon juice
Good pinch of ground ginger
300ml (¼pt) chicken stock

Cut the pork into small dice, trimming off any excess fat or skin. Peel and roughly chop the onion. Peel and finely chop the garlic.

Heat the oil in a large frying pan until really hot then quickly fry the pork until golden brown, stirring frequently so that the pork is evenly cooked. Add the onion and garlic and continue stirring until the onion softens and turns golden brown. Mix the soy sauce, sherry, sugar, lemon juice and ground ginger together and pour over the pork, together with the chicken stock and continue cooking over a low heat for about 20min.

Gado-Gado
(Vegetable Salad with Peanut Sauce)
(Serves 4)

350g (12oz) green beans
225g (8oz) cabbage or spinach
225g (8oz) beansprouts, washed
2 carrots
½ cucumber
3 large potatoes, boiled
2 hardboiled eggs
6tbsp crunchy peanut butter
175ml (6fl oz) water
2tsp soft brown sugar
3tbsp light soy sauce
Juice of ½ lemon

This is unusual in that it combines both raw and cooked vegetables , and is a very popular Indonesian salad.

Cut the beans into diagonal bite sized pieces, and cook in lightly salted boiling water until just tender. Drain and refresh under cold running water. Remove the tough stalks from the cabbage and shred the leaves. Blanch in boiling water for 1min, drain and refresh under cold running water. Peel the carrots and cut into matchstick strips. Thinly slice, but do not peel, the cucumber. Cut the potatoes into thick slices, and the hardboiled eggs into wedges.

In a small saucepan combine the peanut butter, water, brown sugar, soy sauce and lemon juice, and heat gently, stirring all the time until the ingredients are well mixed, adding a little more water if the sauce appears to be too thick; the desired consistency is a pouring sauce. Pour the sauce into a jug and chill well.

Use a large flat platter to arrange the salad; put the cabbage in the centre, and then arrange all the other vegetables in sections around, garnish with hardboiled egg and hand the dressing around separately.

Nasi Goreng (Fried Rice)
(Serves 4)

3 eggs
Salt and freshly ground black pepper
4tbsp vegetable oil
225g (8oz) shelled prawns
350g (12oz) pork fillet
2 large onions
3 cloves garlic
350g (12oz) cooked long grain rice
2tbsp heavy soy sauce
2tsp soft dark brown sugar
1tbsp lemon juice

Beat the eggs and season with salt and freshly ground black pepper. Heat 1tbsp of oil in a large frying pan and pour in the beaten eggs, cook until completely set. Slide out of the pan, without folding, onto a plate and allow to cool. Remove the black vein from the prawns, rinse under cold running water and pat dry on kitchen paper. With a very sharp knife cut the pork fillet into wafer thin slivers, and then into strips no more than 1.25cm (½in) wide.

Peel and roughly chop the onion and garlic and put both into an electric blender or food processor, and process until puréed.

Heat the remaining oil in a wok, or large frying pan, and cook the onion and garlic purée until golden brown, stirring all the time. Add the prawns and pork to the wok, and cook, stirring all the time until the prawns have turned pink, and the pork is cooked through. Stir in the rice.

In a small bowl mix the soy sauce, brown sugar, and lemon juice together, add to the rice mixture, stirring well so that the sauce is evenly distributed, and the ingredients are heated through. Pile the rice mixture onto a warm serving dish. Cut the cold omelette into thin strips, and use to garnish the rice.

Pisang Goreng (Banana Fritters)
(Serves 4)

100g (4oz) plain flour
Pinch salt
200ml (7fl oz) water
6 small ripe bananas
1 egg white
Oil for deep frying
Castor sugar

Combine the flour, salt and water and beat until smooth. Peel the bananas and cut each in half. Beat the egg white until stiff and fold into the batter. Dip the bananas into the batter and deep fry in very hot oil until golden brown and well puffed out. Drain on a generous quantity of kitchen paper and sprinkle with sugar before serving.

I used to buy these sweet, delicious, fritters from any street stall that happened to be selling them when I was in Indonesia and the smell of them cooking still evokes memories of small backstreets in little island towns. In Indonesia the fritters are fried in coconut oil but the flavour of the oil is a little rich for Western taste and it is better to use sunflower oil.

These fritters were very successful when I was running a Christmas charity stall in our local Westcountry market. It was a miserable day and to encourage trade I set up a butane gas burner and wok and fried my *pisang goreng* to hand out free to anyone who spent more than £5 – sales went up very satisfactorily.

Ireland

My grandparents moved from England to Ireland around the turn of the century, and my mother was born and brought up in Dublin. She came from a large family and, when she was old enough, the obvious choice for work was domestic service. She tells many a tale of those days, some with much laughter, others with a whimsical smile on her face. 'Housekeeper, that was the glorious title I was given, it really meant chief cook and general dogsbody' she said, adding in a rather stern voice 'and they wouldn't work today like we did in those days.'

My mother has always been what I would call a good plain cook, using seasonal fresh ingredients, and inexpensive cuts of meat to produce nourishing and tasty meals for our family. After all, raising three children in wartime, and then coping with postwar rationing was no easy task. Now aged 83, she still cooks for herself each day, and she is as particular as ever that the vegetables are fresh and of fine quality, and that the meat is tender and not too fatty; her great indulgence now is occasionally to treat herself to some fillet steak, and this she enjoys enormously.

Country cooking in Ireland is based on use of fresh ingredients, and potatoes remain the staple diet. Many butchers own some sheep and cattle, which they rear and slaughter themselves, and the quality is excellent. Pork is used a lot, roasted, in chops, pies and sausages and *cruibini* is a very popular dish, usually served in a country inn accompanied by hunks of soda bread and a glass of creamy-topped Guinness. Cruibini or pig's feet crubeens use the hind feet of the pig since they are more meaty than the trotters. They are made simply by simmering in water with onion and root vegetables and a few herbs until the meat is really tender. Then the feet are removed from the pot, allowed to cool and eaten with the fingers.

Seafood from the coastal waters around Ireland and freshwater fish, such as trout and salmon, are caught in the rivers and many lakes dotted throughout the country. Fish is

138

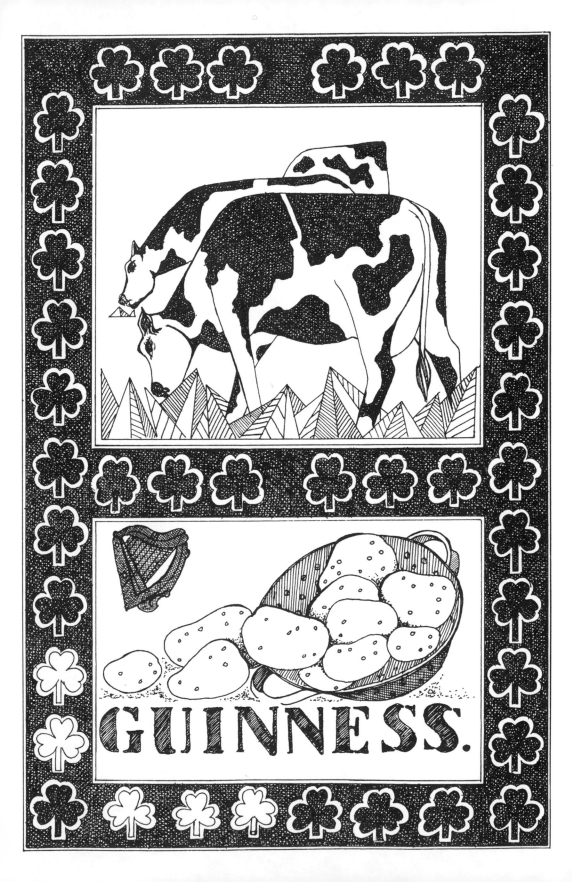

usually cooked quite plainly, and served perhaps with parsley sauce or flavoured butter. Lobster, crabs, mussels and the famous Dublin Bay prawns are often served cooked in crisp light batter.

Country folk always kept poultry, not just for the meat, but for the eggs; chickens are as popular today, and feature frequently in recipes for pies, stews, casseroles and roasts.

Root vegetables and brassicas are the basis of most Irish vegetable dishes; cabbage features in some classic dishes, such as colcannon, which ideally should be made with kale.

Large field mushrooms are there for the picking in many districts, flavoursome with a good 'meaty' texture, they are used in soups.

Many dessert puddings incorporate fresh fruit – apples in particular. A favourite dish is *apple charlotte*, where bread-crumbs mixed with butter and sugar line a pie dish, lightly stewed and sweetened apples are spooned in, which is then topped with more of the breadcrumb mixture. In Ireland it would traditionally be served with warm cream, but it is equally good with custard.

The food of Ireland, outside the cities, remains true country cooking; to sit down to a pot of strong tea at a scrubbed kitchen table and to bite into thickly buttered wedges of *barm brack*, a scrumptious homebaked fruited yeast bread, is truly to experience Irish country cooking.

Trout with Lemon Butter
(Serves 4)

100g (4oz) butter
Grated rind and juice of a lemon
1tbsp finely chopped fresh parsley
4 fresh trout
25g (1oz) melted butter
Freshly ground black pepper

Soften the butter and beat until creamy. Add the lemon rind and chopped parsley and mix well. Mould the butter into a sausage shape, wrap in foil and chill in the refrigerator until hard.

Gut and wash the trout, patting dry on kitchen paper. Place the fish on a grill pan, and brush with the melted butter mixed with the lemon juice, season the fish with freshly ground black pepper and grill under a medium heat for about 6min each side. Serve the trout with slices of lemon butter.

Ireland

Dressed Crab
(Serves 4)

---

1 cooked crab
2tbsp fresh breadcrumbs, white or brown
2tsp lemon juice
Salt and freshly ground black pepper

Lay the crab on its back and twist off the legs and claws. Lift up the flap curving under the body, push and remove the shell. If you find it difficult to pull apart use a teaspoon to pry open the shell. Remove the spongy appendages, known as 'dead men's fingers', and the stomach sac, which should come away neatly and looks as though it is packed inside a plastic bag.

Separate the crabmeat. Using a teaspoon, scoop the brown meat from the shell onto a plate and mix this with the breadcrumbs and lemon juice, seasoning with salt and freshly ground black pepper. Break the claws and legs, using a crab cracker or a hammer, and remove the white meat – a skewer is helpful at this stage. Crack the body and pick out any more white meat.

Wash the crab shell under cold running water, and break off the edges at the clearly defined grooves, and you will be left with a neat shell in which to arrange the crabmeat.

Arrange the brown meat down the centre, in a neat strip, and the white meat either side. Serve with mayonnaise.

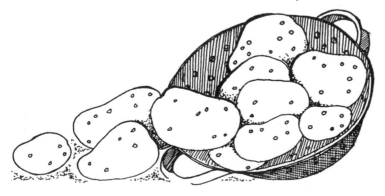

Ireland

Probably the best known Irish dish, economical but nutritious and warming.

Irish Stew
(Serves 6)

2kg (2¼lb) neck of lamb
675g (1½lb) potatoes, peeled
2 large onions
4 carrots
Salt and freshly ground black pepper
1tsp mixed herbs
1tbsp finely chopped fresh parsley
1*l* (1¾pt) stock, or water and stock cubes

Trim any excess fat from the lamb, then cut the meat into neat pieces. Cut the potatoes into thick slices. Peel and thinly slice the onions and carrots.

Layer the potatoes, meat, onion and carrots in a large ovenproof casserole, seasoning each layer with salt and freshly ground black pepper, and a sprinkling of the mixed herbs and fresh parsley. Finish off with a layer of potatoes. Pour over the stock and cook in a preheated oven at 150°C (300°F, Gas mark 2) for 2hr.

Kathleen's Spiced Beef
(Serves 6–8)

When I visited Ireland as a child and teenager, my cousin would always prepare this very festive dish to welcome the family home, and it would be followed by a rousing singsong with one of my younger cousins playing the accordion – what the Irish call a real 'hoolie'.

2kg (4½lb) rib of beef, boned and rolled
100g (4oz) coarse seasalt
1tsp ground cloves
1tsp ground mace
½tsp allspice
½tsp ground cinnamon
50g (2oz) soft dark brown sugar
4 juniper berries, crushed
225g (8oz) carrots
2 medium onions
2 sticks celery
Water or stock
Bouquet garni

142

Place the meat in a nonmetal dish. Mix together the seasalt, ground cloves, mace, allspice, cinnamon, brown sugar and juniper berries and rub into the meat very thoroughly; sprinkle any leftover spice mixture into the bottom of the dish under the meat. Cover the dish with clingfilm and put in the bottom of the refrigerator. Turn the meat at least 2 or 3 times a day for the next 3 days.

After 3 days it is time to cook the beef. Peel and slice the carrots and onions, and chop the celery and put into a large flameproof dish, lay the meat on the top, pour over enough water or stock to cover and add the bouquet garni. Bring to the boil, then lower the heat as much as possible, and let simmer slowly for around 4hr, or until the meat is tender.

The meat can be served hot, though it is equally popular served cold, thinly sliced accompanied by a green salad.

Chicken and Leek Pie
(Serves 4)

4 large leeks
675g (1½lb) cooked chicken
Salt and freshly ground black pepper
75g (3oz) butter
1½tbsp plain flour
600ml (1pt) chicken stock
½tsp mixed herbs
1tbsp finely chopped fresh parsley
Grated rind of a lemon
225g (8oz) puff pastry
1 small egg

Trim and wash the leeks, removing any grit and dirt, thinly slice and arrange in the bottom of a pie dish. Roughly chop the chicken and arrange on top of the leeks, season with salt and freshly ground black pepper.

Melt the butter in a saucepan until it begins to foam, and mix in the flour, stirring all the time; gradually stir in the chicken stock, until the sauce comes to the boil and is thick and smooth, add the mixed herbs, parsley and lemon rind, and pour the sauce over the chicken and leeks, moving these ingredients with a fork so that the sauce is evenly distributed.

Roll out the pastry on a lightly floured board and use to make a pastry top to the pie, use any trimmings to decorate the top. Cut a small slit in the centre of the pie. Beat the egg and brush over the pastry. Bake at 200°C (400°F, Gas mark 6) for 5min, then lower the heat to 180°C (350°F, Gas mark 4) for about 35min, when the pastry should be golden brown.

Colcannon
(Serves 4)

675g (1½lb) potatoes
Salt
1 cabbage
Pinch of bicarbonate of soda
1 onion
40g (1½oz) butter
300ml (½pt) milk
Freshly ground black pepper
Pinch of nutmeg

Peel the potatoes and boil until tender in plenty of lightly salted boiling water. Chop the cabbage quite finely and cook in about 5cm (2in) of boiling salted water to which a small pinch of bicarbonate of soda has been added.

Peel and finely chop the onion. Melt 13g (½oz) butter in a saucepan and gently fry the onions until soft and transparent, not browned. Put the remaining butter and milk in a saucepan, and heat gently. Meanwhile, drain the potatoes and cabbage.

Mash the potatoes, add the warm milk and butter, mix in the cooked onion and mix in the cooked cabbage, then season with freshly ground black pepper and nutmeg. Pile into a warmed serving dish.

Mother's Boxty Potatoes
(Potato cakes)
(Makes approximately 12)

450g (1lb) potatoes, peeled
Salt and freshly ground black pepper
100g (4oz) plain flour
A little milk

Spread a piece of muslin over a large mixing bowl, and grate the potato onto the muslin. When all the potatoes are done, gather up the ends of the muslin and squeeze the juices from the potatoes; leave the juice to settle for a while and the starch will sink to the bottom of the bowl. In a clean bowl put the grated potato, together with the starch from the potato liquid (use a spoon to scrape this from the bowl), season with salt and freshly ground black pepper and mix well. Add the flour to the potato mixture and mix well. Gradually beat in some milk a little at a time to produce a firmish dough (firm enough to roll).

On a well floured board roll out the potato mixture and using a small round cutter, cut out into small cakes. Refrigerate for 15–20min.

Lightly oil a heavy bottomed frying pan, and heat until a haze starts to rise, then cook the cakes a few at a time, about 5–6min each side until golden brown.

Ireland

The method of making these potato cakes varies considerably throughout the different regions of Ireland, but this is my mother's recipe, which she recommends served with crispy bacon for breakfast, or as a supper dish with grilled herbed sausages.

Barm Brack

350g (12oz) mixed dried fruit
100g (4oz) demerara sugar
300ml (½pt) hot strong tea
225g (8oz) self-raising flour
½tsp mixed spice
Pinch of ground nutmeg
1 egg
A little milk

Though traditionally made with yeast, this is my mother's recipe, and she recalls making this when she was growing up in Ireland.

Mix the dried fruit and demerara sugar together in a mixing bowl, and pour over the hot tea. Leave to soak overnight.

Sift the flour and spices together and fold into the fruit and tea mixture, beat the egg and mix in well. Add sufficient milk to produce a pouring consistency. Pour the mixture into a lightly oiled loaf tin and bake for 1–1¼hr at 180°C (350°F, Gas mark 4). Test with a skewer to ensure that the cake is cooked.

This is best served sliced and buttered. It also keeps exceptionally well.

Rome, the eternal city: whenever I think of Italy and Italian food, it is the first place that comes to mind. Some twenty years ago, returning home on leave after a two year posting in Pakistan, I managed to grab a few days in this fascinating city. Soaking up the sights, I visited the Colosseum then waited with thousands of others for the Pope to appear on the balcony of St. Peter's. I sat outside a little cafe, drinking cappuccino, in one of the many piazzas with a tinkling fountain, revelling in the sights, sounds and smells of Italy. My all too short visit culminated in an evening visit to the Apian Way, high above the city where little stalls were selling freshly roasted suckling pig (I can recall the delicious aroma even now), which was eaten with the fingers with a chunk of fresh bread, and then washed down with Frascati, that delicate fruity wine of Rome. As I partook of that simple fare, the sun, like a great red shining ball, set slowly over the city casting a golden aureola over the ancient and beautiful buildings below; it is a memory that I cherish.

Rome was for centuries the food centre of Italy, where cooks would strive to create exciting foods for famous folk; Italian chefs went to the court of Louis XII to teach the French the art of fine cooking and they introduced artichokes, haricot beans and other vegetables, until then unknown outside Italy, but which are today an essential part of French *haute cuisine.*

Italy stretches almost a thousand miles from the mountains in the north to the hot and dry southern 'tip of the toe', and the food changes, quite dramatically, throughout the various regions. In the mountainous northwestern Italy the staple foods are rice and *polenta*, made from cornmeal. *Risotto*, made with locally grown round rice originated in this area. To make risotto, melt some butter in a large pan and sauté the rice until all the butter is absorbed and the grains turn opaque, then add some stock, perhaps a little wine and a few herbs, cover and cook until the grains are soft – a risotto should always be quite moist, never dry.

On the northeast coast lies Venice; again, a city I managed to visit during my travels. Evenings in Venice spring to mind – sitting in one of the many restaurants in St. Mark's, enjoying good food, good wine and conversation while an orchestra played in the background. I found it produced a strange feeling of unreality in me; perhaps it was being surrounded by so much water! One of the best known regional dishes is *fegato alla veneziana* – slivers of calf liver, cooked with onions; add a little sage to this dish – it makes all the difference. Some excellent vegetables grow in this region, wild mushrooms, and the famous *Bassano del Grappa* asparagus, which is eaten cold with lashings of mayonnaise.

South of Venice is Bologna, the only region where cream is used lavishly in cooking; in this area grow the delicious black and white truffles that are incorporated into sauces for pasta.

Tuscany, with its green valleys, meandering rivers, and vineyards, is one of Italy's main agricultural areas and the cookery of this region is based on good economical use of the abundant local produce. Tuscan pork is renowned for its excellence.

Sweet chestnuts, grown on enormous trees, are made into chestnut flour for use in many desserts, and here, too, pine nuts grow, an essential ingredient for the famous Italian *pesto sauce*. Olive trees feature in the landscape of Southern Italy, and produce the oil essential to many Italian dishes. The famous oil from Lucca in Tuscany is light and makes superb salad dressings.

With one of the longest coastlines in Europe, Italy has a plentiful marine harvest; prawns, crabs and baby clams, squid, sea bream, swordfish and sole are sold in local markets and incorporated into famous dishes, such as *fritto misto*, comprising morsels of fish and shellfish, dipped in a light batter and deep fried until crisp and golden, then served with wedges of lemon.

One thread that runs through Italian cookery, no matter what the region, is pasta, in all its shapes and forms. Ribbon noodles such as *fettuccine* and *tagliatelle* are used in central Italy, while in the south *ziti*, *rigatoni* and *penne*, tube pastas are more popular. The variety of pastas ranges from the strips of *lasagne* and matchlike *tonnellini* to stuffed pastas such as *ravioli, anolini* and the *tortellini* of Bologna. *Spaghetti*, however, is eaten throughout Italy.

Legend has it that Marco Polo introduced pasta to Italy, but it is more probable that pasta was eaten by the Romans. Italians adore pasta; most of them eat it every day and many enjoy nothing more than pasta tossed in olive oil and liberally sprinkled with freshly ground black pepper.

Many Italian housewives make their own pasta daily; it is delicious and to my mind bears no resemblance to the dried variety obtainable at supermarkets. Making pasta dough is simple, but the rolling does require practice; there are several inexpensive pasta machines on the market to make things easier. To make pasta dough, lightly beat 4 large eggs and mix with 4tbsp cold water in a large mixing bowl. Add 100g (4oz) plain flour to the mixture and beat with a wire whisk, add 350g (¾lb) flour, and (this is the fun bit) work the mixture using your hands into a soft dough; you can add more flour if the dough is too sticky. You should knead the dough for about 10min or so on a well floured board, then let it rest for 30min in a covered bowl. Roll out the dough on a well floured board until very (and I do mean very) thin, and cut into strips or shapes as desired – this is where one of the little pasta machines is very useful. Fresh pasta only needs to be cooked for about 7–8min. If you want to make coloured pasta, then about 225g (8oz) finely chopped cooked spinach, well drained, added to the dough will produce a green pasta, or *pasta verdi* as it is known; the addition of 2tbsp of concentrated tomato paste will produce a pink pasta, or in Italian *pasta rosa*!

Italy is a fruitful country, and the Italian housewife buys fresh produce in season at the daily markets. A veritable array of vegetables such as red and green peppers, aubergines, courgettes, spinach, broccoli and young broad beans, glistening with freshness are usually served as an hors d'oeuvre. Tomatoes, synonymous with Italian cooking, are grown throughout the country and used lavishly. A family meal usually consists of a selection of cold meats, *antipasti*, or perhaps a soup or *risotto*, followed by a pasta course with a sauce; then follows the main dish, usually meat or fish with fresh vegetables or maybe just a salad. The meal finishes with fresh fruit or icecream. When an Italian family gathers for the main meal (usually taken midday), it is a time for relaxation, conversation and pleasure for all members of the family.

Italy

Vegetable omelettes in Italy are included in an *antipasti* (appetizer or first course). Cut into wedges and served hot, warm or cold, they also make excellent picnic foods. This is one of the most simple varieties but no less delicious for that.

Frittatina de Cipolle (Small Onion Omelette)
(Serves 4)

1 large mild onion
4 eggs
½tsp salt
3tbsp olive or sunflower oil

Peel and very thinly slice the onion and divide into rings. Beat the eggs with the salt until smooth.

Heat the oil in a large, heavy, nonstick pan. Add the onion rings and cook over a medium heat, stirring until the onion is soft and transparent. Pour on the eggs and cook until the bottom has become a light golden crust and the omelette is *just* set. Slide the omelette from the pan, add a little more oil to the frying pan and when it is hot turn the omelette over into the pan and continue to cook until the second side is crisp and golden. Serve cut into wedges.

A stunning everyday Italian dish that has evolved over the centuries. Various flours used to make a simple background starch dish finally developed into a more complicated dish of maize flour or cornmeal made like a cake and served in wedges or, even better, fried to accompany meat and vegetable dishes.

Polenta is served with a sauce, with meat, vegetables, fish and a tomato sauce or it can be more simply presented with grated cheese or butter. In any form it is an inexpensive sustaining form of starch which acts as a base for more expensive ingredients. Polenta flour, maize flour or cornmeal can be bought from specialist food shops. The flour must be a rich strong yellow.

Polenta
(Serves 6–8)

1.2*l* (2⅕pt) water
Salt
500g (1lb 2oz) polenta flour
3tbsp oil

Bring the water to the boil and stir in 1tsp salt. Add the flour, a little at a time, to the water whisking over a low heat until the mixture is smooth. Cook the mixture over a low heat, stirring every now and then to prevent sticking. Turn the polenta into a well buttered baking dish, pressing it down firmly and leave to get cool. Chill in the refrigerator for 30min and then turn out of the dish and cut the polenta into 1.5cm (¾in) thick slices about 15cm (6in) long.

Heat the oil in a frying pan until a haze rises from the oil. Add the slices of polenta and cook over a high heat, turning half way through until the polenta is crisp and golden brown on both sides. Serve hot.

Ragu Bolognaise
(Serves 6–8)

2 rashers streaky bacon
50g (2oz) lean ham
1 onion
2 cloves garlic
2 sticks celery
4 ripe tomatoes
15g (½oz) butter
2tbsp sunflower oil
350g (12oz) lean minced beef skirt or rib
100g (4oz) lean minced pork
150ml (¼pt) chicken stock
150ml (¼pt) dry white wine
2tbsp tomato paste
Salt and freshly ground black pepper
Pinch ground nutmeg and cloves
75g (3oz) firm button mushrooms
2 chicken livers
300ml (½pt) single cream

Remove the rinds from the bacon and finely chop or mince the rashers. Very finely chop the ham. Peel and finely chop the onion and garlic. Very finely chop or mince the celery. Cover the tomatoes with boiling water for 3min, drain, slide off the skins and chop the tomatoes.

Heat the butter and oil in a heavy casserole. Add the bacon and ham and cook over a low heat until the bacon fat has melted, add the onion, garlic and celery and cook over a low heat until the onion is soft and transparent (stir to prevent sticking). Raise the heat, add the beef and pork and stir over a high heat until the meat is browned. Add the tomatoes, chicken stock, wine and tomato paste, season with salt, pepper, nutmeg and cloves. Bring to the boil and simmer, uncovered, stirring every now and then until the liquid has evaporated. Add 150ml (¼pt) water and continue to simmer very slowly for 30min. Thinly slice the mushrooms. Finely chop the chicken livers. Add the mushrooms and livers to the sauce and cook over a low heat for 10min. Stir in the cream and check seasoning before serving.

One of the most delicious dishes in the world and a far cry indeed from the liver and onions of nursery days. You have to use calves' liver and you have to either get your butcher to cut it in the thinnest of wafer thin slices, or chill a whole piece of liver in a deep freeze for 45min and then slice it yourself into almost transparent thin slices against the grain. You must also use fresh sage leaves which can now be bought from good greengrocers or supermarkets.

The liver should be served with fried slices of polenta.

Fegato alla Veneziana
(Serves 4–5)

450g (1lb) calves' liver
6 small onions or shallots
4 leaves fresh sage
25g (1oz) butter
3tbsp olive or sunflower oil
Salt and freshly ground black pepper
1tbsp finely chopped parsley
1tsp lemon juice

Slice the liver as thinly as possible and about 5cm (2in) wide. Peel the onions, slice them very thinly and divide into rings. Very finely chop the sage.

Melt the butter with the oil, add the onions and cook over a high heat, stirring, until the onions are lightly browned. Push the onions to the side of the pan, add the liver and cook over a high heat, turning and tossing the meat for 1½min. Add the sage, season with salt and pepper and continue to stir the meat over a high heat for 30sec. Mix in the parsley, sprinkle over the lemon juice and serve at once.

Agnello e Fagioli
(Lamb with Beans)
(Serves 6)

The Italians make good use of lamb. A great many of the dishes have the addition of rich tomato sauces but this is a rather more unusual and subtle marriage of lamb with tomatoes and white beans with peas.

225g (8oz) dried white beans
2 cloves garlic
900g (2lb) leg of lamb boned
1 sprig rosemary
Salt and freshly ground black pepper
425g (15oz) tin Italian peeled tomatoes
4tbsp olive oil
175g (6oz) fresh or frozen peas

Cover the beans with cold water and leave to soak overnight. Drain and cover with fresh water, bring to the boil and boil without salting for 1hr or until tender (adding salt to the beans while cooking results in them becoming tough). Drain the beans. Peel the garlic and cut the cloves into thin slivers. Cut small nicks in the lamb and press the slivers of garlic and the needles of rosemary into the nicks. Rub the meat with salt and pepper. Remove the core and seeds from the tomatoes, but save the tomato juice.

Heat the oil in a heavy iron casserole. Add the meat and brown on all sides over a high heat. Add the tomatoes and enough warm water to come halfway up the meat. Cook, covered, over a low heat for about 1½hr until the meat is tender. Add the beans and peas and cook for a further 6min until the beans are hot through and the peas are tender.

Remove the meat and cut into thin slices. Return the slices to the sauce and vegetables, heat through and serve at once with plain rice.

Fagioli al Forno (Baked Beans)
(Serves 4)

350g (12oz) dried white beans
450g (1lb) belly of pork
2 leeks
4 cloves garlic
5 firm ripe tomatoes (or tinned Italian tomatoes)
Pinch oregano or marjoram
Salt and freshly ground black pepper

Some Italian country style recipes are wonderfully inexpensive and robust. Out of very little can be made delicious dishes that are so suitable for summer main courses. The food should be cooked in an earthenware casserole – these are not expensive and proper earthenware will give the dish the authentic flavour.

Soak the beans overnight in cold water and drain well. Remove the rinds from the pork belly and immerse the rind in boiling water for 1min. Scrape any hair from the rind and cut the rind and the meat into thin strips. Clean and thinly slice the leeks. Peel and crush the garlic. Cover the tomatoes with boiling water for 3min and slide off the skins; remove the core and seeds and roughly chop the flesh, saving as much of the tomato juice as possible.

Combine the beans, pork belly, leeks, garlic and tomatoes in an earthenware casserole, mix in the herbs and season with salt and freshly ground black pepper. Add enough water to cover the ingredients by 2.5cm (1in), stir well, cover really tightly (wrap in foil before adding the lid to make a tight seal) and bake in a moderately hot oven 180°C (375°F, Gas mark 5) for 2½hr.

If anything, the baked beans are better if they are left to get cold and then reheated the next day.

Each family has its own recipe for *risotto*, a basic nourishing meal that is inexpensive but full of goodness. A sprinkling of freshly grated Parmesan cheese is an essential finish to this dish. Proper risotto rice can be bought from Italian delicatessen shops.

Risotto alla Paesana
(Country Risotto)
(Serves 4)

50g (2oz) dried mushrooms
1 medium onion
1 stalk celery
1 young carrot
4 leaves fresh basil
275g (10oz) fresh or frozen young peas
5 firm ripe tomatoes
50g (2oz) streaky bacon with rinds removed
1 small courgette
125ml (5fl oz) olive oil
350g (12oz) risotto or long grain rice
2tbsp dry white wine
1.1*l* (2pt) water
2 beef stock cubes
Salt and white pepper
2tbsp finely chopped parsley
25g (1oz) butter
50g (2oz) freshly grated Parmesan cheese

In Italy risotto is not served with vegetables but you can follow the dish with salad or a mixed platter of vegetables as a separate course.

Soak the mushrooms in warm water for 30min. Peel and finely chop the onion. Finely chop the celery, scrape and finely chop the carrot. Finely chop the basil leaves. Cover the tomatoes with boiling water for 3min, slide off the skins and discard the core and seeds, finely chop the flesh. Finely chop the bacon and blanch in boiling water for 2min, drain well. Chop the courgette.

Heat the oil in a large, heavy, saucepan, add the onion, celery and carrot and cook over a low heat, stirring to prevent sticking, until the onion and vegetables are tender. Add the tomato, courgettes and peas and stir over a low heat, without browning, for 15min. Add the rice and mix well. Add the wine and cook until it is absorbed. Add 600ml (1pt) boiling water and the crumbled stock cubes, mix well and cook over a moderate heat until the water had been absorbed. Continue to add 150ml (¼pt) water at a time, cooking for about 20min until the water has been absorbed each time and the rice is tender but almost dry. Season with salt and pepper, stir in the basil and parsley, add the butter and cheese and toss over a moderate heat until the butter and Parmesan have melted. Serve at once.

Insalata Capricciosa
(Salad of Celeriac and Cold Meats)
(Serves 4 as a starter)

2 celeriac roots
1tbsp lemon juice
100g (4oz) smoked cooked tongue
50g (2oz) lean cooked ham or prosicuitto
100g (4oz) firm button mushrooms
2 cucumbers
300ml (½pt) mayonnaise
Salt and white pepper
Cos or Webbs Wonderful lettuce
3 anchovy fillets

In Italy this is served as an *anti pasta* or first course; elsewhere the dish makes a delicious supper or light dinner main course for the summer. It is also the perfect picnic food.

Peel the celeriac roots, cut them into thin slices and then into thin matchstick strips. Cover the celeriac with cold water and the lemon juice until ready to use. Cut the tongue and ham into very thin slices and then into very thin matchstick strips. Very thinly slice the mushroom caps, discarding any tough stalks. Peel the cucumbers and cut them lengthwise into 8. Scoop out the seeds, sprinkle the cucumber with salt and leave in a sieve or colander to sweat for 30min; shake well to remove excess moisture and pat dry on kitchen paper.

Season the mayonnaise generously with salt and pepper. Add the celeriac, tongue, ham, mushrooms and cucumber and toss lightly to coat the ingredients with mayonnaise, pile onto a serving dish and garnish with young, crisp, leaves of lettuce.

Cut each anchovy fillet in 3 lengthwise. Make a crisscross pattern over the dish and serve chilled.

My delight in the less complicated Italian food from the countryside lies in its simplicity. This is a typical such recipe, lovely for a summer lunch starter, reasonably inexpensive and thoroughly satisfactory if the potatoes are new and waxy and the tuna fish is of good quality.

Tonno e Patate Salata
(Tuna and Potato Salad)
(Serves 4)

450g (1lb) waxy new potatoes
Salt and freshly ground black pepper
5tbsp olive oil
1 mild onion
1tbsp finely chopped capers
2tbsp finely chopped parsley
1 tin tuna fish (200g [7oz])
3tbsp white wine vinegar

Scrub the potatoes and boil them in salted water in their skins until they are just tender. Leave until cool enough to handle and remove the skins. Slice the potatoes and season with salt and pepper. Lightly mix in the olive oil while the potatoes are still warm so that they absorb the oil.

Peel the onion, cut into very thin slices and divide into rings. Add the onion to the potatoes with the capers and parsley. Lightly break up the tuna fish with a fork (do not drain the oil from the tin). Add the tuna and vinegar to the other ingredients, toss lightly and serve at room temperature rather than chilling.

Pesto

The sauces of Italy are some of the finest in the world and provide a wonderful flavouring agent for the most simple ingredients. Many of these sauces form the basic essentials of dishes thought of as French *haute cuisine*. One of the best and most interesting is *pesto*. Now that fresh herbs are available on sale it is possible to make this sauce at home and it will keep well in a sealed jar in a refrigerator.

3 cloves garlic
1 bunch fresh basil leaves
25g (1oz) finely grated Parmesan cheese
25g (1oz) pine kernels
Coarse salt
6tbsp olive oil
1tbsp finely chopped parsley

Peel and chop the garlic. Combine the garlic, basil, Parmesan, and pine kernels in a food processor or liquidizer. Process until the ingredients are reduced to a purée, season with coarse salt. With the machine switched on, add the oil, 1tsp at a time, processing until the sauce is thick and shiny. Add the parsley and process to mix.

Pesto can be used as a sauce for spaghetti, tagliatelli or other pastas (it should be mixed into the hot pasta at the last minute before serving together with 25g [1oz] butter cut in small pieces) and it can also be added to minestrone soup or other types of vegetable soups before serving. Pesto with the addition of lemon juice and freshly ground black pepper is an attractive dressing for a cold salad of shellfish or tuna.

Salsa Verde

1 small pickled cucumber
5tbsp finely chopped parsley
1½tbsp capers
1 slice white bread with the crusts removed
3tbsp olive oil
4tbsp white wine vinegar
½tsp castor sugar
Salt and freshly ground black pepper

Another Italian masterpiece which we could use with our own food is this sauce which has a piquant sweet/sharp flavouring and is excellent with plain boiled meats such as tongue, beef, etc, and also delicious with cold salads of tongue, beef or ham.

Chop the cucumber. In an electric food processor or liquidizer combine the parsley, capers, cucumber and bread; process until the ingredients are reduced to a paste. With the machine switched on gradually add the oil and vinegar 1tsp at a time until the mixture is thick and fairly smooth. Add the sugar, season with salt and pepper and process to mix.

My search for the great peasant foods of the world led me to many places, but nowhere else in the world have I come across the cultural shock experienced in the food of Japan. Western Japanese restaurants inevitably have the most highly sophisticated culinary expertise and so is most of the food offered to visitors to Japan. The famous *sukiyaki* for instance, is a relatively modern dish designed to increase meat consumption in Japan; another dish, *tempura*, made from slivers of this and that cooked in a featherlight batter, was introduced by the Portuguese in the sixteenth century. For the ordinary Japanese the origins of traditional food go back far earlier than that.

Only by travelling off the beaten track, through the countryside, through small fishing villages and townships did I begin to discover what it was all about. After winning the Corning Food Writer of the Year Award, I was fortunate enough to travel to several authentic Japanese inns, *ryokans*, which retain the traditional cuisine and Japanese lifestyle.

Fish is Japan's major flavour ingredient; not the fish of exorbitantly priced, specially licensed restaurants which sell the globe fish *fugu* (its glands secrete a poison which could taint the flesh during its preparation), but fish which is sold in the markets. Fish, of a thousand or more varieties from those so small they are mere embryos to the giant tuna, are on sale daily. They are supplemented by smoked, pickled and salted fish of all kinds. Fish are bought with discernment not only by women, but by elderly men, who spend a long time in considering the purchase of a mere few ounces.

In coastal areas cooked crabs, pink and succulent, are sold by street vendors; strange prehistoric looking shellfish become articles of value, their wandering suckers and warty filaments being treated as treasured purchases.

The ethnic cuisine of Japan is far more than just a means of feeding the family. Each meal, even in the most frugal household, is made up of a dozen or more dishes and side dishes; small is beautiful and large is vulgar. Not just the

makeup of the meal is important but so are the containers for each dish. They may be of countrystyle pottery, plastic lacquer or antique porcelain and patinated lacquer, but each dish is designed to complement the food served on it; each covered bowl has a role to play in the relation of soup to fish, vegetables to pickles and each tiny bowl, with its ubiquitous soy sauce, a pattern in the tapestry of even the most simple Japanese home meal.

Japanese soup is all important to any meal (in the same way the language is read in reverse to ours, soup and rice are served in reverse order in a meal, coming at the end). The broth gives sustenance and vigour to even the poorest family. The basic stock, *dashi*, is made from water, dried seaweed (kelp) and *katsuobushi* (dried bonito fish flakes) and has a salty, meaty flavour, often enriched by the addition of chicken carcasses bought in special chicken shops. The soup is further enhanced by herbs and vegetables from the pocket handkerchief gardens in front of houses, or by leaves, grasses and wild mushrooms gathered in the country. The stock is crystal clear, garnished with prawns, thin strands of spring onions, vegetables or herbs, or with the protein-bearing white soya bean curd.

Rice or noodles, thick, thin, flat or round form the staple starch backup. The rice is round grained and fluffy and the noodles usually cooked in stock to give them flavour.

The main meal of the day begins with small quantities of whatever is in season with bowls of almost minute quantities of fresh vegetables, pickles often dyed to a glorious dark red with beetroot juice, slivers of raw fish, smoked roe, salt and pickled fish. The practice of eating with finely pointed, lacquered chopsticks determines that the food is nibbled delicately. At the end of the meal, however, the soup and the rice are attacked more heartily with much slurping, sucking and unembarrassed enjoyment. No bread, no milk or dairy products, seldom any meat and few fried foods form part of the everyday meal.

The Japanese cuisine is a curious one. While most of the world cooks food by methods derived from many culinary traditions, the food tradition of Japan has remained isolated and surprisingly pure with its recipes and lore being handed down through the generations by word of mouth. The food of the people is simple, still based on the frugality of the *samurais*, many of whom were impecunious. Even in the poorest household almost as much attention is paid to food presentation, the order in which it is served, the position of the dishes in relation to each other and to the time of year as is paid to the food itself.

The general stores in even the smallest villages contain an extraordinary range of goods, but, surprisingly, none contains deepfreeze cabinets. The only food that appears to be frozen in Japan is the huge tuna fish caught way out to sea. Even inland fresh fish is always for sale as well as salt, dried, smoked and pickled fish. Also available are pressed seaweed in sheets, bottles of soy sauce in different strengths and flavours, some thin and salty, some thick almost syrupy and sweet, the special fermented *miso*, and other soya bean products like *tofu* (milky bean curd), red and white *miso* bean pastes and special 'silky' bean curd used mainly in soups.

You will find a wide variety of noodles and rice, dried *bonito* flakes (made from bonito fish which has been dried slowly and then shaved into flakes) which provide the main flavouring for the basic stock (*dashi*), and fresh chrysanthemum leaves to use in soups and stews (*chrysanthemum coronarium*). Japanese radish is sold raw or in a green powdered form which has a veritable furnace in its flavour; the robustly flavoured *shiitake* mushrooms, fresh or dried, now successfully farmed, are in every shop.

The day's fresh fruit and vegetables are arranged outside the little shops. Perfectly shaped and matched aubergines, cucumbers and tomatoes are laid out on small baskets in groups of three or four. Cherries look as though they were individually polished, small sweet black grapes glow, and the white peaches are perfection. Any blemished or unmatched produce is hidden and sold cheap, with loss of face to those who buy it, since the shape and appearance of the raw ingredient is as important as its appearance when cooked. On one counter will be a choice of chopsticks; half split sticks of natural wood, thin tapering lacquered sticks and chopsticks in red, black and even gold. Beside them will be a variety of lacquer and china bowls, miniature saucers, little plates, rice bowls and shallow platters shaped like leaves or fish, most of them incredibly cheap and all in the best possible taste.

What almost impressed me most about Japanese food was the husbandry. Vast fields of paddy rice, bright emerald green in immaculate terraces with almost static water reflect the sky and clouds; in the great fruit growing areas every apple, pear and plum is protected by a white or pale brown paper bag encouraging quick growth and preserving the fruit from insect attack; every spare inch of land is cultivated with close growing weedless crops of onion, courgettes, cucumbers, tomatoes, lettuces, aubergines and perfectly formed cabbages.

Food grows up to every door leaving just a tiny space for a flower or *bonzai* garden; even window boxes and hanging baskets contain fragrant herbs.

At home I serve Japanese-style soups at the beginning, rather than at the end, of special dinners in a set of dull reddish brown lacquer bowls with black interiors.

Bonito flakes are hard to find so I make a *dashi* substitute from chicken stock or stock cubes clarified until clear and add, when the soup has been poured into the bowls, cubes of *tofu* (now available in cardboard cartons), a whole prawn and a spring onion cut through ¾ of its length so that it fans out, flower shaped, in the hot liquid. Sometimes I flavour the soup with a little medium dry sherry (in place of the rice wine, *sake*) and soy sauce, garnishing the soup with slices of soaked dried mushrooms, noodles or thin strips of omelette and if my edible chrysanthemum leaves are young and tender I will float a leaf in each bowl.

Today most shops sell electric rice steamers and stock a range of wickedly sharp knives with short handles and rounded blades. For Japanese cuisine on any level, the value of the right knife is of paramount importance. A special knife is used for intricate procedures of cutting, slicing and chopping; the *vote* (a medium blade knife) is used for allpurpose cutting and slicing, the longer *sashimi-bocho* for preparing the almost transparently thin slivers of raw fish and the *deba bocho* with its heavy, almost chopper shaped, blade for cutting off fish heads.

The aim of the Japanese cook is to create food with a natural flavour, cook it in the shortest possible time, stretch ingredients to the utmost and present them with grace and beauty.

Prawn Soup
(Serves 6)

450g (1lb) fish heads, tails and bones
1.7*l* (3pt) water
2tbsp sake
2tbsp light soy sauce
Salt and white pepper
1 small leek or two spring onions
18 prawns, unpeeled

Combine the fish trimmings with the water, sake and soy sauce in a saucepan, bring to the boil and simmer, with the water moving gently for 15min. Strain through 2 layers of muslin, return to a clean pan, season with salt and pepper and heat through. Trim and thinly slice the leek or spring onions. Pour the hot soup into bowls and garnish with the prawns and leek or spring onions.

Fish Soup with Mushrooms
(Serves 6)

450g (1lb) white fish heads, tails and bones
1.7*l* (3pt) water
2tbsp sake
2tbsp light soy sauce
4 spring onions
40g (1½oz) firm button mushrooms
225g (8oz) firm-fleshed white fish fillets with
the skin removed
Salt and white pepper

Combine the fish trimmings with the water, sake and soy sauce in a saucepan, bring to the boil and simmer with the water moving gently for 15min. Strain the stock through 2 layers of muslin and return to a clean saucepan.

Trim and thinly slice the spring onions. Thinly slice the mushrooms. Cut the fish into 0.5cm (¼in) thick, diagonal, slices. Add the spring onions and fish to the stock, bring gently to the boil, season with salt and white pepper, and cook for about 2min until the fish is *just* tender. Serve at once with thin slices of mushroom floating on the top.

Yushiki-Sushi
(Serves 6)

Sushi are normally eaten as appetisers or snacks and make excellent picnic food.

The omelettes
4 eggs, lightly beaten
½tsp salt
Vegetable oil

The Rice
350g (12oz) short grain rice
Salt
2tbsp white wine vinegar
1½tsp sugar

The Filling
50g (2oz) smoked salmon
Omelette trimmings
1 bunch watercress leaves, finely chopped
Thin strips of cucumber
Button mushrooms, thinly sliced
Chopped peeled prawns
French beans, lightly cooked and chopped
Freshly ground black pepper
Soy sauce
English mustard
Spring onions
1 lemon sliced thinly

Season the beaten egg with the salt and mix well. Brush a 23cm (9in) omelette pan with a film of oil and heat well. Pour in just enough of the omelette mixture to form a thin film over the bottom of the pan and cook over a medium heat until just set. Turn over and cook the other side until a pale golden. Remove, cool, and cook the remaining mixture (it should make about 8 omelettes).

Wash the rice in cold running water and put into a heavy saucepan with enough cold water to come 4cm (1½in) above the level of the rice. Season with salt, cover tightly and bring slowly to the boil. Turn down the heat and simmer very slowly for 14min. Remove the lid and stir well, shake the pan over a high heat to remove excess moisture and then cover tightly again and leave to stand on the edge of the stove for 10min. Add the vinegar, sugar and a little more salt, stir with chopsticks or 2 forks and leave to cool. Trim the omelettes to roughly 20.5cm (8in) squares.

Cut squares of foil just larger than the omelettes. Place an omelette square on each piece of foil and spread over a thin layer of rice, leaving a 2.5cm (1in) border all round. Place some chopped salmon, chopped omelette, chopped watercress, cucumber and mushroom in a line across the centre of the rice. Season with a little pepper, a few drops of soy sauce and a little driblet of made English mustard.

Working from one end of the foil, roll up the foil tightly over the filling to make a sausage shape. Seal the edges of the foil and chill in the refrigerator for at least an hour. Unwrap and cut each *yushiki-sushi* into 3. Arrange them on small plates with remaining ingredients and garnish with shredded spring onions and thin slices of lemon. Serve chilled.

Norimaki-Sushi
Follow the directions for making *yushiki-sushi* but use sheets of nori seaweed for wrapping the rice. Crisp the *nori sushi* over a hot electric plate. Foil can be used for rolling the *norimaki-sushi* but it is easier to do with the help of a *sudare* (thin bamboo mat) available from oriental supermarkets.

Grilled Mackerel Fillets
(Serves 4)

2 mackerel fillets
Salt
1 piece *daikon* (Japanese white radish)
about 5cm (2in) long
oil
Thin slices pickled green ginger root
1tbsp light soy sauce

Serve with rice and side dishes of soup and pickled vegetables.

Halve the fillets and rub both cut and skin side with salt. Peel and finely grate the daikon and squeeze out excess moisture. Stand for 5min; rinse in cold water. Pat the fillets dry on kitchen paper. Make 3 diagonal slashes through the skin of the fillets to prevent the fish curling when cooking. Grill the fish skin side down under a high heat about 7.5cm (3in) from the flame (brush the grill rack with oil to prevent sticking) for

3min. Turn the fish over and continue to grill with the skin side up until the skin is crisp and brown.

Serve, skin side up, in 4 small serving dishes garnished with thin slices of pickled green ginger root and mounds of finely grated daikon. Pour the soy sauce over the fish and daikon just before serving.

Egg Glazed Fish Fillets
(Serves 4)

8 small fillets white fish with skin removed
(use sole, plaice, dabs, John Dory etc)
Salt
2 egg yolks
1tbsp *mirin* (or use medium dry sherry)
1 small chilli pepper (optional)
4tbsp light soy sauce
1tbsp sake
1tsp finely grated peeled horseradish
1 salted cucumber thinly sliced
1 lemon thinly sliced

Rub the fillets on both sides with a little salt and leave to stand for 5min. Beat the egg yolks with the mirin (or sherry) until smooth.

Arrange the fillets in a fireproof dish and brush with half the egg mixture, grill under a medium heat for 4 minutes, turn over, brush with remaining egg mixture and grill for a further 4 minutes until golden.

Remove the seeds from the chilli pepper and very finely slice the flesh and combine it with the soy sauce, sake, and horseradish in 4 small dishes.

Serve the fillets on small individual plates with the dipping sauce and garnish the fish with some thin slices of salted cucumber and thin butterfly slices of lemon.

Tempura
(Serves 4)

8 large raw prawns or shrimps
1 small squid
4 fillets sole
4 large fresh firm mushrooms
1 small aubergine
2 small courgettes
1 green pepper
1 large egg
150g (5oz) plain flour
200ml (8fl oz) iced water
3tbsp soy sauce
150ml (¼pt) *dashi* (made from dashi essence available from Japanese food shops)
1½tbsp *mirin* (or use medium dry sherry)
1tbsp finely grated Japanese horseradish
Deep oil for frying

Crisp, deep fried fish and vegetables in a light batter served with a dipping sauce and Japanese horseradish.

Remove the heads from the prawns and take off the shell, leaving the tail on. Cut the prawns ¾ of the way through from the stomach side along the length of their bodies and take out any black vein. Remove the skin from the body of the squid, cut down one side, clean the inside and cut the body into 5cm (2in) squares. Remove the skin from the fish fillets and halve the fish lengthwise. Remove the stalks from the mushrooms. Thinly slice the aubergine. Cut the courgettes into thin diagonal slices. Deseed the pepper and cut into rings. Beat the egg with the flour and water until smooth. Combine the soy sauce, dashi made from the mirin (or sherry) and mix in the horseradish.

Heat the oil until little droplets of batter flicked into the oil form crisp bubbles immediately they touch the oil. Cook the fish first. Dip the ingredients into the batter and deep fry until crisp and lightly golden. Drain on kitchen paper and serve on small dishes lined with rice paper. Continue with the vegetables, cooking in the same way and accompany with small bowls of dipping sauce.

Tempura must be eaten as soon as the ingredients are cooked and may be served as an appetiser or a light main course.

Yakitori
(Grilled Barbecued Chicken)
(Serves 4)

These are served as a starter or as a snack or as a main course with rice and side dishes.

2 boned chicken breasts with the skin removed
3tbsp dark soy sauce
2tbsp soft brown sugar
2tbsp *mirin* or medium dry sherry
1 clove garlic
1cm (½in) piece of fresh ginger root

Cut the chicken into small cubes. Combine the soy sauce, sugar, mirin or sherry, and the garlic and ginger peeled and crushed through a garlic press. Mix the marinading ingredients, add the chicken and marinate for 1hr. Oil small bamboo skewers and thread on the chicken pieces. Grill under a high heat or over a charcoal grill for about 8min, turning frequently and brushing the chicken cubes with marinade as they cook.

Sukiyaki
(Serves 4)

Although this is known as a popular Japanese dish it is too expensive for the average family to produce at home and is usually served only in restaurants. In the home similar dishes are made from noodles and vegetables with, perhaps, some thin slices of pork or chicken. It is essential that this dish is cooked at the table and eaten straight from the pan.

450g (1lb) beef fillet
10 spring onions
6 Japanese dried mushrooms
2 squares bean curd
100g (4oz) young spinach leaves or watercress
350g (12oz) shirataki noodles
(available vacuum packed from Oriental supermarkets)
150ml (¼pt) light soy sauce
150ml (¼pt) *mirin* (or medium dry sherry)
150ml (¼pt) *dashi* (made from dashi essence available from Japanese food shops)
2tbsp sugar
Salt
5cm (2in) piece beef fat

Trim any fat or sinews from the beef fillet and chill the fillet in the freezer for 30min to firm it. Cut the fillet into wafer-thin slices and then into 4cm (1½in) squares. Trim the spring onions and cut them into thin diagonal slices. Soak the mushrooms in cold water for 20min, cut off the tough stems and slice the caps. Cut the bean curd into 1cm (½in) thick slices. Shred the spinach (or remove the stalks from the watercress). Drain the shirataki and cook in boiling water for 1min. Drain and halve the noodles.

Combine the soy sauce, mirin, dashi and sugar and season with salt. Bring to the boil and remove from the heat.

Heat an electric frying pan or heavy frying pan on a gas burner. Rub the beef fat over the surface of the pan until a thin film of fat has been formed. Leave the piece of fat in the pan. Add the beef and cook over a high heat for 1min, push the beef to the side of the pan and add the spring onion, stir for 30sec.

Pour in the sauce, add the noodles, bean curd and spinach (or watercress), stir all the ingredients with chopsticks for 3min and eat at once.

The sukiyaki can be served with a dipping sauce of 1 beaten egg per person served in small bowls with the ingredients being dipped into the raw egg before they are eaten.

Teriyaki
(Serves 6)

**6 fillets of mackerel (you can also use small fillets of
seabass or cleaned squid cut into 5cm [2in] squares)
OR 900g (2lb) fillet steak
6tbsp dark soy sauce
6tbsp *mirin* (or use medium dry sherry)
6tbsp *sake*
1 clove garlic
1.5cm (½in) green ginger root
Oil for frying**

A simple and traditional way of cooking meat or fish. *Teriyaki* forms the main part of a meal and is served with rice, soup and perhaps side dishes of vegetables and pickles.

Cut the fish into roughly 10cm (4in) pieces. (If using meat cut the meat into thin slices and then into 1.5cm (½in) wide strips.)

Combine the soy sauce, mirin (or sherry) and sake, add the garlic and the ginger, both peeled and pressed through a garlic press. Mix well, add to the fish or meat and leave to marinade for 30–60min. Preheat a grill, place the fish on a rack and cook for about 6min brushing the fillets with more marinade as they cook. (For the meat: drain off excess marinade and fry the meat over a very high heat in a thin film of oil for about 4min only until it is just cooked, sprinkle with any remaining marinade.)

Fried Noodles
(Serves 6)

350g (12oz) dried *udon* noodles (or use *tagliatelli*)
Salt
1 onion
2 cloves garlic
4cm (1½in) fresh ginger root
175g (6oz) lean pork
4 spring onions
2 eggs
2tbsp oil
2tbsp dark brown soy sauce

Plunge the noodles in plenty of boiling salted water. Bring to the boil, add 300ml (½pt) cold water, return to the boil and cook for about 5min until the noodles are tender. Drain well. Peel and very finely chop the onion. Peel and very, very finely chop the garlic and ginger root. Cut the pork into wafer thin slices and then into very thin strips. Trim the spring onions and cut them into thin lengthwise strips. Lightly beat the eggs and season with a little salt.

Heat a thin film of oil in an omelette pan, add the eggs swirling them around so that they just cover the bottom of the pan. Cook the omelette over a medium heat until set, turn over and cook until lightly browned on the other side. Leave to cool, roll the omelette up tightly and cut into very thin strips.

Heat 2tbsp oil in a heavy pan. Add the onion, garlic and ginger and cook over a medium heat, stirring, until the onion is lightly browned. Add the pork and stir until it is just tender. Add the noodles and stir over a high heat until lightly browned and slightly crisp. Add the soy sauce and spring onions and stir to heat through. Pile onto a serving dish and top with the omelette strips.

Rice
(Serves 4–5)

450g (1lb) short grain rice
1½ times the quantity of volume of water to rice
Salt

Basic Cooking Method
The rice used in Japanese
cooking is the short
grained variety rather than
the Patna or long grain
rice.

Wash the rice in plenty of cold running water, swirling it round until the water is almost clear. Drain the rice and bring slowly to the boil in a large pan with the water and a little salt. Stir vigorously to separate the grains, cover tightly and cook over the lowest possible heat for 20min. Remove from the heat. Stir vigorously again to separate the grains, cover tightly and leave to stand for 10min before serving.

Sushi Salad
(Serves 6)

50g (2oz) filleted firm white fish (halibut, cod, hake etc)
1tbsp oil
50g (2oz) peeled prawns or shrimps
4 anchovy fillets
50g (2oz) pickled herring or rollmop
4 *shiitake* mushrooms
50g (2oz) bamboo shoots
50g (2oz) lotus root
15g (1oz) sesame seeds
Sushi rice (see page 164)
50g (2oz) fresh bean sprouts
Salt
50g (2oz) small, cooked, peas

Fry the fish fillets in the oil until *just* tender. Drain on kitchen paper and flake the flesh. Cut large shrimps into thin slices. Rinse the anchovy fillets in cold water to remove excess salt, dry on kitchen paper and cut into thin strips. Cut the pickled herrings into thin strips. Soak the mushrooms in cold water for 20min, drain, remove tough stems and cut the caps into thin strips. Very thinly slice the bamboo shoots and lotus root and cut the slices into quarters. Roast the sesame seeds in a hot oven 200°C (400°F, Gas mark 6) for about 3min until they are crisp and golden.

Combine the sushi rice with the fish, bamboo shoots, lotus root, mushrooms and bean sprouts, season with a little salt and mix very lightly together. Pile into a pyramid in a serving bowl and sprinkle with sesame seeds and the peas.

Bean Sprout and Cucumber Salad
(Serves 4)

Vegetable salads are popular in Japan during the summer. Often the vegetables are lightly blanched before being dressed and chilled.

225g (8oz) bean sprouts
1 medium cucumber
Salt
1tbsp white wine vinegar
1tsp sugar
1tbsp sesame seed oil
2tbsp light soy sauce
1tbsp sesame seeds
Schichimi-togarashi (seven flavour spice)

Rinse the sprouts in cold running water and blanch them for 30sec in fast boiling water. Drain well and refresh in cold running water.

A sheet of seaweed (*nori*) crisped over a high heat for a few seconds and crushed may also be sprinkled over the salad. Similar salads may be made by combining lightly blanched young asparagus spears or very small French beans and combining them with bean sprouts.

Peel the cucumber, cut it in half lengthwise and remove the seeds. Cut the cucumber halves into thin slices, place them in a sieve or colander and sprinkle the slices with salt. Leave to stand for 20min, press off excess liquid and dry on kitchen paper. Combine the wine vinegar, sugar, oil and soy sauce and mix well. Toss the bean sprouts and cucumber in the dressing. Roast the sesame seeds in a hot oven 200°C (400°F, Gas mark 6) for 3min until golden brown and leave to cool.

Divide the salad between 4 small bowls, sprinkle over the sesame seeds and serve chilled.

172

Pickled Vegetables
(Serves 6)

2 small white turnips
2 carrots
4 inner, crisp, white cabbage leaves
225g (8oz) small, crisp, French beans
2tbsp salt
2tsp lemon peel

Pickled vegetables in one form or another are served with almost every Japanese meal. Often these vegetables are quickly pickled and have a relatively short shelf life. In this recipe the pickles are mixed, but individual vegetables may be salted and fermented on their own.

Hot pickles can be made by sprinkling the vegetable layers with a little finely chopped chilli pepper with the seeds removed.

Peel and thinly slice the turnips and cut the slices into thin sticks. Peel and cut the carrots into very thin matchstick strips. Shred the cabbage leaves. Top and tail the beans. Sprinkle ½tbsp of salt over the cabbage leaves and leave to stand for 20min. Shake off excess liquid and pat the cabbage dry on kitchen paper. Arrange the ingredients in layers in an earthenware bowl, sprinkling each layer with salt and lemon peel. Press the vegetables down firmly, cover with a weighted plate and leave in a cool place for 24hr before using. Keep leftover pickles in the refrigerator.

Malaysia and Singapore

I was an avid reader of Somerset Maugham even before visiting Malaysia and as a result knew something of the British who lived there in colonial days; their romances, murders, adventures and nightmares but I discovered little about how anyone else, especially the Malays themselves, actually kept body and soul together. There were descriptions of *tiffin* (lunch), of course, and how house boys served *stenghas* (whisky and soda) before dinner but there was nothing about the life of the average Malay, the daily food, its preparation and origins.

In the end I had to go there myself to answer my questions and, while I never visited Kuala Lumpur, the capital of Peninsular Malaysia, I was in the magical city on the fringe of the Federation, Singapore, spent quite a while in the Malaysian provinces of Sabah and Sarawak on that enormous island, Borneo, to the east of mainland Malaysia and ate heartily in Kuching, the capital of Sarawak. What is more, for two and a half months, I cooked for a multi-disciplinary Royal Geographical Society expedition to the rain forests of Sarawak, a task that involved not only cooking but also shopping in local markets, the best way ever to get to know regional food.

Malaysia is an exciting country from a gastronomic viewpoint because of the varied cuisines that make up the national dishes, the variety of fruit and vegetables produced there, the extraordinary wealth of its shores and the creativity of its people in preparing the food.

The basic Malaysian cuisine is founded on rice, rice and more rice: dry, fluffy white rice, golden brown fried rice or thick, glutinous and sticky. The rice is enhanced by fresh vegetables, a small amount of meat, fish or poultry, high seasonings, spices and herbs, rich sauces that often have a sweet/sour taste and a wealth of fresh fruit to end the meal.

Peanut oil or coconut oil are usually used for cooking although I find these too strongly flavoured for my taste and

174

in my kitchen the fairly innocuous sunflower oil predominates. Salt fish is invaluable to Malaysian dishes; small, medium and even large fishes, tiny shrimps and larger prawns are salted and left to rot in the sun (this process smells as revolting as you might imagine and pervades many South East Asia coastal towns and villages) before being pounded into pastes or deep fried and crumbled like Bombay duck over savoury rice or other dishes. Pickled or fresh vegetables are served at every meal and a standard Malaysian style supper will probably (apart from the basic boiled or fried rice dish) consist of 4 or 5 dishes which may well have an Indonesian, Indian, Chinese or highly individual and entirely Malaysian flavour to them.

Water or beer is usually served with meals except in the heart of the forests of the mainland or Borneo where you are more likely to find shades of World War I with a peculiar chocolate-flavoured drink called Milo which I believe was popular then. In the interior you are also likely to come across some lethal alcoholic brews made from fermented rice and often stored in exquisite Chinese jars.

Hospitality features in all Malaysian entertaining; a housewife goes to great lengths to make food look appetising and the guest is unbelievably pampered.

Fish, chicken and pork are the major ingredients of savoury dishes. Most people living outside the larger cities will keep chickens and, providing they are not Muslims, a pig or two even if they have only a small back yard. Among the tribal, longhouse, and other groups, standing in the community is denoted by how many pigs a man owns. When it is past laying all parts of a chicken are used (legs, feet and carcasses make stock, the meat itself is stretched to make dish after dish and the giblets are considered the best part of the bird). Eggs play a large part in the diet too; added to soups and made into as many different omelettes as there are in French cuisine. Pork is salted, pickled and preserved; bones are used for stock and all offal is put to good use. Small pigs, usually roasted over an open fire or in pits over hot coals form part of any respectable festival.

Soups which are served at most Malaysian meals with the rice and side dishes depend on a good stock or broth base. Often they contain small amounts of almost raw vegetables, or thinly sliced meat, fish or poultry, and they are flavoured with spices or with coconut milk. Soup garnishings often consist of a few rings of seeded green or red chilli peppers or a scattering of chopped, fresh coriander leaves. Coriander, by the way, is frequently used for flavouring in South East Asian cookery. You can grow it easily from seed (Suttons can

supply these) and then use the pungent green leaves as you would parsley before harvesting the dried seeds in autumn.

While considerable use of the curry spices, turmeric, cardamom, cumin, coriander, nutmeg, cinnamon, garlic, fresh root ginger and chilli show the Indian influence on Malay cooking, Chinese influence shows in the way ingredients are chopped, sliced or shredded with a metal cleaver (what we would call a meat chopper). Malays use cleavers for everything, from chopping a piece of garlic to slicing a chicken breast. Most cooking is done in a *kuali*, a version of the Chinese round bottomed *wok*, over a simple hearth, a kerosene stove or a Calor gas ring. Malay kitchens are simple but every cook has a pestle and mortar for grinding spices, a good grater for grating coconut and a large fireproof, earthenware pot for making long-cooking curry type dishes.

Penang, in the north, boasts some sensational chicken dishes in one of which, *inche kabin*, pieces of chicken are cooked in deep oil at least 3 times. The chicken pieces are marinaded in a mixture of ground red chillies, salt, pepper and oil, fresh ginger root, lemon and turmeric and left to stand for 30min. The marinade is drained off; the chicken is deep fried in very hot peanut oil until brown and then removed and well drained. When the pieces are cool they are deep fried again over a moderate heat until cooked. Finally they are recoated in the marinade and just wafted through very hot oil to give them a final and ultimate crispness. *Inche kabin* is served with sauce made from mustard, a little sugar, lemon or preferably lime juice and, would you believe, that good old standby, Worcestershire sauce. Try this for a summer buffet party with boiled, fluffy, rice and a salad of cucumber and tomato – it's a stunner.

Around the coastal areas and in small towns located on the banks of larger rivers, fish is always available. The fresh crabs are delicious and the varieties of prawns you get throughout the Federation are superb. The best I ever ate were in a small town called Miri in Sarawak where they were grilled with a little crushed garlic and grated fresh ginger root, and at other times served floating in clear chicken stock amongst finely shredded vegetables, paper thin slices of ginger root and chrysanthemum flower petals. Fresh ginger root, by the way, can be found quite easily here now and will keep for weeks in the bottom of a refrigerator.

As in all Asian countries the Malays stretch their ingredients by cutting them into waferlike slivers or slices. Most people have never been able to afford the joints of meat we in this country, are used to. A dish I use frequently now for summer parties is called *dendeng*, probably a hand down

from the hunter gatherers of the rainforest who preserved game by this method. Paper thin slices of rump steak are cut against the grain. (I buy 450g (1lb) of rump in a piece from my butcher and chill it in the freezer until it is stiff enough to cut transparently thinly but not frozen solid. Rub a little salt into the meat before cutting.) Marinade the slices in a mixture of the juice and grated peel of a lemon pounded to a paste with a grated onion, a 2.5cm (1in) piece of grated fresh ginger root and 2tsp of sugar. Stretch the strips of meat on a cake rack and (if there is any sun!) dry in hot sunshine for about an hour (if there is no sun dry the beef in a moderate oven 150°C (300°F, Gas mark 2) for 10min, turn the meat over and continue to dry for a further 10min until all the moisture has evaporated). Heat some deep oil until a haze rises from it, add the meat (not too many strips at a time) and cook quickly until the beef is brown and crisp. Remove at once from the oil with a wire spoon and drain well on kitchen paper. Serve cold with a beautiful garnish of spring onions, radishes and small mature white turnips cut into flowers and curled in ice-cold water before being used.

I first experienced the delights of the 'Singapore Steamboat' in, of all places, Fiji. You start with a good chicken stock, then add some finely chopped fresh ginger root, chilli pepper and onion and boil the stock fast for about 15min to amalgamate the flavours. Then you strain it into a pan which can be kept hot on a small burner at the table (for a real steamboat you need a pot which looks like an enlarged *savarin* ring with a high central funnel to take away the fumes of burning charcoal placed immediately under the ring).

The simplest steamboat consists of a dish of thinly sliced pork and chicken flesh and a medley of thinly sliced vegetables and bean curd (available fresh from Chinese supermarkets). Each diner picks up ingredients with his chopsticks and drops them into the simmering broth for a minute or two, then retrieves them as they are cooked. For special occasions the plainer ingredients are augmented by slices of firm fish fillets (seabass, bream, halibut etc); slices of rump, sirloin or fillet; strips of cuttle fish or squid; pork fillet and sliced chicken or turkey breast. Sliced, firm mushrooms can be added too and so can strips of green pepper or finely ground fish or chicken flesh balls. There may even be slices of lobster or large shrimp. With the steamboat will be served side dishes of boiled rice and small bowls of soy and chilli sauces. At the end, once all the main ingredients have been cooked and eaten, raw eggs are broken into the stock, stirred with a wire whisk and the stock is drunk as a rich and nutritious soup – what a dish.

Malay Chicken Soup
(Serves 4)

450g (1lb) raw, boneless and skinned chicken
1 clove garlic
2 medium onions
2 medium potatoes
2 tomatoes
2 carrots
1 stick celery
12 peppercorns
3 cloves
5cm (2in) stick cinnamon
25g (1oz) butter
2tbsp vegetable oil
1*l* (1¾pt) chicken stock
1 small onion

Cut the chicken into small dice. Peel and crush the garlic. Peel and chop the 2 medium onions. Peel and dice the potatoes. Cover the tomatoes with boiling water, let stand for 3 minutes then slide off the skins, deseed and chop the flesh. Peel and slice the carrots, thickly slice the celery. Tie the peppercorns, cloves and cinnamon in a piece of muslin.

In a large saucepan heat the butter and 1tbsp of oil and fry the garlic until golden. Add the diced chicken and cook for a further 3min, stirring continually. Add the vegetables, and mix well. Pour over the chicken stock, add the bag of spices and cover the pan and let simmer until all the vegetables are cooked.

Very finely slice the small onion, and fry in the remaining oil until golden brown and crisp. Remove with a slotted spoon and drain on kitchen paper. Serve the soup in warmed bowls with a sprinkling of the crisply fried onion as garnish.

Malayan Omelette
(Serves 2)

A really spicy start to the day is this typical Malay breakfast dish. Evaporated milk is very popular with Malays.

3 standard eggs
2tbsp evaporated milk
Salt and freshly ground black pepper
1 large onion
1 fresh red chilli
25g (1oz) butter
Soy sauce

Beat the eggs lightly, with a fork, just enough to break the yolks; beat in the milk and season with salt and freshly ground black pepper.

Peel and thinly slice the onion. Finely chop the chilli (you can remove the seeds if you don't like your omelette too hot). Melt the butter in an omelette pan and cook the onions until soft and transparent, add the chilli and cook for a further minute. Spread the onion and chilli mixture evenly over the bottom of the pan and pour over the egg mixture. When the egg has set fold omelette into 3, or you can divide into 2 separate pieces before serving with a sprinkling of soy sauce.

Ikan Bilis (Seasoned Whitebait)
(Serves 6)

Spoon into small pottery bowls and serve as an accompaniment to drinks.

1 large onion
3 green chillies
25g (1oz) soft dark brown sugar
1tsp ground cumin
10 peppercorns
Oil for deep frying
450g (1lb) whitebait
1tbsp peanut oil

Peel and roughly chop the onion and put into a food processor or electric blender with the chillies, sugar, cumin and peppercorns and process to a paste.

180

Heat the deep oil until a haze rises, then fry the whitebait, in batches, until crisp (keep the cooked whitebait warm in the oven on kitchen paper).

In a large frying pan heat the peanut oil and cook the spice and onion mixture over a medium heat for 3–4min, until the mixture starts to dry. Add the whitebait, stirring all the time, so that the mixture is evenly distributed.

Singapore Steamboat (or Boiling Fire Pot)
(Serves 6)

3l (5½pt) chicken stock
2.5cm (1in) fresh ginger root
1 red chilli
175g (6oz) fillet of pork
100g (4oz) fillet steak
100g (4oz) chicken breast fillet, skinned
175g (6oz) fresh king prawns, shelled
225g (8oz) firm flesh white fish fillets
225g (8oz) fresh egg noodles
1 Chinese cabbage
Chilli sauce
Soy sauce
6 eggs

The name of this dish derives from the charcoal heated pot with a central funnel which heats up the circular trough that surrounds the funnel. The trough is filled with boiling stock, and a selection of meat, poultry, vegetables, fish, noodles etc, are cooked individually, using either chopsticks or small wire baskets. When all the ingredients have been used, eggs are broken into the stock to poach, then the whole lot is eaten as a soup – it's a totally different way to eat, and is great fun.

Put the stock into a large saucepan. Peel and finely chop the ginger, thinly slice the red chilli; add to the stock. Bring to boil and simmer for 10min, and pour into the steamboat. Cut the pork, steak, and chicken into thin slivers, using a very sharp knife and divide equally amongst 6 plates, arranging attractively. Divide the prawns in the same way. Cut the fish into diagonal slices and distribute evenly. Arrange the noodles and cabbage in the same way. Pour the chilli and soy sauce into small individual dipping bowls.

When the stock in the steamboat starts to bubble, cooking can commence. Each person selects the desired ingredient and cooks it as required then dips the food into the sauces.

Once all the ingredients are used, break the eggs very carefully into the remaining stock, and poach lightly. Ladle the now enriched and well flavoured soup into bowls.

These patties make a delicious snack.

Meat and Lentil Patties
(Serves 4)

100g (4oz) lentils, washed and drained
225g (8oz) cooked beef, pork or lamb
1 small onion
2tbsp vegetable oil
2tbsp mild curry paste
2 eggs
Salt and freshly ground black pepper
Flour

Cook the lentils in plenty of lightly salted boiling water until tender (about 30min), drain and allow to cool. Finely mince the cooked meat, and then the lentils, season with salt and pepper and mix together.

Peel and very finely chop the onion, and fry in 1tbsp vegetable oil until golden brown and soft, add the curry paste and mix well. Add this mixture to the minced meat and lentils. Beat the eggs, and add enough to the meat mixture to form 1cm (½in) thick patties. Put the patties in the refrigerator for 30min to firm up. Dip the patties in the remaining egg, and then in a little flour and fry in the remaining oil until golden brown.

Serve with a topping of crisply fried onion rings, some thinly sliced and skinned tomatoes or 1tsp of sweet pickle.

Kurmah
(Serves 4)

Coconut milk is used in many Malay dishes (see basic recipe on page 129), imparting its own very distinctive flavour.

1 small onion
25g (1oz) butter
2tbsp vegetable oil
2.5cm (1in) fresh ginger root
½tsp ground cloves
2 cardamoms
Grated rind and juice of ½ a small lime
1tsp ground coriander
½tsp ground anise
1tsp ground cumin
450g (1lb) chuck steak
600ml (1pt) coconut milk

Peel and thinly slice the onion. Heat the butter and oil in a large frying pan and cook the onion until soft and golden brown. Peel and finely chop the ginger root and add to the pan. Mix all the spices and add to the pan together with the grated lime rind, and mix well. Cook for 2min.

Trim the meat and cut into thin slivers, add to the pan, tossing until browned all over. Lower the heat, and cover the pan and cook for 10–15min. Add the coconut milk and simmer over a very low heat for about 1hr. Add a squeeze of lime juice to the dish just before serving with fluffy boiled rice.

Fried Curry Puffs
(Makes approximately 24)

1 large onion
2tbsp vegetable oil
2tbsp hot curry paste
225g (8oz) cooked beef or pork
2 large cooked potatoes, skinned and diced small
225g (8oz) plain flour
½tsp baking powder
100g (4oz) soft margarine
1 egg, beaten
Deep oil for frying

Peel and finely chop the onion. Heat the oil in a large frying pan and cook the onion until soft and transparent, mix in the curry paste, together with 1tbsp water. Finely mince the meat, add to the pan, together with the diced potato. Mix well. Allow to cool.

Sift the flour and baking powder into a bowl, add the margarine, cut into small pieces and use the fingertips to rub the fat into the flour until the mixture resembles fine breadcrumbs. Mix in the beaten egg, using a palette knife; add enough water to form a soft elastic dough. Turn onto a well floured board and roll out thinly. Using a round cutter about 10cm (4in) diameter, cut out pastry circles. Put 1tsp of the filling onto each circle, moisten the edges with water and seal well, pinching the edges together and folding over for a double seal.

Heat the deep oil until a haze rises, then deep fry the puffs, a few at a time, until golden brown. Serve at once.

Serve the pancakes with a sprinkling of sugar and a squeeze of fresh lime or lemon juice.

Malay Banana Pancakes
(Serves 4)

2 eggs
150ml (¼pt) milk
175g (6oz) self raising flour
25g (1oz) castor sugar
4 bananas
4tbsp vegetable oil

Beat the eggs until light and frothy, then beat in the milk. Put the flour in a large bowl, make a well in the centre and gradually add the egg and milk mixture, beating well until the batter is smooth. Mix in the sugar. Peel and mash the bananas until puréed then beat into the mixture.

Heat the oil in a heavy bottomed frying pan, and quickly fry tablespoonsful of the batter mixture until golden brown, flipping over with a palette knife to cook both sides an even brown.

Spicy Pot Roasted Duck
(Serves 4–6)

2tsp ground coriander
12 black peppercorns
½tsp ground cloves
½tsp ground cinnamon
2tsp soft brown sugar
4tbsp rich dark soy sauce
2kg (4½lb) duck
1 medium onion
2 cloves garlic
3tbsp vegetable oil
450ml (¾pt) duck or chicken stock
Salt

Combine the coriander, peppercorns, cloves and cinnamon with the sugar and soy sauce in a blender (or food processor) and process to mix well; brush the mixture all over the duck.

Peel and very finely chop, or mince, the onion and garlic. Heat the oil in a flameproof casserole and cook the onion and garlic until soft and golden brown. Add the duck, pouring over any of the spicy mixture left, and brown the duck lightly all over. Add the stock, seasoning with a little salt, cover and cook over a low heat for 1hr; remove the lid and allow to cook until most of the liquid has evaporated and the duck is tender.

Malaysia and Singapore

Captain's Curry
(Serves 4–6)

1.5kg (3½lb) chicken
8 black peppercorns
2.5cm (1in) fresh ginger root
1tsp ground coriander
1tsp ground turmeric
300ml (½pt) coconut milk (see page 129)
Juice of 1 lime
Salt and freshly ground black pepper
2 cloves garlic
1 medium onion
1tbsp vegetable oil

Chop the chicken into small pieces (about 5cm [2in] sq), and put into a large heavy bottomed frying pan, or saucepan. Put the peppercorns, peeled ginger root, coriander and turmeric into a blender or food processor and process until well mixed. Add the coconut milk and lime juice, and season with salt and freshly ground black pepper, process to mix. Pour the mixture over the chicken pieces and cook, over a medium heat, covered, until the chicken is tender.

Meanwhile, peel and thinly slice the garlic and onion and fry in the oil until crisp and golden brown; sprinkle over the chicken.

Mexico

While researching the cuisine of Mexico, I found little to draw on among the thousands of cookery books published in Britain; I had to turn to the North American list of gastronomic books and features and found a wealth of material. In the United States, Mexican cookery is all the vogue both in the home and, especially near the border, in restaurants. In London there is, to my knowledge, only *one* Mexican restaurant. On a recent visit to America I found *chilli* in one form or another on the menu of almost every small diner; *tacos* are almost a must at smart drink parties; Mexican snack bars are sweeping east from the border in the same way that the Chinese and Indian invasion of restaurants hit this country ten years ago and *tortillas* are fast becoming as popular as hot dogs and hamburgers.

So why, I wondered, was there so little interest here in one of the oldest cuisines? Could it be our distrust of foods that are 'hot and spicy'? Could it be cost? Surely that couldn't be the problem because, like other countries with a high peasant population and despite the present oil boom, Mexican food tends to be economical if not downright cheap. Could it then be the difficulty of getting the right ingredients? Again this argument does not hold water; it is nearly always possible to improvise and, in any case, many of the better delicatessens and supermarkets now stock items such as tinned tortillas, tacos, tinned green tomatoes and bottles of hot chilli sauce.

In Mexico, as in most hot countries, great care is taken to cook meat, fish and poultry soon after they have been killed; herbs and spices are used to protect the fresh food rather than to disguise bad ingredients and, in Mexican cooking especially, a balanced use of herbs and spices is considered an aid to good health. So far we in Britain use only one form of Mexican food, the *barbacoa* (the original barbecue) but I feel there is scope, especially with today's economic climate, to experiment with many more of their interesting and economical recipes.

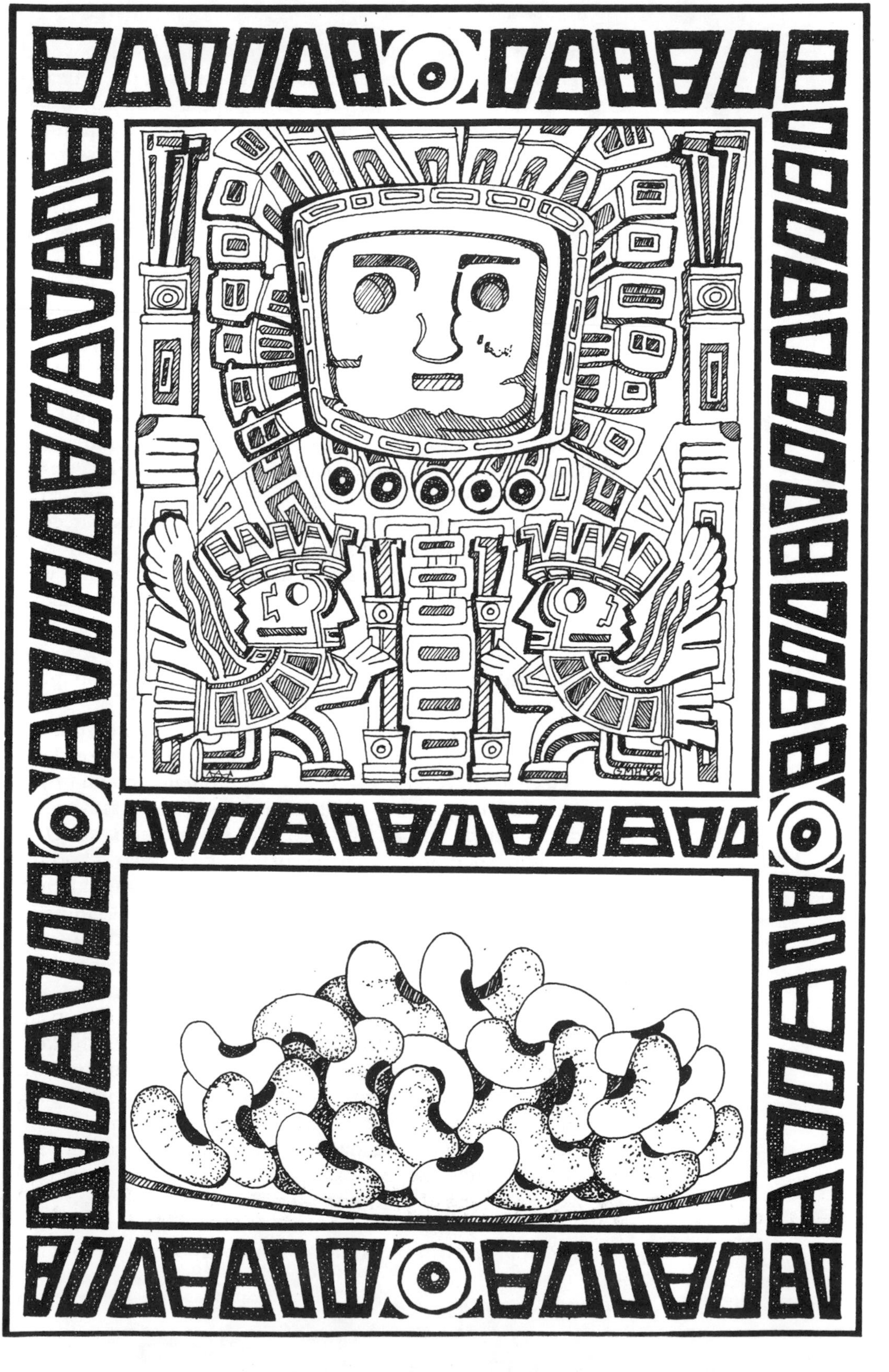

Mexican cuisine is very old. Mexican Indians discovered and grew the tomato; they learnt the greatness of the avocado and cultivated a dazzling variety of peppers and squashes. With the conquistadors came meat, poultry, and a multitude of European dishes, and game and fish have always been abundant. Despite regional diversifications, a strong culinary pattern has survived in Mexico with many traditional dishes deriving from the Aztecs. Mexican cooking, while being realistically economical, is rich and colourful and stands up well the saying *La comida debe entrar primero por los ojos que por la boca*, 'food goes through the eyes before it enters the mouth'.

The main meal in Mexico is taken at lunchtime. Even in the poorest of peasant families this is an occasion to get together and even if the ingredients are simple, a nourishing and colourful meal can be produced from a tomato and chilli, some rich beans and a little protein. Lunch may start with an *entremes*, a snack sold by vendors at every Mexican street corner. *Tacos, tamales* and *tortillas* come in this category often in the form of a spicy, little filled package. These nibbles known as *antojitos Mexicanos* can be anything from fiery to extremely mild. Tortillas are softly cooked maize pancakes; tacos, the same pancakes fried until crisp; *churupas*, pancakes stacked with savoury fillings; *chilaquiles*, small pieces of tortilla fried until crackling crisp and *enchiladas*, soft pancakes wrapped round a meat or cream filling.

The entremes is followed by a soup dish which despite its richness costs little and satisfies the appetite. Many of these soups have the *recaudo*, a basic sauce of tomato and onion, as the foundation; most benefit from the use of herbs and nearly all rely on stock for flavour. To make a recaudo, soften a finely chopped onion, 2 cloves of garlic, 2 finely chopped small hot chillies (I grow these in pots on my kitchen windowsill with great success) in about 3tbsp groundnut or sunflower oil, add 450g (1lb) (or a 425g [15oz] tin) peeled and mashed tomatoes, season with salt and pepper, add a little oregano and coriander and simmer for 30min.

Stock and other flavourings are added to this basic soup which can be served with meatballs, with pieces of chicken, ham and garlic sausage, with rice and a little ham or with vegetables. Fruit is sometimes added to the soup or with pork ribs it becomes more like a stew.

The main course is usually a meat or poultry dish; the poorer the family the less meat is used and bulk is produced by well-flavoured vegetables and beans.

The famous *chilli con carne* is far richer than any American or English facsimile; the meat is not minced but cut into small 1cm (¼in) cubes, and boiled with soaked beans until both are tender (salt is not added at this time – by the time of the Aztecs it was realised that salt had a hardening effect on beans). Onions, tomatoes, garlic, chilli with oregano, sage, cumin and chilli powder are then added and the stew is cooked for a further hour (see also the US version on page 255).

Steaks are lightly marinaded in wine vinegar and flavoured with garlic and chilli powder to produce Mexico's answer to *steak au poivre* (I served this dish with amazing success recently to the most conservative of guests – after an 8hr marinade chuck steak was almost as tender as rump).

Estofada, a versatile meat stew, uses cuts of pork, lamb or beef (or even a mixture of meats) with tomatoes, herbs and sweet peppers for a dish that can be made in advance and that benefits from reheating.

Pork is cooked with oranges and sherry. Layers of meat often are stewed slowly with vegetables, beans and green bananas to produce an almost ambrosial meal. Chicken, turkey or game cooked in a *mole* sauce are dishes that are especially served at fiestas. Lavishly flavoured richly aromatic dishes with chillies, onions, garlic, almonds, raisins, herbs and spices and dark chocolate are surprisingly inexpensive because the many ingredients add a rich taste.

With the main course comes traditional bean (*frijoles*) dishes; white beans, black beans, beans cooked with rice, red kidney beans cooked in earthenware pots with onions, garlic and lard and plenty of seasoning. Nothing is wasted; if the beans are not eaten at that meal they are fried in more lard with additional chopped onion for another meal. But my favourite Mexican dish is *ceviche*, which made from the inexpensive mackerel, produces one of the most sophisticated first courses I know. *Ceviche* usually is served as an appetiser. Any firm fleshed fish will do. The fillets are cut into cubes or strips and marinaded in fresh lime juice for 4hr until the flesh becomes opaque. Onion rings, slices of pepper, chopped tomato flesh and a seasoning of salt and pepper and some oregano are mixed in and the ceviche is served well chilled with straight tequila or a Marguerita cocktail – unbelievably delightful.

Mexican soups divide into two categories; those that are light and very much a first course and those that are a main course in their own right when times are hard. This is one of the light, vegetable varieties flavoured with chicken liver and enhanced by the bright green of young peas. It isn't, I hasten to add, light in the way that a consommé is light but then Mexicans have hearty appetites.

Sopa de Pollo Bigado
(Serves 4)

1 small onion
225g (8oz) firm ripe tomatoes
225g (8oz) courgettes
25g (1oz) butter
1tbsp sunflower oil
1tbsp flour
900ml (1½pt) chicken stock
Pinch oregano
Salt and freshly ground black pepper
2 chicken livers
1½tbsp sunflower oil
1 egg yolk
300ml (½pt) single cream
100g (4oz) fresh or frozen young green peas
1tbsp chopped fresh parsley

Peel and finely chop the onion. Cover the tomatoes with boiling water for 3min, drain, slide off the skins and discard the seeds and cores, reserving the juice. Coarsely grate or finely chop the courgettes.

Heat the butter and ½tbsp oil in a heavy saucepan, add the onion, tomatoes and courgettes and cook over a low heat, stirring to prevent sticking until the onion and courgettes are tender. Purée the vegetables through a sieve, food mill or electric food processor.

Heat the remaining oil in a saucepan, add the flour and mix well. Add the vegetable purée and mix well. Gradually blend in the stock and add the oregano, stirring until the soup comes to the boil and is thick and smooth. Simmer for 15min and season with salt and pepper.

Remove any fibres and yellowy parts of the chicken livers. Cook the livers in 1½tbsp of sunflower oil until firm (about 5min), drain on kitchen paper, cool, and rub through a coarse sieve. Beat the egg yolk with the cream and chicken livers.

Cook the peas in boiling salted water until just tender, and drain and add to the soup together with the chicken liver mixture. Check seasoning and heat through without boiling. The soup can be garnished with finely chopped parsley.

Sopa de Pescado
(Serves 5–6)

2 large onions
450g (1lb) fish heads (cod, halibut, hake etc)
3 cloves garlic
4 whole peppercorns
2 bay leaves
Sprigs of thyme and marjoram
2.3*l* (4pt) water
2 leeks
5 medium potatoes
2 medium carrots
6 leaves spinach
4tbsp cooking oil
1 large tin (425g [15oz]) tomatoes
Salt and freshly ground black pepper
100g (4oz) cooked long grain rice
1 small lime

The countries I have been writing about are often those that have cuisines where people cannot afford to use ingredients lavishly, but that does not mean that they cannot produce delectable food on an extremely tight budget. This is a case in point where a couple of fish heads make a delicious soup.

Peel and roughly chop 1 of the onions. Combine the fish heads, chopped onion, 1 clove garlic, peppercorns, bay leaves, thyme and marjoram in a large saucepan and cover with 2.3*l* (4pt) water, bring to the boil and simmer for 1½ hours.

Pass through a fine sieve pressing gently to strain out all the goodness.

Peel and crush the remaining garlic. Peel and chop the remaining onion. Wash and thinly slice the leeks. Peel the potatoes and cut into small dice. Peel and cut the carrots into small dice. Remove the leaves from the spinach stalks and shred the leaves and finely chop the stalks.

Heat the oil in a large heavy saucepan, add the onion, garlic, potato, carrot and leeks and cook over a low heat stirring to prevent sticking to soften the vegetables without browning. Add the tinned tomatoes and stir over a medium heat to break them up. Add the fish stock, season with salt and pepper, bring to the boil and remove any scum from the surface, simmer uncovered for about 40 minutes until the vegetables are tender. Add the spinach for the last 10min, and the rice for the last 5min. Serve the soup with thin slices of lime in each bowl.

For those who like it, serve a strong hot tomato and chilli sauce on the side (you can get this from specialist food shops).

191

Albondigon (Meat Loaf)
(Serves 8)

A typical country range type dish which varies from home to home and depends on what goes in it as to what happens to be available. The loaf is served with a rich *escabeche* and a tomato sauce. It is usually garnished in the very Mexican way with salad ingredients. The classic accompaniment is, of necessity, a dish of *frijoles refritos* (refried beans).

3 *chorizos* (spiced sausages)
450g (1lb) lean stewing beef
450g (1lb) lean pork
2 large onions
100g (4oz) stoned green olives
3 pickled peppers (these can be bought in jars or tins)
1 chicken breast
100g (4oz) fine fresh white breadcrumbs
4 eggs
Salt and freshly ground black pepper
2tsp ground chilli pepper
450ml (¾pt) white wine vinegar
2 cloves
1 sprig thyme, marjoram and oregano
3 bay leaves
450g (1lb) firm ripe tomatoes, sliced
3 firm ripe avocados, peeled, stoned and sliced
muslin

Remove the skin from the *chorizos*, combine with the beef and pork and mince or finely chop the meat in an electric food processor. Peel and very finely chop the onions. Mince the olives and very finely chop the pickled peppers and the chicken meat. Combine the above ingredients with the bread and eggs and mix to a firm paste, season with salt, pepper and chilli and mix well. Form into a thick sausage shape, wrap tightly in muslin, and secure with string into a tight package. Place enough cold water in a saucepan to cover the muslin wrapped loaf, add the vinegar and herbs to the water and bring to the boil, put in the meat loaf and simmer gently for 2hr. Remove the loaf from the water and leave to stand for 10min. Remove the muslin and turn the loaf onto a serving dish. Garnish with slices of tomato and avocado.

Biftecs (Braised Hamburgers)
(Serves 4)

450g (1lb) topside beef
450g (1lb) pork sausage meat of good quality
Freshly ground black pepper

Tomato sauce
2 cloves garlic
225g (8oz) firm ripe tomatoes
1 small green chilli pepper
¼tsp coriander seeds
1 small onion
5tbsp sunflower oil
Salt
Pinch cayenne pepper

So often cheap meat can be helped by the addition of a more expensive item to provide a reasonably priced tasty dish. In this recipe pork meat combined with good beef is braised in a classic sauce and, quite honestly, is far better than a poor quality beef steak or one that has been massacred by overcooking.

Coarsely mince the beef and sausage, or process the meat in a food processor until it is finely chopped. Season with freshly ground black pepper and, using your hands, shape the meat into 4 firm patties, and chill in the refrigerator while making the tomato sauce for braising.

Peel and crush the garlic. Cover the tomatoes with boiling water for 3min, drain, slide off the skins and discard the seeds and cores, reserving the juice. Finely chop the green chilli pepper. Crush the coriander seeds. Peel and very finely chop or coarsely mince the onion.

Heat 3tbsp oil, add the garlic, onion and coriander, cook over a medium heat, stirring to prevent browning, until the onion is soft and transparent. Add the chilli pepper and the tomatoes, season with salt, pepper and cayenne pepper, bring to the boil and cook over a low heat, stirring for 5min until the sauce is fairly smooth and thick.

Heat the remaining 2tbsp sunflower oil in a large heavy frying pan until the oil is really hot and a haze rises from the surface. Add the patties and cook over a high heat (I cover the pan with a saucepan lid to prevent spitting) for 3min on each side until well browned on both sides. Arrange the patties in a shallow baking dish just large enough to take them; add the tomato sauce to the juices in the saucepan, stir to incorporate the sediment and then pour the sauce over the patties. Cover with foil and bake in a moderately low oven 140°C (275°F, Gas mark 1) for about 40min.

This, of course, is the basic dish. You can titivate it by garnishing with fried or raw onion rings and slices of pimento stuffed olives, and you should serve the meat with thick, very crisp potato chips.

193

A rich vinegary sauce used for pickling meat, poultry or fish or served cold as a robust accompaniment for all manner of dishes.

Escabeche
(Serves 6–8)

6 medium pickled peppers
2 green peppers
2 onions
2 cloves garlic
150ml (¼pt) olive or sunflower oil
2 bay leaves
600ml (1pt) white wine vinegar
Salt
Pinch ground cumin, oregano and freshly ground
black pepper

Drain, rinse and slice the pickled peppers and remove the core and seeds. Remove the core and seeds of the green peppers and cut the flesh into thin strips. Peel and thinly slice the onions. Peel and crush the garlic.

Heat the oil, add the pickled and green peppers and the onion and garlic and cook over a low heat, stirring to prevent sticking, until the onion is soft and transparent. Add the bay leaves, vinegar, salt, cumin, oregano and pepper, bring to the boil and cook for 5min. Remove from the heat and leave to cool. Keep if possible for 24hr before using.

Refritos (Refried Beans)
(Serves 4)

Such a simple dish but one that is so good that you can't help making your right thumb and forefinger into a circle in the universal gesture of excellence. In Mexico the beans used are the large Mexican red beans, the pintos or the black beans, but red kidney beans are a useful substitute.

450g (1lb) red kidney beans
1 large onion
75g (3oz) lean bacon
Salt and freshly ground black pepper
2tbsp olive or sunflower oil
3tbsp grated Parmesan cheese
Stock, if necessary

Cover the beans with cold water and leave to soak overnight. Peel and finely chop the onion. Remove the rind and cut the bacon into small pieces.

Place the beans in an earthenware crock or casserole with the water the beans have been soaked in together with the onion and bacon and cook over a moderate heat (first bring to the boil, and boil for a minimum of 10min) for about 4hr until tender. Season the beans with salt and pepper and leave to cool.

Heat the oil in a heavy casserole, add the beans and cook over a moderately high heat and mash them with a potato masher as they cook, sprinkling over a little of the Parmesan cheese until the beans are fairly smooth and reasonably dry but not mushy (if the beans become too dry as they cook, stir in a little stock).

Chicharos
(Green Peas with other Vegetables)
(Serves 6)

2 large carrots
450g (1lb) waxy potatoes
2 medium onions
75g (3oz) butter
Salt and freshly ground black pepper
2 bay leaves
Sprigs of oregano and thyme
900g (2lb) young, podded, peas
Pinch of bicarbonate of soda
1tbsp flour
300ml (½pt) single cream

Some of the best vegetables in Mexico grow in the valleys of rivers such as the Santa Maria which rises in the Sierra, and their bounty is such that there is often no need to use expensive meat, fish and poultry. In many other places there is a larder of rich milk and honey and, in prosperous times, cream and butter enhance the vegetable dishes of the region.

Peel the carrots and cut them into very thin lengthwise strips. Peel the potatoes and cut into small dice. Peel and finely chop the onions. Melt the butter in a flameproof casserole, add the carrots, potatoes and onions and cook over a low heat, stirring to prevent sticking, until the onion is soft and transparent. Season with salt and pepper, mix in the herbs, cover tightly and cook over a low heat for 15min.

Add the peas to a saucepan of fast boiling water, to which a little bicarbonate of soda has been added to preserve the colour. Cook for 6min and drain well. Add the peas to the rest of the vegetables, stir in the flour and mix in the cream, stirring gently over a low heat until the sauce is rich and thick and all the vegetables are cooked.

Pesadumbre
(Mixed Vegetable Salad)
(Serves 6)

Mexican salads are extra special, particularly those salads made from vegetables. One of the great delights of Mexico is to visit the vegetable markets, even in the smallest town or roadside village. They are fantastic and vegetables are especially used during the summer months. This salad is made in advance and generally kept for 2 days to mature the flavours of the vegetables. This can go with meat dishes (in Mexico salads are frequently served with hot dishes) but I serve it as a first course.

450g (1lb) small firm courgettes
450g (1lb) firm young carrots
450g (1lb) waxy new potatoes
225g (8oz) fresh or frozen peas
3tbsp chilli powder
1 clove garlic
1tsp cumin
½tsp dried thyme
150ml ¼pt white wine vinegar
1 bay leaf
Salt
1 medium mild flavoured onion
50g (2oz) sharp flavoured Cheddar cheese
3–4tbsp olive oil

Cook the courgettes in boiling salted water for 5min, and drain well. Peel and cook the carrots in salted water for about 20min until just tender but still crisp. Wash and cook the potatoes in salted water until just tender; peel when cool enough to handle.

Cut the courgettes into 1cm (½in) slices and drain in a sieve. Cut the carrots and potatoes into small dice. Cook the peas in boiling salted water until just tender and drain well.

Combine the chilli powder, crushed garlic, cumin, thyme and vinegar, add to the warm vegetables, add the bay leaf and sprinkle with salt. Cover and leave to stand in a cool place rather than a refrigerator for 24–48hr. Peel and thinly slice the onion and divide into rings, cut the cheese into thin strips.

Remove the bay leaf from the vegetables, add the oil to the vegetables and mix lightly. Garnish with the onion rings and cheese strips.

Guacamole (Avocado Dip)
(Serves 6)

2 large ripe avocado pears
2tbsp lemon juice
3 cloves garlic, peeled and crushed
Freshly ground black pepper
Pinch paprika pepper
Few drops Tabasco sauce

Avocados, ripe and mashed, can be used in place of butter, as a base for soups and in savoury dips and sauces. *Guacamole*, a creamed avocado mixture, is often served as a filling for *tortillas* or *tostadas* or as an appetiser or snack with pieces of *tostadas* being dipped in the strongly garlic flavoured mixture.

Peel and halve the avocados, remove the stones, roughly chop the flesh and put in a bowl; sprinkle with lemon juice. Mash the avocado with the crushed garlic (or you can process with a liquidizer or food processor). Season with freshly ground black pepper, paprika and a few drops of Tabasco sauce and mix well. Serve chilled.

Salsa Verde (Green Tomato Sauce) and Salsa Cruda

Salsa Verde
375g (12oz) green tomatoes
1 clove garlic
2 spring onions
1 small green chilli pepper
2 sprigs fresh coriander (or use parsley)
Pinch sugar
Salt
75ml (3fl oz) water

These sauces make their appearance on most Mexican tables whenever tomatoes are in season. The sauces are eaten with any savoury dish and are usually made fresh each day. In Mexico of course the sauces are usually made in a *molcajete* (pestle and mortar) but an electric liquidizer or food processor makes puréeing the sauces much easier.

Cover the tomatoes with boiling water, leave to stand for 3min, drain and peel off the skin and chop the flesh cutting out any hard cores. Peel the garlic. Trim the green from the spring onions. Remove the seeds from the chilli pepper and roughly chop the flesh. Combine all the ingredients in an electric liquidizer or food processor until the ingredients are reduced to a coarse purée. Serve at room temperature.

Salsa Cruda
225g (8oz) firm, ripe tomatoes
2 small green chilli peppers
1 small shallot or onion (or 2 spring onion bulbs)
1tbsp finely chopped coriander leaves (or use parsley)
Salt
Pinch sugar
45ml (3tbsp) cold water

Cover the tomatoes with boiling water for 3min, drain and slide off the skins. Roughly chop the tomatoes. Remove the seeds from the chillis and roughly chop the flesh. Roughly chop the onion. Combine all the ingredients except the water in a liquidizer or food processor until the ingredients are all chopped, but not puréed. Add the water, taste for seasoning and serve at room temperature.

Tortillas
(Makes 12 *Tortillas*)

A classic food from Mexico. Large pancakes are sold in the street or made at home to be filled with meat, vegetables or salads. Maize flour can be bought from specialist food shops and health food shops.

100g (4oz) maize flour
150g (5oz) wholewheat flour
1tsp salt
150ml (¼pt) cold water

Combine the flours in a bowl, mix in the salt and then add enough water to make a firm, pliable but not sticky dough. Turn onto a floured board and knead to make a smooth, elastic dough. Form into a roll, cut into twelve slices and then roll each piece of dough into a ball. Roll out the balls into thin circles about 20cm (8in) in diameter.

Heat a large, heavy, frying pan without oil until very hot. Add one of the tortillas and cook over a moderate heat, pressing the tortilla down with the back of a wooden spoon for 2 minutes, turn it over and continue to cook until it is firm but not browned. Transfer to a dish and cover with a cloth to prevent drying while cooking the rest of the tortillas.

Tostadas
Cooked tortillas are overfried until crisp and crunchy. The

crisp tortillas are topped with salad or meat mixtures or broken into quarters to serve with savoury avocado or tomato mixtures.

Heat a thin layer of sunflower oil in a frying pan until smoking. Add a tortilla and cook over a high heat until crisp and golden on both sides. Drain well on kitchen paper and keep warm while frying the remainder.

Crisp Fried Golden Bread
(Serves 4)

4 thickly cut slices white bread
2tbsp runny honey
1 egg
Deep oil for frying
Quarters of lemon

Cut each slice of bread into 4 fingers. Beat the honey with the egg until smooth. Heat the oil until a haze rises from it. Dip the fingers of bread into the honey and beaten egg and drop them into the hot oil cooking them until crisp and golden brown. Remove with a slotted spoon and drain on kitchen paper. Pile the fingers onto a napkin and serve at once garnished with lemon quarters.

I was given this delicious golden crisp fried bread as a pudding by a Mexican friend who spent his life bewailing the fact that he was living in New York. 'Why', he would ask, 'do I go on living here instead of in beautiful Mexico?' One had only to see how much money he was making to know why he stayed in a cold country, but he said he still ate the real food of his family, food of the hot *sierra*. Living in a cold country myself, it is a pudding I have made with success; in Mexico I seemed only to eat fruit dishes for puddings.

Served with cream or sour cream on the side this is scrumptious!

New Zealand

I can think of no better way to start this chapter than to introduce you to Hugh Fullerton-Smith, or Pancho as his friends know him. Pancho left New Zealand in 1966 to travel round the world, eventually settling in Cornwall to farm sheep high up on Bodmin Moor. Here he and his Cornish wife Jan live in a farmhouse with their two young daughters, Sarah and Katie.

In January 1986, after an absence of 10 years, Pancho returned to New Zealand with his family, on a Nuffield Scholarship, to study breeding methods in New Zealand and Australia.

New Zealand has a backbone of mountains, the most rugged being in the South Island, where snow can be quite heavy in the winter. Many Scots settled in Dunedin and Christchurch, and even today one can hear a distinctive roll of the 'r' in the accents of the people. The Scottish ancestry is reflected in the popularity of porridge and nourishing casseroles and stews. During the summer months long hours of sunshine compensate for the long hard winters.

Arriving in New Zealand in January, one is greeted by warm sunny weather. Almost the first thing Pancho did on arrival at his parents' home at Ohope Beach on the Bay of Plenty, was to go fishing with his father Bill, a very active 75 year old. They set up a net across a tiny estuary while the tide was coming in, left it and went cockling. Upon their return an hour or so later they found 15 plump flounders caught in the net. Lunch that day was cooked on the barbecue in the garden; in fact during the summer months all food is cooked outdoors with the exception of dishes baked in the kitchen oven.

With the barbecue really hot, a small sheet of corrugated iron is placed over the coals and fresh cockles are laid in the ridges of the iron and cooked until they 'pop'; immediately they are given a good dash of pepper sauce and consumed with great gusto. Flounder is laid on buttered foil, seasoned with freshly ground black pepper and a squeeze of lemon,

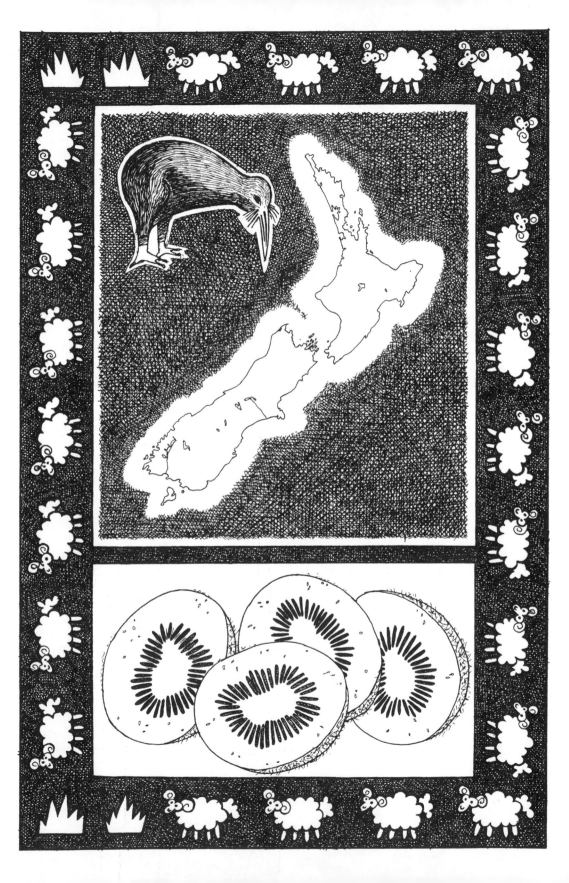

then sealed into a parcel and cooked over the coals — simple food at its best.

Most rural New Zealand homes have a garden, where fruit and vegetables grow abundantly. The housewife takes great pride in her stock of bottled peaches, apricots, beans, corn and tomatoes that share the shelves with preserves and pickles. As with most countries, home baking is popular in rural areas and a favourite teatime recipe is pikelets, little drop scones which are cooked on a griddle. In the cities much entertaining is done by eating out; in the country however, most people entertain at home, and on a regular basis. Summertime dinner parties often take the form of barbecues, while in winter they can be quite formal indoor affairs. The older generation still prefers to have a midday main meal and an evening high tea with sandwiches, cakes, biscuits, and tray bakes. The younger generation, however, usually eats dinner at night and has a light lunch. Agriculture is important to most New Zealanders, whether they farm or work in industries dependent on primary produce; 3.5 million people and 65 million sheep give an idea of the ratio.

The arrival of the shearing gang is seen twice yearly at sheep stations. On a big station this can be as many as 8 shearers, 3 shed hands (who deal with the fleeces as they are removed from the sheep), and a cook. They will move into the 'batch', usually a shed, lean-to, or caravan, and the farmer will provide meat and vegetables, and the cook will produce the meals. From 5am until early evening there is the continuous buzz of electric shears, with breaks only for food and drink. I met several shearers who clip Pancho's sheep, far from their homeland, in Cornwall and they seemed a very happy bunch of men, who enjoy their work.

Until the 1960s, deer were culled in New Zealand as they were considered a threat to forestry, a very important part of the country's economy. Then some New Zealanders decided to farm deer, and this has now become a thriving industry. Farmed venison has a unique flavour, is low in cholesterol and fat, thus making it a very healthy and popular food, the demand for which is steadily increasing. Unfortunately the prohibitive costs of deer fencing preclude fast expansion, but that does ensure the continuing popularity of lamb and beef.

I was also surprised to learn that deer horn is much sought-after, usually by Far East countries, for its great medicinal and, so it is said, aphrodisiac qualities.

A New Zealand custom that Pancho has brought to England is the *hungi*, a popular outdoor form of eating, usually for a crowd of friends on a special occasion. Its origins lie in Polynesian cookery, as many Pacific Islanders cook various foods in a pit in the ground. This method of long, slow, cooking produces moist, steamed, ingredients.

First dig a pit, a large oval one, not too deep (that, Pancho told me is where amateurs go wrong, they usually make it much too deep). Having dug your pit, light a big fire in it and let it burn for about an hour before piling river stones or firebricks in a wire basket and placing them on the fire. As the fire sinks, the stones or bricks will become white-hot. Meanwhile the ingredients are prepared. Lamb being inexpensive and plentiful is most used for the hungi, and it needs to be cut into portions and placed in a large wire basket. Another basket is piled with vegetables, onions, carrots, cauliflower and *kumrah* (the Maori potato) and lots of wild watercress which the Maoris call pouha (it grows in abundance, and a Maori, when cooking a hungi, will liberally scatter it through the meat). A 'pillow' of mixed herbs is then laid on top.

The embers are raked out of the pit, and the baskets of ingredients lowered onto the hot stones. A wet sheet is laid over the baskets and tucked down the sides of the pit; then heavy sacking, probably a clean woolsack, is thrown over the top and finally all the earth dug out of the pit is piled over the sack to seal everything and ensure that no steam can escape. In New Zealand everyone would then go to the beach, or to the pub. When they returned some three or four hours later the hungi would be ready, the pit opened up and platefuls of moist, tender meat and vegetables accompanied by big bowls of salads and a selection of sauces would be served. While there is no definite New Zealand cuisine it certainly does not lack imagination and good use is made of the excellent local produce.

Toheroa is a shellfish which is found buried in the sands of many of New Zealand's beaches, and it must be dug out by hand. You can also use clams, mussels or oysters in this recipe.

Toheroa Soup
(Serves 4)

25g (1oz) butter
25g (1oz) plain flour
300ml (½pt) fish or chicken stock
300ml (½pt) milk
175g (6oz) finely chopped toheroa, clams, mussels or oysters
2tsp lemon juice
Salt and freshly ground black pepper
4tbsp natural yoghurt
1tbsp finely chopped fresh parsley

Melt the butter in a medium sized saucepan, and stir in the flour mixing well until the flour is cooked. Mix the stock and milk together and gradually stir into the roux, over a medium high heat, until the soup comes to the boil and is thick and smooth. Add the toheroa or other fish, and mix well together with the lemon juice. Season with salt and freshly ground black pepper. Ladle into warmed soup bowls, and garnish with 1tbsp of natural yoghurt topped with a generous sprinkling of finely chopped fresh parsley.

Foiled Fish
(Serves 4)

Just about any fish is suitable for this dish. The last time he was in New Zealand, my friend Pancho cooked several flounder in this way on the barbecue, and he assures me the dish was outstanding.

25g (1oz) butter
450g (1lb) fish fillets, skinned
1 lemon
1 onion
2 ripe, firm, tomatoes
4tbsp white wine
Freshly ground black pepper
1tbsp finely chopped fresh parsley

Butter 4 pieces of foil. Divide the fish equally on each piece of foil. Thinly slice the lemon and lay on top of the fillets, peel and thinly slice the onion and put on top of the lemon. Cover the tomatoes with boiling water, stand for 3 minutes, slide off the skins, and slice thinly, arrange on top of the onion. Drizzle a little wine over each portion. Season with freshly ground black pepper, and sprinkle over the chopped parsley. Fold over the foil and seal each into a parcel. Place over white-hot coals on the barbecue and cook for about 20min. Serve in the foil on a plate, slitting the foil with a sharp knife in a cross, so that it can be turned back to expose the fish and the delicious aroma.

NZ Fish Pie
(Serves 4)

450g (1lb) smoked fish
1tbsp lemon juice
50g (2oz) butter
40g (1½oz) flour
300ml (½pt) milk
2tbsp finely chopped fresh parsley
Salt and freshly ground black pepper
2tbsp thick cream
1 medium onion
4 hardboiled eggs
200g (7oz) frozen puff pastry, thawed
1 beaten egg

Fish pie is a favourite family dish which contains either fresh or tinned fish. Home smoking is very popular and this pie therefore uses smoked fish.

Put the fish into a large deep frying pan, cover with water, add the lemon juice and poach gently until the fish starts to flake; drain and allow fish to cool.

Melt the butter in a saucepan, and over a medium high heat stir in the flour, until smooth. Gradually add the milk stirring all the time until the sauce comes to the boil and is thick and smooth. Stir in the chopped parsley and season with salt and freshly ground black pepper, remove from the heat and stir in the cream.

Peel and thinly slice the onion and divide into rings. Peel and roughly chop the hardboiled eggs.

Flake the fish into a lightly greased pie dish, spread the onion rings evenly over the top. Sprinkle the chopped egg over the onions. Pour over the sauce, moving the layers with a fork to ensure that the sauce is evenly distributed.

Roll out the puff pastry on a well floured board and cut a long strip about 2.5cm (1in) wide, using a little water fit this

around the edge of the pie dish. Use the remaining pastry to make a lid to fit the top of the dish, moistening with water so that it can be sealed around the edges. Flute the edges and use any pastry trimmings to decorate. Brush the pastry all over with beaten egg. Bake in the oven at 200°C (400°F, Gas mark 6) for 25–30min or until the pastry has risen and is golden brown.

Venison Casserole
(Serves 4)

Deer farming has increased over the last few years, and although venison is still a luxury dish, it can be stretched when combined with vegetables and served in a tasty sauce.

1kg (2¾lb) braising venison
Seasoned flour
25g (1oz) butter
2 medium onions
150ml (¼pt) robust red wine
150ml (¼pt) chicken stock
400g (14oz) tin tomatoes
2tbsp tomato purée
1tsp dried thyme
1tsp dried oregano
2 bay leaves
Salt and freshly ground black pepper
100g (4oz) button mushrooms

Trim the venison and cut into 2.5cm (1in) cubes, and roll in the seasoned flour.

Heat the butter in a heavy (preferably cast iron) flameproof casserole and brown the meat. Peel and finely chop the onions and add to the dish, mixing in well. Add the other ingredients except the mushrooms; season well with freshly ground black pepper and a little salt. Cover tightly and cook in a preheated oven at 170°C (325°F, Gas mark 3) for 1½hr. Wipe over the mushrooms. Remove the casserole from the oven, add the mushrooms, and check seasoning. Return to the oven for a further 30min.

Honey Roast Lamb
(Serves 4)

2 cloves garlic
1.5kg (3½lb) leg of lamb
Freshly ground black pepper
3tbsp clear honey
1tbsp light soy sauce

One of the many lamb
dishes of New Zealand
where local wild honey
would be used, but any
clear honey will make it
just as delicious.

Peel and thinly slice the garlic. With a sharp, pointed, knife,
make small slits all over the lamb and insert the slivers of
garlic, then season generously with freshly ground black
pepper. Stand the lamb in a roasting tin, on a rack. Put the
honey and soy sauce in a small pan and heat gently to
amalgamate; pour evenly over the lamb and roast in the oven
preheated to 180°C (350°F, Gas mark 4) allowing 25min/
450g (1lb) and basting occasionally with the juices in the
roasting tin.

Homemade Tomato Sauce

3kg (7lb) ripe, but firm, tomatoes
1kg (2¼lb) apples
3 onions
1l (1¾pt) light vinegar
25g (1oz) salt
450g (1lb) sugar
1tsp ground cayenne pepper
5cm (2in) fresh ginger root
1tsp black peppercorns
1tsp allspice
½tsp ground cloves

Jars of preserves can be
seen in most New Zealand
homes, where any glut of
home produce is used in
sauces, chutneys, jams
and jellies.

Cover the tomatoes with boiling water, let stand for 3min
then slide off the skins, chop the flesh and put into a large
saucepan. Peel core and roughly chop the apples and add to
the pan. Peel and finely chop the onions and add to the pan.
Pour over the vinegar. Mix in the salt, sugar and cayenne
pepper. Peel and finely chop the ginger root and add to the

pan together with the peppercorns, allspice and cloves. Bring to the boil over a gentle heat, then lower the heat to simmer and cook until very soft. Purée in a blender or food processor (this will have to be done in batches) and spoon into hot, clean, jars. Seal and label.

Sweet Potato Bake
(Serves 6)

Kumara (or sweet potato) is available for most of the year, and is a popular vegetable.

450g (1lb) **kumara**
Salt
300ml (½pt) **apple sauce**
50g (2oz) **soft dark brown sugar**
Juice of ½ lemon
25g (1oz) **butter**
25g (1oz) **mixed chopped nuts**

Wash the kumara, but do not peel, and cook in lightly salted boiling water until tender. Drain and allow to cool. Peel off the skin, cut into ½cm (¼in) slices and arrange in a lightly greased shallow ovenproof dish.

Mix the apple sauce, sugar and lemon juice together with half the chopped nuts and pour over the kumara. Sprinkle the remaining nuts on the top and dot with butter. Bake at 190°C (375°F, Gas mark 5) for 20min.

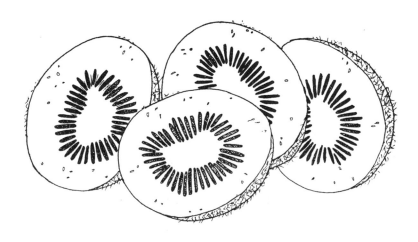

Kiwi Pavlova
(Serves 6–8)

4 egg whites
½tsp salt
225g (8oz) castor sugar
4tsp cornflour
½tsp vanilla essence
2tsp vinegar
4 kiwi fruit
100g (4oz) strawberries
300ml (½pt) whipping cream

Australians and New Zealanders argue over the origins of the pavlova, but this recipe contains the delectable New Zealand kiwi fruit, indigenous to that island. Kiwi fruit look rather like browny furry eggs, but when sliced they are a beautiful iridescent green, with a unique sugary texture and a tangy flavour – definitely a favourite.

Whisk the egg whites, with the salt, until stiff. Whisk in the sugar a spoonful at a time and continue whisking until the mixture is very stiff. Beat in the cornflour, vinegar and vanilla essence. Spoon the mixture onto a baking sheet lined with baking parchment on which is drawn a 23cm (9in) circle. Using the marked circle as a guide, build up the sides and hollow out the middle slightly to form a basket shape. Bake for 1¼hr in an oven preheated to 140°C (275°F, Gas mark 1). Turn off oven and leave to cool.

Peel and slice the kiwi fruit. Hull and halve the strawberries. Whip the cream until it is thick, not stiff, and fold in the fruits. Spoon the mixture into the pavlova shell. Serve at once.

Walnut Slices

100g (4oz) soft margarine
100g (4oz) sugar
2 standard size eggs (medium)
100g (4oz) wholemeal flour
75g (3oz) chopped walnuts
50g (2oz) butter
50g (2oz) soft brown sugar

Slices, or traybakes, are eaten at coffeetime and teatime in New Zealand.

Cream the margarine and sugar together until fluffy, then beat in the eggs. Gradually beat in the flour, then stir in the walnuts. Spread the mixture over a greased shallow baking tin about 25cm (10in) square. In a small saucepan melt the butter, add the soft brown sugar, mix well and pour over the mixture in the tin.

Bake in a preheated oven at 190°C (375°F, Gas mark 5) for about 25min. Leave in the tin until cool and then cut into slices.

Pikelets
(Makes about 18)

A lot of New Zealand cookery has its origins in Britain, and pikelets, I have no doubt, derive from Scotch pancakes, or drop scones.

450g (1lb) plain flour
2 rounded tsp baking powder
1tsp salt
40g (1½oz) butter
300ml (11fl oz) milk
2 eggs
50g (2oz) castor sugar

Put the flour, baking powder and salt into a large mixing bowl and mix well together.

In a small saucepan melt the butter, then pour into the milk and whisk together. Beat the eggs and sugar together until pale yellow and frothy and beat into the milk mixture.

Make a well in the dry ingredients and gradually pour in the liquid, beating with a wooden spoon until the mixture is smooth. Lightly grease a heavy bottomed frying pan, and fry tablespoonsful of the mixture, until the tops begin to bubble; flip over with a spatula and cook the other side until golden brown. Keep warm in a medium oven until all the mixture is used up.

Pikelets can be buttered and served with a dollop of jam.

Pear Chutney

2kg (4½lb) pears
450g (1lb) onions
450g (1lb) tomatoes
2 green peppers
225g (8oz) raisins
450g (1lb) demerara sugar
5ml (1tsp) salt
2 cloves garlic
Good pinch cayenne pepper
5ml (1tsp) ground ginger
1l (1¾pt) pickling vinegar
6 whole cloves
15ml (1tbsp) pickling spices

An excellent way of making good use of any 'windfalls'.

Peel core and finely chop the pears. Peel and finely chop the onions. Cover the tomatoes with boiling water, let stand for 1min, then slide off the skins; roughly chop the flesh. Deseed the peppers and cut into small dice. Put the chopped ingredients into a large saucepan, cover and cook, without the addition of any extra liquid, over a gentle heat for 20min. Add the raisins, sugar and salt to the pan together with the garlic, finely chopped, cayenne pepper, ground ginger and vinegar.

Tie the cloves and pickling spice in muslin and add to the pan. Cook over a gentle heat for about 1½hr, stirring occasionally to prevent sticking, until the chutney becomes thick.

Ladle the mixture into clean warm jars, cover with waxed paper, seal and label. Store for at least 2 weeks before use.

Start asking about Russian peasant food and, at first you come up against something like a brick wall. Russians will tell you that the peasant was usually so poor, his life so hard, communications so difficult and the winters so long and rough, that he scratched what he could from the soil and existed rather than ate. It was the wealthy, you are told, who ate what is known as Russian cuisine today, who wallowed in caviar, whose chefs excelled in the roasting of sucking pigs, perfected *boeuf Straganov* (a recent innovation this, invented in the last century and named after Count Straganov) and moulded and chilled the famous chicken Kiev so that garlicky, herbed, melted butter spurted from the boned chicken when a knife pierced it. These chefs developed the sensational *zakuski* (hors d'oeuvres) which before the 1917 Revolution was served regularly in most large houses and comprised a dozen or more cold dishes to tempt and restore any visitor upon arrival.

Russian peasants lived, I was told, off soups and bread, the thin beer, *kvas* and *kasha*, buckwheat, fried and then soaked in boiling water, pickled cabbage in winter, and not much else. Then, gradually, I discovered the picture of Russian country cuisine wasn't all that black. The soups may have been simple but many are masterpieces of taste, colour and texture; bread wasn't just the harsh, almost black ryebread, there were other varieties as well. *Maslemitsa* (butter week), the last days before Lent, saw the making of light buckwheat pancakes and *paskha*, the richest of all cheesecakes, and *kulich*, a delicious golden cake. The great feast of Easter saw the painting of eggs, serving of buttery *blini* and a feast of exotic food. Fresh fish from the rivers were made into soup or used in *piroqi* or *pirozhki*, large and small *koulebiaka* which are light puff pastry casings stuffed with rice and vegetables as well as fish or, sometimes, spiced meat. Although, perhaps these pies might be more simply made in a peasant home than those served to the aristocracy (where they might well contain sturgeon or salmon) they were nonetheless delicious.

212

Since the winters were hard and long, vegetables were stored, dried and salted. Cabbage and cucumbers were pickled, fresh fish salted and dried, and mushrooms, gathered by the thousand in early autumn were dried to provide a flavouring for the lean days. The mushroom markets were the first to flourish when free markets began again after the revolution. In September and October not just the country people, but town dwellers too, take to the woods all over Russia to gather edible fungi. At weekends everyone is seen wearing stout boots and carrying baskets overflowing with red, yellow, grey, orange and brown fungi on the backs of bicycles, in trams, on trains and on buses. Mushrooms are served with the delicious pancake *blini*, incorporated into the *kasha* used in soups, served with fish and any meat there may happen to be and spiced with sour cream and dill as a course in their own right.

The use of *smetana*, or sour cream, in Russian cookery is something we could well use. Basically the smetana is cream exposed to the sun to sour and thicken. If you cannot get commercially soured cream, which is excellent and can be bought from supermarkets, you can thicken and sour double or single cream by adding 1tbsp of lemon juice to 125ml (5fl oz) of cream, or by mixing the liquid from a carton of cottage cheese with the cream and leaving it in a warm place overnight. The cream is swirled into vegetable soups, used as a dressing for salads and cold dishes, incorporated into sauces for chicken fish and meat, mixed with fruit and used in rich cheesecakes. I love it as a topping for hot or cold soups when seasoned with salt, pepper and paprika or cayenne and flavoured with a little dried or fresh chopped dill.

Ivoroq, the national cheese, is a dry smooth curd cheese which hardly tastes of cheese and is used widely as a filling for both sweet and savoury pastries and pancakes and is incorporated into the small dumplings which are often served in soups.

Most people, when they get drunk for the first time prefer to forget about it. Paradoxically I, when I first drank too much liquor and had to be driven home in a taxi and put to bed, remember the occasion with great delight and gastronomic fervour. I was taken to dinner at the Bortsch N'Tears in Beauchamp Place, London which I am happy to say is still going strong. There I had my first vodka or three or four and fell in love – not with my escort but with my first taste of *bortsch*. Miraculously I woke next day without a hangover but with the flavour of that soup ingrained on that part of my memory reserved for special dishes and I have been making it ever since, in true Russian peasant style, with beetroot for

colouring and flavour but with the bulk made up of available seasonal vegetables. I add finely chopped dill pickled cucumber to my version for that slightly sharp overtone and I crown it with that all important dollop of sour cream, flavoured with salt and cayenne with the addition of a pinch of dried dill soaked until soft in a little lemon juice.

Herbs are an integral part of Russian food. Dill, much underestimated here and a herb that can be grown easily in a garden or windowbox, has a subtle taste that does a lot for fish dishes and soups; oregano may be added to almost any vegetable dish and coriander (again, this is easily grown) goes well with anything from eggs to meat or even sweet dishes. In Southern Russia, where many culinary influences stem from the Middle East, food tends to be spicy with the almost lavish use of garlic and herbs, hot peppers and fruit mixtures being compatible with the warmer climate but farther north the emphasis is on warm, sustaining food for people who live in a cold climate and work hard manually. In the north, therefore, the soups, which I personally enjoy and serve in our own damp and chilly climate, come into their own.

As in most farming communities, the main meal of the day is in the evening after the workers have returned from the fields. Amongst poorer Russians, soup and bread only may form the meal together, of course, with vodka which raises the spirits and warms the heart. The best known Russian soup is *bortsch*, basically made from vegetables coloured and flavoured with beetroot. Like all peasant food the charm of this soup is that it varies with regions and families; into it goes what is available, and it is spiced or seasoned according to the whim of the cook. If times are good the stock may be based on meat or poultry making a richly flavoured soup. In summer the dark redness comes from whole baby beetroot rich in juice, iron and flavour. When times are hard a little beetroot and the tops of the beetroot add the colouring and the bulk of the soup will come from cabbage, potatoes, turnips and wild herbs. This form of food is for all seasons. Beetroots store well and last throughout the winter; in summer the soup is served cold and well laced with *kvass* and topped with dollops of rich, seasoned *smetana*.

In the southernmost part of Russia, bordering on Turkey, Iran, the Black and Caspian seas, is the most fertile part of the Soviet Union, with perfect growing conditions. The food of the Caucasus is exciting, exotic, richly flavoured and rich in tradition as well. It has been influenced by the Greeks, Romans, Persians, Arabs, Asians and Turks, is highly aromatic, succulent and unusual and probably forms the most healthy diet eaten anywhere.

Lamb, chicken and veal are kebabed and grilled out doors over charcoal and when served are accompanied by spicy, sauces, sliced pickled cucumber, slices of fresh tomatoes and lemons. Yoghurt is substituted for the sour cream *smetana* and some people attribute to this the longevity of many Georgians and Armenians.

Nuts, particularly walnuts and almonds, are widely used for both sweet and savoury dishes; onion, garlic herbs and spices are all used lavishly but with discretion in almost every savoury dish. In Georgia you will find buckwheat (*bulghur*) used as a staple starch; in the Caucasian East, rice comes into its own with many dishes being very similar to those of the Middle East.

Salads form a large part of the staple Caucasian diet (another reason why, perhaps, they are so healthy – their ingredients read like a vegetable cookery book.) Salads of tomatoes, cucumber, peppers and fresh herbs dressed with oil and lemon juice, salads of cooked vegetables (the original Russian Salad) dressed with sour cream or yoghurt, salads with the addition of chopped walnuts and of raw spinach, all may be served as a first course, main course or as a vegetable side dish.

Russian Vodka

Vodka is the Russian national drink. Usually it is served ice cold and knocked back in one large gulp, but for parties and special occasions there are variations on the vodka theme. Lemon vodka is made by adding a little sugar and thinly pared lemon rind to a bottle of vodka and refrigerating it for about a week before drinking. Mint is also used as a flavouring in the same way, so are various berries and a wellknown cure for colds is 'pepper' vodka or 'garlic' vodka both of which will lift your head off, even if they do not cure your cold! To make 'pepper' vodka add a red chilli pepper, pricked all over with a darning needle, or for 'garlic' vodka, a large, plump clove of garlic to a bottle of vodka and leave to infuse in a refrigerator for one week before drinking.

Yagodni (Fruit Soup)
(Serves 6)

225g (8oz) blackcurrants, redcurrants or raspberries
75g (3oz) sugar
1.4l (2½pt) water
450g (1lb) ripe peaches
1tbsp cornflour
6tbsp sour cream

Place the currants (or raspberries) in a pan with the sugar, add the water, bring to the boil and simmer until the berries are soft. Rub through a fine sieve to remove seeds and return the juice to a clean pan. Halve the peaches, remove the stones, roughly chop the fruit, add to the fruit syrup and simmer for about 20min until the peaches are soft. Lift out the peaches with a slotted spoon and purée through a food mill, return the purée to the pan, add the cornflour and mix over a moderate heat until the soup is thick and glossy. Leave to cool. Serve the soup really well chilled, with a swirl of sour cream over each serving.

The Russians enjoy fruit soups. Served chilled in the summer these soups are made from whatever fruit is in season. Russians like their fruit soups to be thick and sweet; for Western taste it is probably preferable to cut down on the sugar, but either way they make delicious summer starters and look attractive with a swirl of sour cream mixed in just before serving. In fruit growing areas peaches are often combined with other fruit to make an especially good cold starter.

Accompany with slices of dark ryebread.

Okroshka (Chilled Vegetable Soup)
(Serves 6)

2 hardboiled eggs
2 medium sized boiled potatoes
4 radishes
2 dill pickled cucumbers
6 spring onions
100g (4oz) cooked lamb, ham or chicken
1.1l (2pt) dry light cider
Salt and freshly ground black pepper
3tbsp sour cream

Peel and chop the hardboiled eggs. Cut the potatoes into small dice. Thinly slice the radishes. Cut the pickled cucumbers into small dice. Finely chop the spring onions including the tops. Thinly slice the meat and then cut into

Cold soups with cooked vegetables and, perhaps, a little leftover meat or poultry, are popular for outdoor summer eating. The soups are rich and sharp with a dill flavouring. In Russia they are made with kvass (a thin fermented beer) but this is time consuming to make and does tend to overferment and burst its bottles. I recommend that you substitute a light dry cider for the kvass.

On very hot days add ice cubes to the soup to keep it well chilled.

very thin matchstick strips about 4cm (2in) long. Combine all the vegetables and meat and chill. Add the cider, season with salt and pepper, stir and serve well chilled with some sour cream added to each serving.

Rassolnik (Sorrel and Kidney Soup)
(Serves 6)

Another meal in a bowl soup with plenty of nourishment and warmth. If you find it impossible to find sorrel (in Russia it is picked from the hedgerows) you can substitute spinach and add lemon juice to provide the essential tartness of the dish.

450g (1lb) lamb kidneys
1 onion
1 stick celery
900g (2lb) sorrel leaves
100g (4oz) spinach or chard leaves
1 dill pickled cucumber
3tbsp sunflower oil
1tbsp finely chopped parsley
1.7l (3pt) beef stock (or stock cube and water)
Salt and freshly ground black pepper
Flour
1tbsp pickled cucumber juice
1 egg yolk
150ml (¼pt) sour cream

Skin the kidneys, remove the cores and slice the flesh into thin slices. Soak in cold water for 30min to remove some of the sweet flavour. Drain and dry the slices well. Peel and finely chop the onion. Thinly slice the celery with the leaves. Pick over the sorrel, wash and dry; if necessary, remove any tough stalks and shred the leaves. Pick over the spinach, wash and dry and shred the leaves. Halve the dill pickled cucumber, discard the seeds and cut the flesh into small dice.

Heat 2tbsp oil in a large heavy saucepan. Add the onion and celery and cook over a low heat, stirring to prevent sticking until the onion is soft and transparent. Add the cucumber, parsley, sorrel and spinach and stir in the beef stock. Bring to the boil, season with salt and pepper and simmer gently for 15min.

In a clean pan heat the remaining oil, dredge the kidney slices in seasoned flour, and brown them over a high heat, stirring until browned on all sides. Add a little of the stock, stirring to incorporate all the bits which adhere to the pan and stir in the remaining soup. Bring to the boil and simmer for 4min (do not overcook as this will toughen the kidneys).

Beat the egg yolk lightly in a bowl, add the pickled cucumber juice and mix well. Gradually stir in 150ml (¼pt) of the hot stock stirring until smooth. Add this mixture to the soup and stir over a moderate heat, without boiling, until the egg is incorporated. Stir in the sour cream, heat through and serve at once.

Shchi (Cabbage Soup)
(Serves 6)

1 small cabbage
1 large onion
1 carrot
1 stick celery
2 potatoes
225g (8oz) sauerkraut
1.7*l* (3pt) beef stock
4tbsp tomato purée
Salt and freshly ground black pepper
2 bay leaves
1tbsp sunflower oil

This classic peasant soup is found amongst all the poorer Russian families. Like all such soups it is made with what happens to be handy at the time; in winter fresh cabbage is augmented by pickled sauerkraut which provides a spicy flavour. Soups like this are cheap, warming and nourishing and make a substantial meal with thick slices of bread enhanced perhaps by a glass of vodka on special days. Spinach, herbs and chopped hardboiled eggs may be added to *shchi*.

Shred the cabbage. Peel and finely chop the onion. Peel the carrot and cut into small dice. Thinly slice the celery with the leaves. Peel the potatoes and cut into small dice. Place the sauerkraut in a basin. Cover with cold water and leave to stand for 30min. Drain well.

Heat the oil in a large saucepan, add the onion, carrot, celery and potatoes and cook over a low heat until the onion is soft and transparent, and the oil has been absorbed into the vegetables. Add the sauerkraut and cabbage, pour over the stock, stir in the tomato purée, season with salt and pepper, add the bay leaves, bring to the boil and simmer for 1hr. Remove the bay leaves before serving.

Note: The stock can be made from an inexpensive cut of meat like brisket in which case the meat will be eaten separately from the soup. You can also thicken the soup with a browned roux made from frying 2tbsp flour until nutbrown in 2tbsp sunflower oil, stirring in some of the stock, adding the rest of the soup and then stirring until thickened.

Bortsch is usually a country style soup made with what vegetables are to hand but without the use of expensive meat or duck stock. Made with chicken stock it is most delicious and one which can be served again and again.

Postni Bortsch
(Serves 6)

1 clove garlic
1 onion
Half a small cabbage
3 small beetroot and beetroot leaves
3 carrots
1 small parsnip or turnip
3 medium potatoes
2tbsp oil
6tbsp tomato purée
1.7*l* (3pt) chicken stock (or use water and stock cube)
Salt and freshly ground black pepper
6 tbsp sour cream

Peel and finely chop the garlic. Peel and chop the onion. Finely shred the cabbage. Peel and coarsely grate the beetroot and shred the beetroot leaves. Peel and coarsely grate the carrots and parsnip or turnip. Peel and dice the potatoes.

Heat the oil in a large heavy pan. Add the garlic, onion, beetroot, carrots and parsnip and cook over a low heat, stirring to prevent sticking, until the onion is soft and transparent. Add the cabbage, beetroot tops, potato and tomato purée; pour over the stock, mix well, season with salt and pepper, bring to the boil, cover and simmer for 1hr until all the vegetables are tender. Adjust seasoning and serve in deep bowls with a swirl of sour cream on the top.

Kasha (Flavoured Buckwheat)
(Serves 6)

Kasha is an all purpose accompaniment that can be served with any main course dish and is nourishing and sustaining. Kasha is also added to some soups to give more body and nourishment. In Russia wild mushrooms would be used for this dish when they are in season.

175g (6oz) butter
175g (6oz) coarse buckwheat
450ml (¾pt) boiling water
Salt
1 large onion
225g (8oz) firm button mushrooms
150ml (¼pt) single, or sour, cream
Salt and freshly ground black pepper

Melt 50g (1oz) butter in a heavy saucepan or fireproof casserole. Add the buckwheat and turn over a moderately high heat until the buckwheat is lightly browned, add the water, season with salt and bring to the boil. Cover tightly and cook over the lowest possible heat for 2hr or until the water has all been absorbed and the buckwheat is dry and fluffy. Stir well, cover again, and stand off the heat for 10min. (*Note*: if the water is absorbed before the buckwheat is cooked a little extra water should be stirred in.)

Peel and finely chop the onion. Thinly slice the mushrooms. Heat the remaining butter in a saucepan, add the onion and cook over a low heat until the onion is soft and transparent. Add the mushrooms and stir gently for 2min. Raise the heat to high and cook the mushrooms for a further 4min. Add the onion and mushrooms to the buckwheat, stir in the cream, season with salt and pepper and turn into a baking dish and cook in a moderate oven 180°C (350°F, Gas mark 4) for 20min.

Russia

Blinis
(Serves 4)

450ml (¾pt) milk
1tsp sugar
40g (1½oz) yeast
175g (6oz) plain flour
150g (5oz) buckwheat flour
25g (1oz) butter
Pinch salt
2tbsp sour cream
3 eggs, separated
Oil
150ml (5fl oz) sour cream

Small, light pancakes are served hot everywhere in Russia, topped with caviar, salmon roe, smoked fish, chopped hard-boiled eggs mixed with finely chopped spring onions, or simply butter or sour cream. Buckwheat flour can be bought from health food shops.

Heat 300ml (½pt) milk until hand warm. Add the sugar and mix in the yeast. Leave in a warm place for about 5min until frothy on top. Sieve the flour and half the buckwheat flour into a bowl, add the yeast mixture and beat until smooth. Cover with a cloth and leave in a warm draughtless place, for 1½hr until doubled in bulk. Add the rest of the buckwheat flour and beat again until smooth. Cover again and leave to stand in a warm place for 2hr.

Melt the butter, add the remaining milk and warm to hand heat. Beat the egg yolks until smooth, and add together with the butter and milk, 2tbsp sour cream and a good pinch of salt to the dough, and mix until smooth. Whisk the egg whites until stiff, fold into the dough, cover and leave in a warm place for a further 30min.

Rub a heavy frying pan with a thin smear of oil. When the oil is smoking put in 2tbsp of the dough, press it down gently to about 0.5cm (¼in) thick and fry until golden. Turn over and continue to cook on the other side until brown.

Georgian Salad
(Serves 4)

Georgia produces the most wonderful salad ingredients. During the growing season you can see Georgian farmers flying to Moscow on the inexpensive internal flights, their battered suitcases bulging with tomatoes, lettuces and herbs. Despite the cost of the flight they find it worthwhile to take these glorious fresh ingredients to the city's markets. The range of salads is wide and many include top quality walnuts.

1 small cucumber

2 tomatoes

2 sticks celery

1 crisp lettuce heart

1 Cos lettuce heart

50g (2oz) shelled walnuts

1 clove garlic

2tbsp finely chopped onion

2tbsp finely chopped coriander or ¼tsp ground coriander

Salt and freshly ground black pepper

Pinch cayenne pepper

3tbsp sunflower oil

1tbsp white wine vinegar

Peel the cucumber, cut it in half lengthwise, scoop out the seeds and thinly slice the flesh. Cover the tomatoes with boiling water for 3min, drain well, remove the cores and seeds and chop the tomato flesh. Very thinly slice the celery sticks and the leaves. Trim the lettuce and coarsely shred the leaves. Combine the walnuts, garlic, onion and coriander in an electric liquidizer or food processor. Season with salt and pepper, add the oil and vinegar and process until smooth.

Arrange the cucumber, tomatoes, celery and lettuce in a salad bowl, pour over the dressing and toss lightly to coat the salad ingredients with the dressing.

Trout with Walnut Sauce
(Serves 4)

4 trout
Salt and freshly ground black pepper
100g (4oz) shelled walnuts
1tbsp sugar
3tbsp white wine vinegar
2tbsp finely chopped mixed coriander leaves and parsley
(or use parsley only)
1tbsp finely chopped mint
2 cloves garlic
3tbsp fish stock

Trout are much enjoyed in Armenia and Georgia. This delectable dish is, like so many great recipes, based on simplicity. The delicate flavour of the trout is balanced by the excitement of the sauce. As with all fish dishes, it is of paramount importance that the trout should be fresh – the best way to ensure this is to buy your trout live from a fish farm.

Place the cleaned and gutted fish in a shallow pan, season with salt and pepper and pour over enough cold water to come ⅓ of the way up the fish. Bring slowly to the boil, cover and cook over a low heat for about 10min until the fish is just tender. Remove the fish with a fish slice on to a heated serving dish and keep warm while making the sauce.

Combine the walnuts, sugar, vinegar, herbs, garlic and fish stock in an electric liquidizer or food processor and process the ingredients until the sauce is thick and creamy.

Bitki
(Serves 4)

Bitki are small, everyday, meatballs which form the basis of many Russian dishes. Their charm lies not so much in the meatballs themselves but in the sauces that are served with them, which may vary from a dill and sour cream sauce to a rich and aromatic tomato sauce.

100g (4oz) fresh white breadcrumbs
Milk
450g (1lb) lean beef
(I use beef skirt, topside or rump if I can afford it)
Salt and freshly ground black pepper
Pinch mixed marjoram and thyme
1 egg, beaten
Fine dried breadcrumbs
Oil for frying

Cover the breadcrumbs with milk, soften and squeeze out excess milk. Very finely mince or process the meat until it is

223

reduced to a coarse paste. Season the meat with salt and pepper and mix it to a firm paste with the breadcrumbs and herbs. Chill the meat in a refrigerator for 1hr and then, using dampened hands, shape the meat mixture into small balls about the size of a walnut. Dip the balls into beaten egg, then roll in breadcrumbs.

Heat 0.5cm (¼in) of oil in a large heavy frying pan until smoking, add the meatballs and cook over a high heat, tossing the pan, until the balls are browned on all sides (this takes about 8min). Drain on kitchen paper and serve with a sauce of hot sour cream, finely chopped dill pickled cucumbers, salt and pepper, or with a rich tomato sauce.

Russian Cherry Pudding
(Serves 4)

This lovely pudding appears frequently in Russia and is made with any available berries or fresh fruit. In late spring, cherries give it a bittersweet flavour that is truly delightful.

450g (1lb) morello cherries
100g (4oz) sugar
1 egg
1 carton 150ml (5fl oz) sour cream
1tbsp flour
Pinch cinnamon and ground nutmeg

Stone the cherries, sprinkle with 50g (2oz) sugar and leave to stand for 30min. Combine the remaining sugar with the egg, sour cream, flour and spices and beat until smooth. Place the cherries in a lightly buttered baking dish, pour over the batter mixture and bake in a moderately hot oven 190°C (375°F, Gas mark 5) for 30min until the top of the pudding is golden brown.

Serve hot with extra sweetened sour cream on the side.

Syrniki (Cottage Cheese Fritters)
(Serves 4)

Russians like sweet things and many dishes are more suited to serve as a sweet rather than a savoury. This version of *syrniki* though, is served as a sweet course with sour cream and stewed soft fruit, such as currants or raspberries.

350g (12oz) cottage cheese
2 eggs
50g (2oz) butter
2tbsp sugar
6tbsp flour
Butter or sunflower oil for frying.
Castor sugar

Place the cottage cheese in a sieve, cover with a piece of muslin, weight it with a plate to remove excess moisture and leave to stand for 3hr or until the cheese is really dry. Rub through a fine sieve into a bowl, add the eggs and beat well. Melt the butter, add it together with the sugar and flour to the cottage cheese mixture and mix to a fairly firm batter (add a little extra flour if necessary).

Heat a thin film of oil in a frying pan, add the batter a tablespoonful at a time, pressing into circles about 3mm (⅛in) thick. Cook until firm and golden brown underneath, turn over and cook until the other side is golden brown (this should be about 3min each side). Slide onto a hot serving dish and keep warm while making the remaining fritters. Sprinkle with sugar and serve with lemon juice or sour cream.

Russia

Compote of Dried Fruit with Rice Pudding
(Serves 6)

450g (1lb) mixed dried fruit (apricots, peaches, apples, pears, raisins, figs and prunes)
2tbsp honey
350g (12oz) round grain pudding rice
225g (8oz) blanched coarsely ground almonds
1.1*l* (2pt) boiling water
3tbsp sugar

The quality of dried fruit in the Caucasus is first class and puddings of dried fruit appear regularly on winter menus. The combination of dried fruit and rice pudding is often seen around Christmas time.

Soak the dried fruit in water overnight. Drain and roughly chop the fruit. Combine the fruit, honey and enough water to cover in a saucepan; bring to the boil and simmer gently until the fruit is tender (about 30min).

Cover the almonds with the boiling water and leave to steep for 2hr. Drain through a sieve, pressing down the almonds to release their flavour. Combine the almond liquid with the rice in a saucepan and add the sugar. Bring to the boil and simmer for about 30min until the rice is soft and tender and the liquid has been absorbed. Serve the rice with the fruit. Both these dishes can be served hot or cold.

Scandinavia

Marika always maintained that her interest in and love for food and cookery came from her Swedish mother, and when one looks at the food of Scandinavia her love is easy to understand. All five Scandinavian countries, Denmark, Norway, Sweden, Finland and Iceland, enjoy the cold table, but it is by its Swedish name, the *smörgåsbord*, that it is commonly known.

In this chapter I have included recipes from Denmark and Sweden only, not to demean the foods of the other countries, but because to cover those would require another complete section.

Scandinavians are famed for fine glass, stainless steel cutlery and tableware and their flair for interior and furniture design, and I feel this is very much reflected in their cookery and presentation of food.

The smörgåsbord is an elaborate and stunningly attractive buffet, usually prepared for a large number of people and there are several theories as to its origin, though it probably began with a gathering of friends who each brought something to go on the table. At a smörgåsbord, all help themselves, changing plates for the different courses. Traditionally a fish course starts the proceedings; marinated herrings; herrings in dill and the well known herrings in sour cream; there may also be some *gravlax* – boned, halved fresh salmon which has a layer of coarse seasalt, dill and maybe brandy, sandwiched between the two halves. It is weighted down and left for a number of days before being served thinly sliced. This is also an excellent way to serve mackerel. Smoked cod roe and Danish style caviar or lumpfish roe as it is better known are inevitably found among the fish dishes, as well as fresh peeled shrimps and lobster salad – it already sounds a feast in its own right, but of course every dish is sampled in small portions only.

Following the fish course come the hot dishes, or *smavarmt*, which literally translated means 'the small warm dishes', and here you could find Swedish meatballs, medallions of pork, and Danish egg cake with bacon. To follow

there is an almost infinite array of cold meats and pâtés (home made liver pâté is one of the most popular), smoked pork loin, roast beef with horseradish, steak tartare with raw yolk of egg garnished with capers, and ox tongue. There is also a wide variety of salads, which the Swedes in particular like to toss in mayonnaise, together with bowls of pickles, cucumber, beetroot and gherkins.

Breads and biscuits accompany the cheeseboard, which almost certainly includes Herrgard, Samso and Danbo and the famous Danish Blue (I have found that deep freezing a large piece of this cheese changes the texture completely and it becomes beautifully creamy – when I spoke to the Danish Agricultural Producers Association they were quite surprised as they apparently do not recommend freezing – but it really does produce the most delicious texture.)

Ice-cold aquavit, a spirit with a distinctive caraway flavouring distilled from potatoes, is traditionally drunk with the smörgåsbord, possibly followed by a chaser of lager. But there is much more to Scandinavian cookery than smorgasbord.

Perhaps because Danes and Swedes are so hardy, the working day starts much earlier; schools and businesses open at 8am. Breakfast of coffee or tea and rolls, is followed midday by lunch. In Denmark lunch consists of a selection of open sandwiches and everywhere are take-aways containing an amazing selection of *smørrebrød*, with tasty toppings of cold meats, salad, eggs or fish. In Sweden, however, a light cooked lunch is usually served, perhaps an omelette or *pytt i panna*, made from diced leftover meat and vegetables, added to a pan of thinly sliced sautéed onions. Served straight from the pan it can be topped with a fried egg, and tomato ketchup or Worcester sauce.

Midafternoon is the time for coffee, usually accompanied by biscuits or cakes, and some of those delicious Danish pastries.

The main meal of the day (and it is a real family gathering), usually eaten around 7pm, starts with a soup, followed by a fish or meat course. Desserts are eaten only on special occasions, parties and suchlike, and are not part of the daily diet.

In winter Yellow Pea Soup with Pork is often served. It is made from dried yellow peas, seasonal vegetables and one of the less expensive cuts of pork and makes a filling and nourishing meal with the pork, sliced, and served separately on side plates. It is usually followed by pancakes and jam.

In summer the foods are much lighter; crayfish, cooked in salted water with plenty of fresh dill (a herb much used in

Scandinavian cooking), is frequently used for outdoor parties, served cold and eaten with the fingers.

Festivals and holidays are the time for regional specialities and in Sweden goose is eaten on St. Martin's Eve (in honour of Martin Luther). In Denmark lightly poached cod served with a hot mustard sauce is traditional on New Year's Eve, and in Sweden ling cooked in a white sauce, is usually eaten on December 24.

I was fascinated when I learnt the traditions associated with the celebration of the Feast of St. Lucia on December 13 (and again I found Marika's strong links with Sweden, in that her daughter is called Lucia). In memory of the saint who was surrounded by fire but remained untouched, a young girl wearing a crown of spruce with seven lighted candles wakens the rest of her family in the very early hours of the morning with a tray of saffron buns and hot coffee. Later in the day children choose a Lucia to bring more buns in the schools. These winter festivals were very welcome in earlier times when the days were short and the weather cold and Scandinavian food reflects the marrying of unusual ingredients to produce nourishing and exciting dishes.

Yellow Pea Soup with Pork

350g (12oz) yellow split peas
1kg (2.2lb) pork shoulder
3 leeks
1 onion
3 sticks celery
4 carrots
2tbsp finely chopped fresh parsley
1tsp dried thyme

The best known Scandinavian soup, this is traditionally served with Schnapps.

Thoroughly wash the peas and soak overnight in plenty of cold water. Put the peas and water in a large saucepan and bring quickly to the boil; remove any scum and allow the peas to simmer covered for 1½hr, or until they are tender. Purée through a food processor or electric blender. Place the pork in a clean large, heavy bottomed, saucepan. Wash and trim the leeks and cut into chunks. Peel and roughly chop the onion. Wash the celery and chop thickly. Peel and slice the carrots.

Usually the soup is served in bowls with slices of the pork served separately on side plates. Accompany with some good strong mustard.

229

Add these vegetables to the pork together with the herbs. Cover with water and bring to the boil, lower heat and allow to simmer very gently for about 1½–2hr, skimming off any scum as it forms. When the pork is ready remove it with a slotted spoon onto a warm serving dish and keep hot. Add the puréed peas to the saucepan and mix well.

Poor Man's Gravlax
(Serves 4 as a starter)

True Scandinavian *gravlax* (or *gravlaks*) is made with boned salmon, pickled with lots of sugar, a little salt and seasoned heavily with dill. However salmon today is expensive and mackerel makes a very good alternative.

25g (1oz) coarse seasalt
25g (1oz) granulated sugar
1tsp coarsely ground black peppercorns
1tbsp chopped fresh dill
4 fresh mackerel fillets
1tbsp brandy

Mix the salt, sugar, peppercorns and dill together, and sprinkle a third of this mixture into the bottom of a nonmetal shallow dish, lay 2 mackerel fillets skin side down on top. Sprinkle half of the remaining mixture over the 2 fillets, and lay the other 2 mackerel fillets skin side up on top. Cover with the last of the mixture and sprinkle over the brandy. Cover with cling film, and weight down with a plate and weights. Refrigerate for 3 days, turning the fillets over once a day.

After 3 days remove the fillets from the marinade and using a very sharp knife, slice thinly and serve with lemon wedges and thin slices of buttered brown bread.

Hasselback Potatoes
(Serves 4)

These are excellent served with roast meats.

8 medium sized potatoes
50g (2oz) butter
Salt and freshly ground black pepper
25g (1oz) grated Cheddar cheese
50g (2oz) fresh white breadcrumbs

Peel the potatoes and cut into thin slices ¾ of the way through, leaving a 'hinge', so that the potato is fanlike in appearance.

Melt the butter in a shallow ovenproof dish, put in the potatoes, spooning some of the melted butter over the top; season with salt and freshly ground black pepper and bake in the oven for 40min at 200°C (400°F, Gas mark 6).

Remove from the oven. Mix the grated cheese and breadcrumbs and sprinkle over the potatoes; return to the oven and cook for a further 25min until crispy and golden.

Scandinavia

Burning Passion
(Serves 4)

An intriguing name for what is in fact an oldfashioned country dish from Denmark.

1kg (2.2lb) potatoes
Salt
3 large onions
225g (8oz) streaky bacon
50g (2oz) butter
Pickled beetroot for garnish

Peel the potatoes and cook in plenty of lightly salted water until tender. Meanwhile, peel and thinly slice the onions. Derind and roughly chop the bacon. Melt the butter in a large heavy bottomed frying pan and cook the onions until golden brown; remove with a slotted spoon and keep hot; pour off the butter from the pan and reserve. Cook the bacon in the pan until crisp.

As soon as the potatoes are cooked drain well and mash, incorporating the reserved butter. Pile the potatoes into a hot serving dish. Arrange the bacon down the centre, and sprinkle over the fried onions. Garnish with pickled beetroot.

A favourite dish in
Scandinavia where it is
served on pieces of
buttered ryebread as part
of the traditional
smörgåsbord.

Beef Tartare
(Serves 4)

675g (1½lb) fillet or rump steak
1tbsp brandy
1 medium onion
1tbsp capers
4 egg yolks

Trim any fat from the meat, then finely mince in a food
processor or through the fine blades of a mincer. Mix in the
brandy. Divide and shape into small rounds on 4 individual
plates. Peel and finely chop the onion and divide equally
between the plates, divide the capers similarly. Make a slight
hollow in the top of each meat mound, and break an egg yolk
into each.

Pâté is one of the basic
smörgåsbord ingredients
throughout Scandinavia,
garnished with mustard
and cress, pickled
beetroot or wafer-thin
slices of cucumber.

Liver Pâté
(Serves 6)

450g (1lb) calf liver
225g (8oz) streaky bacon
1 small onion
Salt and freshly ground black pepper
½tsp ground cloves
½tsp allspice
Pinch of paprika
3 anchovies
25g (1oz) butter
25g (1oz) flour
300ml (½pt) milk
2tbsp double cream

Trim the liver of any tubes and membrane. Derind the streaky
bacon. Peel and finely chop the onion. Mince the liver and
bacon together until quite fine; mix in the onion and spices.
Mash the anchovies and add to the mixture. Melt the butter
in a saucepan and stir in the flour over a medium high heat,
gradually add the milk, stirring all the time until the sauce

comes to the boil and is thick and smooth. Take off the heat, allow to cool slightly then stir in the cream.

Pour the sauce over the liver mixture, and mix well, seasoning with a little salt and generously with freshly ground black pepper. Transfer the mixture to a lightly oiled loaf tin, place in a larger tin filled with sufficient water to come half way up the sides of the loaf tin. Cook in a preheated oven at 170°C (325°F, Gas mark 3) for 1–1½hr. When a skewer inserted into the middle of the pâté comes out clean it is cooked. Leave to cool completely before turning out of the tin.

Stuffed Fillet of Pork
(Serves 6)

350g (12oz) **prunes**
300ml (½pt) **white wine**
1kg (2.2lb) **pork fillets**
Salt and freshly ground black pepper
50g (2oz) **butter**
300ml (½pt) **chicken stock**
300ml (½pt) **double cream**

A popular dish for a special occasion, fillet of pork is one of the most versatile cuts of meat and is used extensively in Scandinavian cookery.

Soak the prunes overnight in the wine, drain and stone, reserving liquid.

Trim the pork fillets and use a sharp knife to make 'pockets' by cutting the meat ⅔ of the way through lengthwise. Roughly chop the prunes and use them to stuff the pockets, seasoning with salt and freshly ground black pepper. Seal the pockets with toothpicks, or tie round with cotton to make neat parcels.

Melt the butter in a large flameproof casserole and brown the fillets evenly all over. Add the reserved liquid from the prunes together with the stock, and cook over a low heat for 30min. Put the fillets with a slotted spoon onto a warmed serving dish and keep hot.

Boil the liquid in the casserole sufficiently to reduce to half its original quantity; remove from the heat, and stir in the cream, check the seasoning. Serve the fillets in diagonal slices, with a little of the sauce drizzled over, and hand the remainder separately.

Swedish Potato, Sausage and Apple Salad
(Serves 4)

If you mix the salad while the potatoes are just warm, they will soak up more of the dressing, and the salad will be even tastier.

675g (1½lb) new potatoes
Salt
225g (8oz) frankfurter sausages
6 radishes
1 stick celery
1 crisp eating apple
1tbsp chopped chives
50ml (2fl oz) salad oil
25ml (1fl oz) white wine vinegar
1tsp mustard
Few drops of lemon juice
Salt and freshly ground black pepper

Peel the potatoes and cook with salt until just tender, drain and leave to cool. Slice the frankfurters into 1.25cm (½in) thick slices. When the potatoes have cooled cut into small dice. Wash and slice the radishes, chop the celery. Wash, core and dice the apple.

Put the sausage, potato, radish and celery into a salad bowl and mix lightly together. Sprinkle over the chopped chives. Mix the oil, vinegar, mustard and lemon together in a screw-top jar, season with salt and freshly ground black pepper, mix again, and pour over the dressing. Chill well before serving.

Red Wine Jelly
(Serves 4)

Commercial packet type jellies are not eaten in Scandinavia. In Denmark jellies are made either with pure fruit juice or, as in this recipe, with red wine – an elegant dessert which should be served with some lightly whipped cream.

13g (½oz) powdered gelatine
150ml (¼pt) hot water
175g (6oz) redcurrant jelly
175g (6oz) castor sugar
300ml (½pt) red wine
A little lightly whipped cream to decorate

Sprinkle the gelatine over the hot water and stir until dissolved. Put the redcurrant jelly and sugar in a small saucepan, heat gently over a low heat until well amalgamated and the sugar has dissolved. Remove from the heat, add to the gelatine mixture and mix well with the wine.

Pour into glass goblets and refrigerate until set. Decorate with a little lightly whipped cream.

Apple Cake
(Serves 4)

1kg (2.2lb) cooking apples
175g (6oz) granulated sugar
50g (2oz) butter
150g (5oz) fresh brown breadcrumbs
50g (2oz) demerara sugar

Serve the cake with lashings of whipped cream.

Peel, core and slice the apples and put into a saucepan with the sugar and a few tablespoonsful of water, and cook over a low heat until soft. Purée through a food processor or in an electric blender and allow to cool.

Melt the butter in a heavy-bottomed frying pan, add the breadcrumbs and demerara sugar stirring all the time until evenly browned. Remove from the pan and allow to cool.

In a glass dish put a layer of breadcrumbs followed by a layer of apple purée; continue layering until all the ingredients are used, finishing with a layer of breadcrumbs. Chill well and serve.

Scotland

Land of the haggis. That is probably what most people think of the food of Scotland – but my goodness how wrong they would be; Scotland has a long tradition of fine ingredients incorporated into dishes which have more than passed the test of time.

Yes, you will see haggis in most butchers' shops, but it is important to look for one in its natural skin, as, sadly, all too many look like small footballs sealed in synthetic 'skins'.

I remember going with Marika to Glasgow where she was giving a cookery demonstration in aid of the Red Cross. We flew up, loaded with boxes and bags of equipment, and had to shop for the ingredients on arrival. On Sauchiehall Street, surely Glasgow's most famous thoroughfare, a butcher's shop intrigued me with its counter packed with cooked meats, puddings, sausages and pies, including those gorgeous little Scots mutton pies. A variety of square sausage ('how sensible', was my first thought), thickly sliced and fried or grilled – excellent for breakfast together with some of the thin potato pancakes, slice of bread size, of which the Scots are so fond. What struck me forcibly then, was the warmth of the people, and the pride in their traditions, be it in the food or in their city of parks and beautiful buildings.

Of course Scottish food varies depending on the region. Whether it is for the grouse, which is in season from August 12th (the Glorious Twelfth) and which the Scots prefer stuffed with cranberries and roasted, or for the wild deer which still roam the Highlands, Scotland is famed for its shoots. Deer farming is increasing and the meat is quite widely available, providing leaner and more tender cuts than wild venison. Haunch and saddle are generally roasted while other cuts are trimmed and chopped up for use in casseroles and in venison sausages.

One cannot think of Scottish food without thinking of that king of fish, the salmon; fishing in Scotland has become quite an industry with aspiring salmon catchers from all parts of

the world descending on the Tay, Dee, the Spey and the Tweed with their rods and flies.

Marika taught me to cook salmon so that it remained moist and full of flavour. Thoroughly wet about 6 sheets of newspaper (the larger sheets are best) and wrap the salmon, one sheet at a time, ending up with a neat firm parcel. Put in the oven at about 190°C (375°F, Gas mark 5) and bake until the paper dries out completely – this can take up to 1hr, depending on the size of the fish. Once cooked the paper will be quite hard, so cut it with kitchen scissors, then very, very carefully peel the paper off; you will find the skin will come away too and you will be left with a moist and succulent salmon just in need of a garnish of freshly made mayonnaise and wafer thin slices of cucumber. This method works well with other large firm fleshed fish.

A delicacy, renowned throughout the world, is smoked Scotch salmon. The fish is first salted to preserve and bring out its flavour; this process is critical and years of experience guide the curer as to the amount of salt needed for each side. The salmon is then dried and smoked for up to 12hr over gently smouldering wood chips which release a unique aroma, until the flesh acquires a deep, rich pink colour and delicious flavour. Thinly sliced smoked salmon, served with a good wedge of juicy lemon, a grind of black pepper and some thinly sliced and buttered brown bread is guaranteed to set the taste buds tingling.

The fishing industry is still important to Scotland's economy, providing plentiful suppliers of wet fish, such as haddock, whiting and cod which can be baked, fried, poached, or made into pies, and not forgetting the herring which is traditionally rolled in oatmeal before being fried until crisp and golden brown.

The family cook in Scotland is a keen baker, producing savoury 'bridies' (little pastry pasties filled with beef nestling in a good onion flavoured gravy) and the sweet tea breads, tarts, oatmeal biscuits, shortbread and Dundee cakes. A Scottish high tea consists of a main course of fish, sausage, or cold meats, followed by a selection of baked produce, all washed down by lashings of sweet milky tea.

The Scot is a good trencherman and appears to enjoy the fine venison and delicately flavoured salmon as much as the simple haggis, especially when the latter has a tablespoonful or two of Scotch whisky poured over it, and is accompanied by the traditional mashed turnips, or 'neeps'.

238

Scotch Broth
(Serves 4)

675g (1½lb) neck of lamb
1.5*l* (3½pt) water
50g (2oz) pearl barley, soaked overnight
Salt and freshly ground black pepper
2 carrots
3 leeks
1 turnip
1tbsp finely chopped fresh parsley

Trim the lamb of excess fat then chop into small pieces. Put into a large saucepan and pour over the water. Bring to the boil over a gentle heat, removing any scum as it forms. Add the barley, season with salt and freshly ground black pepper and simmer for 35min. Peel the carrots and slice thickly. Trim, wash and thickly slice the leeks. Peel and cut the turnip into small dice. Add the vegetables to the soup and continue simmering for 1½hr, or until the meat is tender.

Use a slotted spoon and remove the bones and meat from the saucepan. Discard the bones, chop the meat finely, then return to the saucepan together with the chopped parsley. Adjust the seasoning as necessary.

Salmon Steaks with Parsley Butter
(Serves 4)

75g (3oz) butter
1tbsp finely chopped fresh parsley
2tsp lemon juice
Freshly ground black pepper
4 salmon steaks (about 2.5cm [1in] thick)
A little melted butter

Scotch salmon, renowned for its flavour and succulence, is very expensive. Salmon steaks, however, are well within the reach of most families.

Soften 75g (3oz) of the butter in a small basin, and with a wooden spoon beat in the chopped parsley, lemon juice and a good seasoning of freshly ground black pepper until well mixed. Shape the mixture into a sausage type roll and put in

Scotland

the deepfreeze to harden (do not allow to freeze). Heat the grill, place the salmon onto a rack, brush with the melted butter and cook for about 5min until lightly browned; turn the steaks over and brush with the remaining butter and continue cooking until lightly browned. Transfer onto a warmed serving plate and garnish with slices of parsley butter.

Saddle of Venison
(Serves 6–8)

2.5kg (5½lb) saddle of venison
60ml (2fl oz) oil
120ml (4fl oz) red wine
1tsp dried basil
2 whole cloves
1 clove garlic
2 leeks
2 carrots
2 parsnips
2 sticks celery
25g (1oz) butter
25g (1oz) plain flour
100g (4oz) streaky bacon

Put the venison in a close fitting shallow dish. Mix together the oil, wine, basil, cloves and crushed garlic, and pour over the meat, turning to coat evenly. Marinate for about 8hr in a cool place.

Remove the venison, reserving the marinade, and pat dry. Trim and thickly slice the leeks, peel and roughly chop the carrots and parsnips, thickly slice the celery. Heat the butter in a frying pan and cook all the vegetables until softened and pale golden, mix in half the flour and brown well. Transfer the vegetable mixture to a roasting tin, spreading evenly over the base, and place the venison on top. Spread the bacon rashers over the top, then pour the reserved marinade evenly over the venison.

Cover with foil and roast in a slow oven, 170°C (325°F, Gas mark 3) for about 2½hr, or until tender. Remove foil and cook for a further 20–30min to brown the venison.

Transfer the venison and vegetables to a serving platter to keep hot. Mix the remaining flour with a little water and stir into the pan juices, scraping up the sediment, and bring to the boil. Strain through a sieve and serve separately.

Scotland

Casserole of Grouse
(Serves 4)

4 casseroling grouse
25g (1oz) flour
Salt and freshly ground black pepper
½tsp mixed herbs
50g (2oz) butter
Bouquet garni
300ml (½pt) chicken or game stock
150ml (¼pt) robust red wine
2tbsp cooking brandy

In season in Scotland from mid-August to December only, they are a much sought-after game bird. Young birds should be roasted, but older birds are excellent cooked in a casserole; ask your butcher to pluck and draw them for you.

Break the grouse into joints. Season the flour with salt and freshly ground black pepper and mix in the herbs. Coat the grouse with the flour.

Heat the butter in a flameproof casserole (a cast iron one is best), and gently sauté the grouse until well browned; add the bouquet garni. Mix the stock and red wine together and pour over the grouse. Heat the brandy in a small saucepan, and set light to it, pour over the rest of the ingredients in the dish. Cover and put in a preheated oven 170°C (325°F, Gas mark 3) for 1¾–2hr.

Serve with game chips (see page 75) and seasonal green vegetables.

These succulent meat filled pasties are similar to the Cornish varieties, but contain only onion, steak and suet.

Scottish Bridies
(Serves 4–6)

50g (2oz) margarine
50g (2oz) lard
225g (8oz) plain flour
Pinch of salt
350g (12oz) rump steak
25g (1oz) beef suet
1 large onion
Salt and freshly ground black pepper
1 small egg

Rub the fats into the flour until the mixture resembles coarse breadcrumbs, add a good pinch of salt and mix well. Add sufficient water to form a firm dough. Roll out on a well floured board and, using a tea saucer or plate, cut out circles of pastry.

Trim the steak of any fat, and cut the flesh into thin slivers. Finely chop the suet. Peel and finely chop the onion. Mix the steak, suet and onion together, season with salt and freshly ground black pepper. Divide this mixture evenly between the pastry circles. Dampen the edges of the pastry, fold over to form a half circle and seal the edges well, then with finger and thumb fold over the edge to give a double seal. Beat the egg and use to glaze the bridies. Place the bridies on a lightly oiled baking sheet and cook in a preheated oven at 190°C (375°F, Gas mark 5) for 40–45min.

Stovies
(Serves 4–6)

675g (1½lb) potatoes, peeled
350g (12oz) cold cooked meat or poultry
1 large onion
50g (2oz) butter
Salt and freshly ground black pepper
150ml (¼pt) water or stock

Slice the potato thinly. Chop the meat or poultry quite finely. Peel and thinly slice the onion.

Use a little of the butter to lightly grease a lidded flameproof casserole. Melt ⅔ of the remaining butter in a frying pan and gently cook the onion until soft and transparent, not browned.

Arrange the potato, meat and onion in layers in the casserole dish, seasoning each layer with a little salt and freshly ground black pepper, finishing with a layer of potato. Pour the water or stock over the layers, and dot the remaining butter all over the potatoes. Bring to the boil, then lower to simmer and cook very gently for about 1hr (shake the pan occasionally to stop the ingredients sticking). Alternatively you can cook the dish in the oven at 180°C (350°F, Gas mark 4) for 1hr.

Scotland

Edinburgh Flan
(Serves 4–6)

75g (3oz) soft margarine
175g (6oz) plain flour
Pinch of salt
50g (2oz) butter
50g (2oz) soft brown sugar
75g (3oz) mixed dried fruit
40g (1½oz) flour
2 eggs

Rub the margarine into the plain flour with the fingertips, add a pinch of salt, and mix with sufficient water to make a soft but firm dough. Roll out on a well floured board and use to line a 20cm (8in) flan dish.

Melt the butter in a saucepan, and stir in the sugar and dried fruit, mix in the 40g (1½oz) flour. Beat the eggs until light and frothy. Remove the pan from the heat and stir in the eggs. Pour into the flan case and bake at 190°C (375°F, Gas mark 5) for about 35min, or until golden brown.

Rich Dundee Cake

275g (10oz) butter
275g (10oz) soft brown sugar
5 eggs
1tbsp treacle
275g (10oz) plain flour
1tsp mixed spice
1tsp salt
350g (12oz) currants
350g (12oz) raisins
275g (10oz) sultanas
13g (1oz) glacé cherries
50g (2oz) mixed peel
50g (2oz) blanched almonds
2tbsp whisky

Cream the butter and sugar together. Beat the eggs then beat them into the fat and sugar mixture and stir in the treacle. Sift the flour, spice and salt into the mixture and mix lightly. Add the fruits, using a metal spoon.

Transfer the mixture to a greased and lined tin, a 23cm (9in) round or a 20cm (8in) square; smooth the top of the cake and arrange the almonds on the top. Bake in a preheated oven at 150°C (300°F, Gas mark 2) for 3–4hr. Test with a skewer inserted in the middle of the cake; when it comes out clean the cake is cooked. Turn out the cake onto a wire rack, and while still warm prick the base with a skewer and spoon over 2tbsp of whisky. Allow to soak for 1–2hr.

Shortbread Fingers
(Makes about 18)

350g (12oz) plain flour
225g (8oz) butter
100g (4oz) castor sugar

Sift the flour into a mixing bowl. Cut the butter into small pieces and add to the bowl. Using your fingertips, rub the butter into the flour, until the mixture resembles fine breadcrumbs. Mix in the sugar, and then knead the mixture until it forms a firm dough. Turn out onto a well-floured board and shape into a square, then very carefully roll out to 5mm (¼in) thickness. Cut into about 18 even-sized fingers, and prick all over with a fork. Place on a greased baking tray and cook for 20min at 180°C (350°F, Gas mark 4) until a light golden brown. Cool on a wire tray, and store in an airtight tin or container.

United States of America

Many people when considering the food of North America are inclined to think, and quite wrongly, that it consists mainly of 'junk' food, take-aways, hamburgers, hot-dogs and the Mexican food take-aways that have sprung up all over the States in recent years.

The regional and country cooking of America, however, is a veritable melting pot of cuisines, rooted in the food cultures of the many peoples who settled this continent.

The Pilgrim Fathers, when they crossed the inhospitable Atlantic Ocean carried a store of salt pork to see them through their first New England winter. The rugged country-side of the region made life rather hard for these early settlers, but the Indians showed them how to use the indigenous vegetables and they discovered an abundance of turbot, sturgeon, mullet and herring together with crabs, lobsters, mussels, oysters and clams (although farther north in Newfoundland, lobster was regarded until quite recently as only fit to fertilize the land).

Undoubtedly the origin of the New England chowder was the result of a pioneering wife hanging a pot over the fire and filling it with whatever fish and vegetables were available.

Today, clambakes are a popular form of outdoor cooking and entertaining and in fact quite a big tourist attraction. A clambake takes place on the beach; a hole is dug in the sand, the bottom is lined with stones or rocks and a large wood fire is lit over the top. When the fire has burnt down, the hot stones are covered in fresh wet seaweed, and ingredients such as chicken, sweet potatoes, lobsters and clams are layered between seaweed and topped by a thick covering of seaweed, then left to cook in the steamy heat.

Thanksgiving, a custom now practised throughout America, celebrated the first year's harvest by the Pilgrims with three days of feasting. Ninety-one Indians joined the settlers, bringing with them contributions to the festival.

Turkey is the traditional meat for the dinner, stuffed with chestnuts and served with cranberry sauce, and the meal is rounded off with a creamy pumpkin pie.

The American Midwest has vast areas of prairieland given over to the growing of corn and wheat. Settlers in this treeless open country depended upon the vegetables they could grow helped out by meat from domestic fowls and animals and prairie wildfowl. Home cookery in this region is very much based on plain but nourishing, tasty but unsophisticated cooking.

Texas is said to have more head of cattle than people and so it is not surprising that beef is eaten in great quantity. Texas beef has the reputation for being the finest and leanest in the land. There is also a plentiful supply of game, rabbits, wild turkeys and pheasants which in the more isolated areas away from the supermarkets will ring the changes for the family cook.

Texans love a barbecue, and have in fact made quite an art of it, barbecuing not just steaks but whole sides of beef on a rotating spit. Accompanied by a wide variety of salads and jacket-baked potatoes, the barbecue is a good way to entertain a large number of people. The influences of Mexico, just across the border, undoubtedly produced chilli con carne which is so popular, though certainly no self respecting Mexican will take responsibility for that dish.

Perhaps it is in the Southern States that the most exciting foods are to be found, where cooking and eating are important to family life. Southern people are proud of their heritage which is strongly reflected in the regional foods. New Orleans cookery is an incredible explosion of flavours demonstrating the Southerner's ability to experiment and create new recipes. Some New Orleans creations are now classic dishes of the world; take for example, Oysters Rockefeller, which was invented at the turn of the century by one of the city's most famous restaurateurs, Jules Alciatore of Antoine's. Oysters placed on the half shell are grilled for 4 or 5min only before being covered in a sauce made from butter, cooked chopped spinach, a little onion and pernod, seasoned with a little anchovy paste and some Worcester sauce; a sprinkling of breadcrumbs and grated parmesan complete the dish before it is quickly browned under the grill or in the oven.

The combination of cultures, the Spanish, French, and the slaves of Africa, play their part in Creole cookery, which is one of the finest in the entire North American continent.

The last state to join the Union was Hawaii and, in contrast to the rest of America, here is found the Polynesian influence.

Feast days are celebrated with much singing and dancing and with a *luau*, when a suckling pig or two and perhaps some chickens will be cooked in the ground while wrapped in banana leaves and corn husks.

In the countryside are vast fields of pineapple; it is, after all, a thriving industry, but other fresh fruits, such as papayas, coconuts and guavas abound. The Pacific Ocean provides an endless supply of seafood, and the Hawaians still use *poi*, a paste made from taro roots, a vegetable found in all the Pacific Islands. I spent a couple of weeks holidaying in Hawaii and though the thriving tourist industry has caused over-commercialisation the warmth of the Polynesian people still shines through.

No matter where you go in America, you will find home cooking is surviving, despite the ready availability of every type of convenience food available to the housewife – it would be such a pity if a land so rich in culinary resources were to lose sight of the richness and diversity of its cuisine.

Robust and filling this soup comes from the Deep South.

Shrimp and Okra Gumbo
(Serves 4)

3tbsp corn oil

25g (1oz) plain flour

75g (3oz) belly pork

2 large onions

2 cloves garlic

1 red pepper

225g (8oz) okra

150g (6oz) tomatoes

1*l* (1¾pt) chicken stock

1tsp Worcestershire sauce

½tsp allspice

Few drops of Tabasco

Freshly ground black pepper

Salt

350g (12oz) shelled and deveined raw shrimps

225g (8oz) hot cooked long grain rice

Heat the oil in a heavy bottomed saucepan and stir in the flour, cook over a low heat, stirring occasionally, until the roux becomes thick and is a rich brown colour (take care not to burn).

Dice the belly pork, and sauté in a heavy bottomed saucepan, until all the fat has run out and the meat is browned and cooked, remove meat with a slotted spoon.

Peel and chop the onions and garlic, deseed and chop the red pepper. Add the onion and garlic to the bacon fat and cook until the onion is soft and transparent, add the red pepper and cook for a further 5min. Coarsely chop the okra and add to the pan, and cook gently for 3 or 4min. Meanwhile put the tomatoes into a bowl and cover with boiling water, let stand for 3min, then slide off the skins, and roughly chop the flesh, and add to the vegetable mixture.

Pour the stock over the vegetables, together with the Worcestershire sauce, allspice and a few drops of Tabasco, stir well, then add the cooked diced pork, and the oil and flour roux, mix well and season with freshly ground black pepper; add a little salt if liked. Cover the pan, and simmer over a low heat for about an hour.

Add the shrimps, stir and cook for 5min. Check seasoning,

then ladle the gumbo into warmed individual soup bowls, topping each bowl with a heaped tbsp of hot cooked rice.

Creole Jambalaya
(Serves 6)

From the Southern States, this makes a delicious family supper.

1 medium onion
2 cloves garlic
25g (1oz) butter
2tbsp oil
100g (4oz) ham
100g (4oz) raw prawns
225g (8oz) tin tomatoes
700ml (1¼pt) chicken stock
350g (12oz) long grain American rice
1tbsp finely chopped fresh parsley
½tsp dried thyme
½tsp dried basil
1 bay leaf
Salt and freshly ground black pepper

Peel and finely chop the onion and garlic. Melt the butter with the oil in a large frying pan, and cook the onion and garlic until soft and transparent. Cut the ham into strips and add to the pan together with the prawns, mixing well. Purée the tomatoes, add to the pan together with the stock. Bring to the boil; add the rice, cover and simmer for 20min. Remove the lid, add the herbs, and season with salt and freshly ground black pepper. Cover again and allow to cook until almost all the liquid has been absorbed; the rice grains should still be moist.

A popular Sunday brunch dish in America, I first sampled this simple but delicious midday special when holidaying in Hawaii and sitting in one of Honolulu's highest restaurants as it revolved very slowly, giving panoramic views of the city and the famous beaches.

Eggs Benedict
(Serves 4)

3 egg yolks
1tbsp lemon juice
Salt and freshly ground black pepper
150g (5oz) unsalted butter
1tbsp white wine vinegar
2tsp malt vinegar
8 standard size free-range eggs
4 wholemeal muffins, split
25g (1oz) butter
175g (6oz) thinly sliced cooked ham

Put the egg yolks and lemon juice into a food processor or electric blender, season with salt and freshly ground black pepper and process until foamy. Melt the butter, together with the white wine vinegar in a small saucepan, until the butter is just coming up to boiling (but is not browning). With the machine switched on, add the butter in a steady stream through the feed tube; the mixture should start to thicken immediately. Pour the sauce into a small bowl, and keep warm over a pan of hot water while you prepare the eggs.

An egg poaching pan is ideal, but if you do not have one, heat a large shallow panful of water with the malt vinegar to boiling point; break the eggs, individually, into a saucer and slide carefully into the water. Cook for 4min, then lift out carefully with a slotted spoon. Trim any ragged edges with kitchen scissors.

Toast the muffins, and butter lightly, and divide the ham equally and place on the muffins, then top with the poached egg, and pour over the sauce. Serve at once.

Southern Fried Chicken
(Serves 6)

6 chicken joints
Garlic salt
Freshly ground black pepper
4tbsp milk
1 egg
50g (2oz) plain flour

Though popular throughout the States, this recipe comes from Arkansas.

Season the chicken all over with garlic salt and freshly ground black pepper. Beat the milk and egg together and dip each chicken joint into the mixture, coating well, then dip into the flour until thoroughly coated. Heat the oil until a haze rises then cook the chicken pieces, 2 at a time, until golden brown and cooked through.

Serve with rice salad (see page 254).

Hash Brown Potatoes
(Serves 4)

450g (1lb) potatoes, peeled
1 small onion
Salt and freshly ground black pepper
25g (1oz) butter
2tbsp sunflower oil

Coarsely grate the potatoes, and put into a colander; squeeze out as much moisture as you can with your hands, then leave to drain for 30min. Peel and finely chop the onion and mix into the potato, season with salt and freshly ground black pepper.

Heat the butter and oil in a 17–20cm (7–8in) frying pan. Spoon the potato and onion mixture into the pan, packing it down firmly, leave a small space all round the base of the pan and cook, over a low heat for 15min, by which time the underside should be golden brown; invert onto a plate then slide back into the pan to cook the other side. Mark the potatoes into 4 wedges with a knife, and cook for a further 10–12min until golden brown.

This is an excellent and traditional accompaniment to Southern fried chicken.

Mixed Rice Salad
(Serves 6)

6tbsp sweet pickle
50g (2oz) pimento
450g (1lb) cooked long grain rice
300ml (½pt) mayonnaise
1tsp prepared mustard
4 hardboiled eggs
Watercress for garnish

Chop the sweet pickle and pimento, and mix into the rice. Mix the mayonnaise and mustard together and fold into the rice mixture. Peel and chop the hardboiled eggs and gently stir into the mixture; be careful not to break up the eggs too much. Chill well, garnish with sprigs of watercress.

New England Baked Beans
(Serves 4)

450g (1lb) red kidney beans
225g (8oz) streaky bacon, derinded
60ml (2fl oz) molasses or black treacle
½tsp hot mustard (English mustard)
Freshly ground black pepper
425ml (15fl oz) hot water
25g (1oz) butter

Soak the kidney beans overnight in cold water. Drain, and put into a pan of lightly salted water. Bring to the boil, and boil hard for no less than 10min (this removes any toxins from the beans). Lower the heat and simmer for 1hr. Drain and put into a deep, lightly greased casserole dish. Chop the streaky bacon into strips and scatter over the beans. Mix the molasses or treacle with the mustard and season with freshly ground black pepper, then add 425ml (15fl oz) hot water, mix and pour over the bacon and beans. Mix well, then dot butter over the top. Cover tightly, and bake at 180°C (350°F,

Gas mark 4) for about 2hr, or until the beans are soft. Uncover the casserole for the last 20–25min of the cooking time to brown the beans.

Chilli Con Carne
(Serves 10–12)

1 large onion
2 cloves garlic
2tbsp sunflower oil
1kg (2lb) minced lean beef
2tsp cornflour
2 tins (400g [14oz]) of tomatoes, puréed
3tbsp tomato purée
1tsp ground oregano
1tsp dried thyme
¼tsp ground cumin
¼tsp ground coriander
3tsp hot chilli powder
2 tins (400g [14oz]) red kidney beans, drained
125ml (4fl oz) red wine
Salt and freshly ground black pepper

Originating in Mexico and Texas, 'chilli' has become popular throughout America, doubtless because it is an economical dish, although I find it excellent for informal supper parties. It can be served with plain boiled rice, or with crusty bread and green salad.

Peel and finely chop the onion and garlic. In a large fireproof casserole (a cast iron one is best) heat the oil and cook the onion and garlic until the onion is soft and transparent. Add the minced beef and brown well. Stir in the cornflour and cook for 1min. Add the puréed tomatoes and tomato purée and stir well, add the herbs, spices and chilli powder and mix well into the meat mixture. Add the kidney beans and red wine, season with salt and freshly ground black pepper. Reduce the heat to simmer and cover and cook on top of the stove for 1–1¼hr.

Traditional fudgy brownies are a favourite with just about everyone.

Brownies
(Makes about 10)

100g (4oz) soft margarine
100g (4oz) soft brown sugar
2 eggs
50g (2oz) plain flour
25g (1oz) cocoa powder
1tsp baking powder
100g (4oz) walnuts, finely chopped

Cream the margarine and sugar together until light and fluffy, add the eggs, and gradually beat into the mixture. Sift the flour, cocoa and baking powder together and fold into the mixture with a metal spoon. Fold in the chopped walnuts. Spoon into a lightly greased 20cm (8in) sq baking tin and bake for about 25min in an oven preheated to 180°C (350°F, Gas mark 4), testing with a skewer, which should come out cleanly. Remove from oven and allow to cool in the tin. When completely cool, cut into squares.

Hawaiian Banana Loaf

This cut-and-come-again loaf keeps beautifully moist and is eaten at breakfast or teatime; sliced and buttered it is delicious.

100g (4oz) margarine
175g (6oz) light muscovado sugar
2 ripe bananas
2 eggs
225g (8oz) self raising flour
1tsp baking powder
2tbsp milk
50g (2oz) macademia nuts

Cream the margarine and sugar together. Mash the bananas and add to the mixture. Break the eggs into the mixture and beat well. Sift the flour and baking powder together and fold into the mixture. Stir in the milk and the macademia nuts. Turn into a greased and lined 1kg (2lb) loaf tin and bake for 1hr in an oven preheated to 180°C (350°F, Gas mark 4) until well risen and golden brown. Turn onto a wire rack to cool.

Shoo-Fly Pie
(Serves 6–8)

75g (3oz) soft margarine
175g (6oz) plain flour
Pinch of salt

For the filling:
75ml (3fl oz) water
100g (4oz) molasses
½tsp bicarbonate of soda

For the topping:
75g (3oz) butter
175g (6oz) plain flour
75g (3oz) soft dark brown sugar
1tsp ground cinnamon
Pinch of ground ginger

United States of America

A very famous Pennsylvania Dutch recipe with its distinctive flavour of molasses.

Rub the margarine into the flour, together with a pinch of salt until the mixture resembles coarse breadcrumbs. Add sufficient water to form a firm dough. On a well floured board roll out the pastry and use to line a 20cm (8in) flan dish.

Put the water and molasses in a saucepan and heat until amalgamated, add the bicarbonate and stir until frothy. Pour into the flan case.

Rub the butter into the flour, until the mixture resembles fine breadcrumbs, stir in the sugar, cinnamon and a good pinch of ground ginger, and sprinkle evenly over the top of the dish. Bake for approximately 40min at 190°C (375°F, Gas mark 5).

This pie is best served warm with some whipped cream.

Wales

As I have not been to Wales for a good many years I went to see John Greenhouse in his sixteenth-century Osborne House Restaurant only a few miles from my Cornish home. Silver haired and standing some 6ft 4in in stocking feet, John is patriotically Welsh, and returns there whenever he can.

As we sat among his Victorian memorabilia he invited me to join him in tasting a truly Welsh dish he had just made – mussels with laver bread. Laver bread, or *bara lawr* as the Welsh call it, is edible seaweed which has been processed by long slow cooking; it is almost black in appearance and if you buy some in Swansea market it will probably be served in oatmeal straight from a big tub.

It was obvious while we talked that country cooking in Wales has long remained unchanged. Years ago, when most country folk had a pig or two, an animal would be slaughtered and used to make bacon. Even now in the big markets in Wales you will see big homecured bacons for sale. Nothing is wasted and the pig's head is made into brawn.

John recalled a favourite dish when he was growing up in Waunarlwyuu (a small village just outside Swansea some 5 miles from Penclawdd and the famous cockle beds) which was always served midmorning on a Saturday. His mother would first pan fry thick slices of gammon, then push them to the side of the pan and add laver bread; finally in would go some cockles. All the ingredients would be arranged on a plate together with slices of bread which had been dipped in batter and fried in lard. A good filling meal for a growing lad.

Bacon joints served with parsley sauce are as popular today served with new potatoes, leeks and seasonal vegetables for a hot dinner, and any leftovers would be served later for tea, together with Welsh cakes, round flat biscuitlike cakes cooked on a griddle. The most famous traditional Welsh dish is *cawl*, which uses lamb, bacon or beef, or a combination of all three. All cooks have their own recipes, and John's mother, he remembers, used only lamb, one of the economical cuts such as breast or neck. The meat was boiled in a

big pan until tender then lifted out and the cooking liquid allowed to become cold so that fat on the surface could be removed. Vegetables would then be added to the pot, and perhaps some dumplings to provide bulk. Traditionally the 'soup' would be served from a tureen and the meat presented on a platter, with everyone carving what they wanted. Usually made early in the week a pot of cawl would last until Friday.

Welsh lamb has an excellent reputation both for its flavour and tenderness. Roasted with rosemary and served with fresh mint sauce, with either new potatoes, or roast potatoes cooked in lard, and some fresh vegetables, including new peas, this is the traditional Sunday lunch in Wales. High tea is served in the evening, and supper is made out of leftover vegetables, chopped up and fried in lard.

Puddings in Wales are derived from simple ingredients; rice pudding is served in a bowl with a good dollop of homemade jam, and the no-nonsense bread and butter pudding remains as popular as ever.

A common thread runs through the cooking of Wales; economy, and the use of seasonal ingredients. Whenever John Greenhouse returns to Wales he visits his nephew's inn especially to recapture a taste of Wales with a generous serving of cawl.

Leek and Potato Soup
(Serves 4)

The leek, probably the best known symbol of Wales, is widely used in regional dishes.

6 leeks
3 large potatoes
50g (2oz) butter
1¼l (2½pt) chicken stock
Salt and freshly ground black pepper

Trim any tough leaves from the leeks then wash carefully, cut into thin slices. Peel the potatoes and cut into medium sized cubes.

Melt the butter in a saucepan and gently cook the leeks and potatoes until lightly golden brown. Pour over the stock and bring to the boil. Season with salt and freshly ground black pepper and simmer for 30–35min, or until the vegetables are tender.

Honeyed Leg of Welsh Lamb
(Serves 4–6)

Sheep farming is a traditional way of life for the Welsh, and they produce some of the best flavoured lamb in the British Isles.

1 small leg of Welsh lamb
Salt and freshly ground black pepper
225ml (8fl oz) clear honey
½tsp mixed herbs
Good sprig of mint
1tsp white wine vinegar

Put the lamb into a roasting tin, and season well with a little salt and generously with freshly ground black pepper and the mixed herbs. Pour over the lamb about ⅔ of the honey and pour a little water round it.

Cook in a preheated oven at 190°C (375°F, Gas mark 5), allowing 30min/450g (1lb). Baste with the honey and water while cooking. When ready remove from the oven and transfer the joint onto a warmed roasting dish, keep warm.

Finely chop the mint and mix it with the remaining honey and the white wine vinegar; just before serving pour this mixture over the lamb.

This dish could quite properly be called the national dish of Wales. In days gone by, large ladles were especially made for serving this nourishing and warming meal; often the ladles would be decoratively carved as well as being practical.

Cawl
(Serves 6)

225g (8oz) swede
225g (8oz) carrots
225g (8oz) leeks
225g (8oz) onion
25g (1oz) butter
675g (1½lb) smoked collar bacon
450g (1lb) brisket or silverside of beef
Salt and freshly ground black pepper
1tsp mixed herbs
2 bay leaves
1*l* (1¾pt) stock (or water and stock cubes)
450g (1lb) new potatoes
1tbsp finely chopped fresh parsley

Peel the swede and cut into medium sized dice. Peel and thickly slice the carrots. Wash and trim the leeks and cut into 2.5cm (1in) chunks. Peel and roughly chop the onion.

Melt the butter in a large flameproof casserole (a cast iron one is ideal) and sauté the vegetables until just beginning to soften. Add the bacon and beef to the vegetables, season well with salt and freshly ground black pepper, sprinkle over the herbs, then pour over the stock. Bring to the boil over a medium high heat, then lower and simmer for about 1½hr. Meanwhile wash and scrape the new potatoes, add to the casserole at the end of the cooking time, and then cook the whole dish for a further 40min.

Remove the bacon and beef from the casserole with slotted spoons, and cut the meat into chunks, then return them to the casserole and heat through. Just before serving sprinkle generously with finely chopped fresh parsley.

Welsh Faggots
(Serves 4)

225g (8oz) pig liver
225g (8oz) pork sausagemeat
2 onions
225g (8oz) fresh white breadcrumbs
75g (3oz) shredded suet
1tsp dried sage
1tsp dried thyme
Salt and freshly ground black pepper

Serve hot with gravy, creamed potatoes and buttered leeks.

Finely mince the liver and mix with the sausagemeat. Peel and roughly chop the onions and drop into a pan of boiling water; cook until tender. Drain and mince finely, and add to the liver mixture. Mix in the breadcrumbs, suet and herbs and season with salt and freshly ground black pepper.

With lightly floured hands divide the mixture into 8 pieces and mould into balls. Lightly grease a shallow ovenproof dish just big enough to take the faggots tightly packed together. Bake in a preheated oven at 200°C (400°F, Gas mark 6) until well browned.

Caws Pobi (Welsh Rabbit)
(Serves 4)

100g (4oz) Cheddar cheese
2tbsp milk
13g (½oz) butter
Salt and freshly ground black pepper
1tsp mustard
4 slices of toast

In the past this would have consisted of toasted barley bread with a chunk of hard cheese, toasted on a fork before an open fire, laid on top. Today it is more usual to make a cheese sauce, which is poured over slices of toast and browned under the grill.

Put the cheese, milk and butter in a saucepan and melt slowly over a gentle heat, stirring all the time, season with salt and freshly ground black pepper and mix in the mustard. When piping hot pour over the slices of toast and brown under the grill. Serve immediately.

Bread and Butter Pudding
(Serves 4)

Butter
4 slices of bread, buttered
50g (2oz) sultanas
25g (1oz) castor sugar
450ml (¾pt) milk
2 eggs
½tsp ground nutmeg

Lightly butter a pie dish. Cut the bread into squares and use some to line the bottom of the dish, sprinkle a few sultanas and a sprinkling of sugar, over the top, then continue layering up the dish, bread, fruit and sugar, until all the ingredients are used, ending with a layer of bread on top.

Gently heat the milk until just below boiling point and remove from the heat. In a basin lightly whisk the eggs until frothy, then pour the hot milk onto them, stirring all the time. Strain the mixture, through a sieve, over the ingredients in the pie dish and sprinkle the nutmeg over the top. Bake for 30min at 180°C (350F, Gas mark 4), when the top should be golden brown.

Welsh Cakes

350g (12oz) self raising flour
175g (6oz) butter or block margarine
100g (4oz) sugar
100g (4oz) currants
2 eggs

Put the flour in a mixing bowl, cut the butter or margarine into small pieces, add to the flour and rub in, with the fingertips, until the mixture resembles breadcrumbs. Mix in the sugar and currants. Beat the eggs and mix, adding sufficient water to form a soft dough. Roll out on a well floured board to about 6mm (¼in) thick. Using a metal cutter, cut into rounds. Lightly grease a griddle and preheat, cook the cakes until golden brown on both sides. Dust with a little castor sugar.

Wales

Shearing Cake

225g (8oz) wholemeal flour
225g (8oz) plain flour
Pinch of salt
2tsp baking powder
1tsp ground nutmeg
225g (8oz) block margarine
350g (12oz) soft light brown sugar
1tbsp caraway seeds
Grated rind and juice of a lemon
2 standard eggs
300ml (½pt) milk

The shearing cake, which has a distinctive caraway flavour, is a favourite at harvest time.

Sift the flours, salt, baking powder and ground nutmeg into a large mixing bowl. Cut the margarine into small pieces and rub into the flour with the fingertips until the mixture resembles coarse breadcrumbs. Add the sugar, caraway seeds, lemon rind and juice and mix well. Beat the eggs into the milk and gradually add to the cake mixture, beating until well mixed.

Pour into a lightly greased 23cm (9in) cake tin. Cook in the centre of a preheated oven at 180°C (350°F, Gas mark 4) for 20min, then lower the heat to 150°C (300°F, Gas mark 2) for 1½–2hr.

Acknowledgements

There are many people to thank when you produce a book. It would be impossible to name everyone and I hope those not mentioned by name will know that they are included. My thanks go particularly to Mrs Jean Knowles of Perth, Western Australia whose research proved invaluable for that section of the book; to John Greenhouse of the Osborne House Hotel in Looe who, despite running a very busy restaurant, found time to help me in the Welsh section, and Jean Claude and Tessa Denat of 'Clarets' for advice on Brittany. Special thanks to my German friend, Kristina Kruse, and to my mother who, having spent her childhood in Ireland, helped me with the section on Irish country cooking.

Finally my thanks to Toshiba for lending me their equipment for recipe testing.

Rosa Mashiter

Index

Index